NO MAGIC

A Natural Explanation of CONSCIOUSNESS

Hugh Noble

Best Wishes Hugh

Tartan Hen Publications
Creachan, Portnacroish, Appin, Argyll, Scotland
http://www.tartanhen.co.uk

Copyright © Hugh Noble 2012
All rights reserved

ISBN: 978-0-9576666-0-3

NO MAGIC

ACKNOWLEDGEMENTS

Thanks are due to my wife Joyce who forbore and to Ben du Boulay who was patient, listened over the years and asked pertinent questions.

In the distant future I see open fields for far more important researches. Psychology will be based on a new foundation, that of necessary acquirement of each mental power and capacity by gradation. Light will be thrown on the origin of man and his history.

Charles Darwin - "The Origin of Species"

It is difficult to get a man to understand something when his salary depends upon his not understanding it.

Upton Sinclair

CONTENTS

INTRODUCTION

In the Oxford Dictionary of Philosophy, Simon Blackburn described consciousness as -

"Possibly the most challenging and pervasive source of problems in the whole of philosophy." [Blackburn 1994]

When one considers the volume of literature on the subject and the almost total lack of consensus, it is hard to disagree. For aeons, since the time of the Greek philosophers, and from probably even earlier than that, the discussion about consciousness has been dominated by metaphysical speculations and elaborate philosophical intuitions.

Only in the last half-century or so, has that changed. The invention of brain-scanning equipment now offers us the prospect of hard third-party-accessible evidence that mental activity takes place in certain circumstances. It also yields information about where within the brain that thinking takes place.

The same technology also shows us that many of the mental experiences, which have great and persuasive influence on the intuitions, which some people have, can be mimicked by the ingestion or injection of neuro-active substances. Scientific experiment is creeping up on the problem of how the brain operates. The space left for metaphysical speculation is shrinking.

But knowing where in the brain our thinking occurs, does not tell us much about how we do it. This book is about how. To understand the way that information can be manipulated we need to turn to the insights and the terminology offered us by computer technology. The solution I offer is speculative but I think it is also plausible. Unusually for a book, which approaches this subject from a strictly materialist standpoint, I will not dodge or try to fudge the issue of how and why consciousness is associated with what we call a "*subjective*" experience. It seems to me that if we do not have an explanation for that, then we do not have an explanation at all.

My approach to the problem of consciousness was a backward journey. It began when I was a post doctoral research fellow in the Department of Artificial Intelligence at Edinburgh University. I worked there on a project to develop a computer aided learning system and became convinced that a really successful system could be built only if it was possible for a computer to understand natural language - and I mean "understand", not simply do a few tricks with strings of words.

In 1988 I published a book called "Natural Language Processing" [Noble 1988]. Into that book I put the start of my ideas. A second book, "Operational Consciousness", was published in 2005 [Noble 2005]. I argued in both books in favour of a concept-based approach to language understanding and did so despite being aware (and being made aware) that my ideas stood in contradiction to the received wisdom of the time.

In the 1970s the views of Noam Chomsky ruled supreme. According to his doctrine, the central problem in linguistics is to discover why human speakers of a natural language can discriminate between grammatical and ungrammatical speech patterns. He also held that an innate knowledge of syntax was the foundation for our facility for language - and so was born the idea of "deep grammar" and the techniques of generative grammar [Chomsky 1971].

I disagreed then and still disagree with all of that. I take the view that any explanation of human behaviour, as is true for everything biological, has to start with evolution, carry on with evolution and end with evolution. The trouble with the Chomskian approach is that it is just not compatible with evolution.

To be compatible with evolution, our ability to use language has to provide us with a survival advantage. The likelihood is that that advantage is linked to the ability to communicate - to share ideas. The need to communicate means that the advantage can not be realised unless several people all have the same or similar ability at the same time. Language is no use at all, to a single person, living in isolation, and able only to talk to him or herself.

So how could Chomsky's deep grammar come about? A wave of a magic wand and then everyone started speaking in tongues? I don't think so.

In an effort to rehabilitate the Chomskian approach, his disciple Steven Pinker suggested that the first person who had the new gene, which enabled language to be used correctly, could have conversed with

"... the fifty percent of brothers and sisters and sons and daughters who shared the new gene by common inheritance".

[Pinker 1994 p 365]

That is a slipshod argument. The fifty percent rule applies only to the inheritance of a single gene and I do not think even Pinker would claim that something with the complexity of deep grammar could be the product of a single mutational change. Furthermore, if the single new gene was indeed a common inheritance, the implication is that one parent would need also to have that special gene, and that parent would then have trouble finding anyone to chat to. A few sentences later Pinker also makes a startling admission -

"... neighbours could have partly understood what the mutant was saying even when they lacked the new-fangled circuitry just using overall intelligence." [my emphasis].

With those words Pinker has undermined his whole case. He has admitted that there must have been a way in which people could have discussed things without the need for any form of grammar. Calling it *"overall intelligence"* does not wish that mechanism out of existence. What I am trying to do here is to explain how that overall intelligence method operates and to describe how it could have evolved gradually, small step by small step, into a full blown language facility.

To overcome the problem of how the Chomskian idea could have started, while retaining the primacy of language, some have suggested that some form of internal language is an essential tool for the thinking process (of an individual person). A person cannot think properly, according to this idea, unless he or she can talk to him/herself.

There is still a problem, however, about how even an internal language could have got started if it had to conform to the way evolution works. Change must come gradually, one step at a time, with each step offering some small tangible advantage.

A language facility based on the grammatical classification of words is useless if you do not have a lot of words which are classified in a variety of ways. So once again we have the problem of how those words and their meanings came to us. Singly? In a miraculous multitude?

There has to be an alternative mechanism which enables the components of thinking to be formed and accumulated before thinking started. That is, these components had to be accumulated in a way that was divorced from thinking altogether. There had to be a way of using them that had nothing at all to do with thinking or with language.

I think concepts came before language. I think we formed concepts for a reason which was not directly related to thinking. We acquired a sizeable collection of them. And then, (and only then) we started thinking consciously with those concepts

We had, I guess, already been communicating using body language. We read one another's facial expressions, followed the gaze of another, focused our attention on and thought on whatever he or she was looking at, read the gestures and the tone of voice, anticipated the actions.

And then we paid attention to the sounds that others made. We applied the same techniques to these sounds as we had used for other perceptible features of the landscape and formed that experience into sound-concepts or word-concepts. We could not help doing that. The mechanisms were there and waiting to be applied to everything we experienced. And the sound of these words became the "handles" or "labels" which were attached to the components of the on-going thinking process.

Then we could talk.

We could talk by using those word-handles. Saying them to each other. We started slowly. One word per utterance. Then two words, and so on. Language crept up on our species. It must have done so - unless you discount the theory of evolution.

I am not prepared to do that. Evolution is not a nuisance. It is not an awkward thing that has to be shown to be compatible with our explanations. It is the explanation.

But what was the mechanism of that creep? What pathway did it follow? The question which haunts the Chomskian approach is this - What could be the survival advantage to the human species if it had only a partially developed deep grammar – before it was transformed into some kind of natural language which presumably did not even exist at the outset? Arriving at your destination before you have started on your journey, without passing through any intermediate stages, is a clever trick.

I began at the end of the evolutionary story and worked backwards to the beginning. At each stage, as I contemplated some development, I asked myself this question - How could *that* have come about? What must have come before that? What condition or facility provided the mechanism with some advantage, and which could then change into the next functioning arrangement, by taking a single small advantageous step?

Forty years is how long it took me to complete my journey. Not so long really in comparison to the journey the evolution of the brain took. That is measured not only in millions of years but quite possibly in billions of years. Most particularly the main bit of that evolution took place during the six hundred million years, or so, that have elapsed since the end of the "Snowball Earth" period.

Forty years, however, is not long provided it gets somewhere - to an explanation of consciousness. That problem is as ancient as Aristotle. In this book I will re-tell the story of that speculative evolutionary journey, but I will tell it in the forward direction.

Most books about consciousness begin by apologising for not being able to tell the reader what consciousness really is. But I will not do that. I will not do that because I am going to tell you what consciousness is, how it works and why it works that way. In a deliberate and, I admit, a mischievous break with that tradition, I will tell you what consciousness is - in the very first sentence of the very first chapter. In the text and chapters, which follow, I will tell you how it works. Consciousness, in my view, has nothing at all to do with the supernatural.

I will deal also with some related issues and explain why those who talk about "An Explanatory Gap", and "The Hard Problem" or claim that a natural explanation of consciousness is impossible, have got it all profoundly wrong.

Consciousness is a natural process.

When I say "process" I mean that literally. Consciousness is not a mental state or a static condition. It is an intensely active thing.

Consciousness has observable consequences. To be able to produce of consequences requires the expenditure of energy. That implies that consciousness cannot be a static thing. It must take the form of an on-going process.

It is quite a complicated process, to be sure, but there is nothing in my explanation, which defies understanding and nothing which requires us to suppose the existence of hitherto unobserved phenomena related (for example) to quantum mechanics. I will argue that the so-called "Explanatory Gap" and the "Hard Problem" are irrelevant. They are based on irrational misconceptions.

And now I will tell you my story again in the forward direction. Reading it will require some perseverance, but I promise that the reading of it will not take you forty years.

CHAPTER 1

A BRIEF OUTLINE OF THE EXPLANATION

What is consciousness and how does it work?

01.01

Consciousness is a procedure performed by a brain to explain itself to itself. Consciousness is not, as is often claimed, "*a mental state*". By that I mean, it is not something that is static or a condition of the whole brain. It is something which is part of what the brain does. The activity within a brain is a variety show and consciousness is just one of the many acts within the whole brain performance.

My explanation in a nutshell

01.02

A creature with an intelligent brain is able to predict the future. By doing that it is able to anticipate important events and situations before they happen. That gives it forewarning, and thus a little extra time, to take avoiding action or to take action that will make good events more likely to occur. Indeed, the ability to predict the future is a useful and practical way to define intelligence.

Predicting the future requires many factors to be taken into account. But the most perplexing of these factors for an intelligent creature, is the problem of predicting its own behaviour. The reason that that is perplexing is that the choice of action it is likely to make, is dependent upon the future it predicts, but in order to make that prediction, it needs to know what action it will choose to take, since that action could change the future completely.

So it finds itself in an impossible position. It needs to know what choice of action it will take in order to provide the information that it will need in order to make that choice of action.

Clearly, some compromise is required.

The compromise, which appears to be possible, can be described as "guesswork". That is, if it foregoes the possibility of making accurate predictions, it can inform its predictions well enough, for practical purposes, by guessing the action that it is likely to take in particular circumstances.

However, it can do that only if it has comprehensive knowledge of its own behaviour in similar previous circumstances.

And that, I claim, is what consciousness is for. Consciousness is a procedure which enables a creature to explain itself to itself, so that it can know and understand itself well enough to anticipate its own reactions to predictable events.

To operate this consciousness mechanism, a creature must observe and analyse its own actions closely. It must attribute to itself various unexplained emotional internal conditions which cause it to take particular types of action. It must do that for two reasons -

(a) It cannot operate a self-simulation procedure inside itself because to do that would be to invite the computational problem called "infinite recursion".

(b) Furthermore, the reasons it has a tendency to take particular actions in response to particular circumstances, have their origins in the evolutionary history of its species. That means that its behaviour is instinctive. There is no way that it could ever re-enact that evolutionary history to discover the reasons for its instinctive behaviour. So it must accept its own reactions to events, as given facts. To anticipate those given facts it must, through observation, construct some arbitrary rules of behaviour.

When a creature makes these close observations of its own actions and apparent motivations, it will find itself operating in a very odd way. It will be, simultaneously -

(i) the thing being represented,

(ii) the thing doing the representation,

(iii) the thing which takes advantage of the information gained in this way, and

(iv) a thing representing itself as a thing representing itself.

My claim is that it is that convoluted multi-role mode of operation, which I believe, constitutes that mysterious phenomenon which we call "subjective experience" and which some people try to explain as a supernatural or metaphysical phenomenon.

Intuition

01.03

Many will find that my explanation of consciousness contradicts their intuition. My response to that is to point out that intuition is itself part of the same conscious brain procedure. It is not a disinterested third-party witness whose testimony can be accepted without question. Intuition has a particular task to perform. It is the explanation of events which consciousness provides. However, intuition would not be able to do that task adequately if it itself became entangled in that complicated multi-role self-observing process. It must therefore stand back and declare itself to be operating as an independent uninvolved observer. And when it acts in that way, it really cannot be telling the truth about itself.

01.04

Voltaire captured the essence of the imbroglio when he said,

"When I can do what I want, there is my liberty for me. But I do not know why I want it."

How did it get to be that way?

01.05

I think the mechanism of consciousness evolved from simple beginnings.

The brain is a device. In the beginning, it, or whatever it was that served the purpose of a brain before it became focused enough to be called a brain, was a mechanism which could detect what is going on in the external world - right now, that is, in the present. It could also tell itself what it should do in response to those external conditions - to run, to jump, to walk about, to hide, to reproduce. It did all that by responding unconsciously. These were actions the species (the species that the owner of the brain belonged to), had learned to do over aeons. It learned all that the hard way. That is, by trial and error. Mostly by error, followed very often by death. Those that did not die, lived on, became the standard model and became the progenitors of the next generation.

The internal world

01.06

In addition to being able to detect what was happening in the external world, a creature's brain could also detect what was going on inside the creature's own body. It could then instruct itself how to act in response to those internal conditions - how, what and when to eat, to drink, to rest, to sleep, to avoid certain conditions, and a lot more besides. That was all a brain was at the start of this story. For some creatures, that is what it has continued to be.

01.07

A brain was once a simple thing. The number of conditions the mechanism could detect was quite limited. So too was the range of actions it could instruct its owner to carry out.

For some species, over time (an enormous length of time), it evolved into something much more complicated. It could then detect a much larger number of conditions and it had a much larger range of possible responses. The things it learned to do were numerous and complicated - how to balance, how to grasp and pick things up, how to judge distance and relate that to the effort involved getting to places in the distance, how to reconcile the view seen by one eye with the one seen by another a few centimetres away. Robot engineers who are trying to reproduce these abilities are finding all that extremely difficult.

Memory

01.08

And then the brain, or some brains at least, evolved a bit further. It became able to remember the past. That helped its owner to survive a little better because the past starts now, and the conditions which happen now and which last for a few seconds or perhaps a few minutes in memory, will continue to exert an influence on what is happening, right now, and to determine what kind of response is needed, right now.

Prediction

01.09

The past has a tendency to repeat itself. The mechanism of the brain, by analysing what had happened in the past, was then able to predict what was likely to happen a short time into the future. That made survival a little easier and a little more likely. The brain could often see trouble coming before it arrived.

Concepts

01.10

Unfortunately, some objects, and some circumstances, on different occasions, present to us what appear to be different patterns of perceptions. For example, an animal can walk about, turn round or lie down. To deal with that, to be able to recognise things even when those changes occur, the brain had to develop more subtle capabilities.

Even if the whole pattern is seldom repeated exactly, there will be bits and pieces within that whole, which are repeated. The trick, therefore, is to be able to chop the whole of a perceived pattern into its constituent parts and to recognise each part individually. The complete pattern can then be recognised as a re-assembly of those parts. We have a name for those constituent parts. They are

16

called "concepts". The brain chops its perceptions of the world into chunks. Concepts are those chunks.

So the next big step in the evolution of a conscious brain is the ability to form these concepts.

But how do concepts ever get started?

01.11

Putting concepts together to re-assemble a recognisable entity or event, is rather like putting the pieces of a jigsaw puzzle together to construct a whole picture. And therein lies a snag. If you are trying to construct a jigsaw picture you will not find that easy if all you have is one piece. At some time, however, in this evolutionary story, there had to be a time when the brain was just beginning to form concepts and all it had was one single concept. So what was the immediate survival advantage that led evolution to keep going in that direction by forming more and more concepts?

Data compression

01.12

My answer is that there had to be some other process, which did provide a marginal survival advantage from the outset, and which created concepts as a side-effect.

The only candidate I could think of, which met those requirements, was data compression. Data compression could allow the brain to store more memories without overwhelming its storage capacity. The procedure identifies chunks of material which occur repeatedly within the memory store. It extracts those chunks, stores one copy elsewhere, and puts a small tag or bookmark into the vacant slot. So it forms chunks of memory material. But the advantage it gains is not associated with the chunks themselves. The advantage is associated with the holes in the memory store, which the chunks leave behind. That is the space that is saved.

Repeated compression

01.13

But simple chunks of repeated memory material do not correspond to concepts - yet. There has to be some additional processing before useful concepts are formed - that is, chunks which can be put together again. The process that I think can do that, is a repeated application of the data compression algorithm - to the original memory store, and to the collection of chunks already formed.

Evolution in steps

01.14

An aspect of evolution that is sometimes overlooked is that we do not need to suppose that a finished end product is formed immediately. The end result can grow and take advantage of what has already been achieved. Each step can take advantage of previous steps.

As chunks are identified and replaced by tags, the presence of those tags will make it easier to identify larger and more complicated chunks because the mechanism will not need to match up the detail of the different chunks which different tags represent.

An example may help. If, within a memory, there are two repeating bits of material - one representing "FIDO barking" and the other representing "ROVER barking" - and if both FIDO and ROVER have already been recognised, extracted and been replaced by tags, the mechanism can then ignore the difference between those two tags and identify a new repeating chunk of material consisting of what we might call "(some TAG) barking".

Memory reconstruction

01.15
There is little advantage to be gained by data compression if there is not also an associated mechanism of memory reconstruction. It must be possible for the extracted chunks to be restored to the locations in memory from which they were extracted and for broken links to be re-built. Doing that, as I remarked earlier, is like constructing a jigsaw picture. But note this, if each concept is formed from several separate incidents, each chunk formed in that way must contain information drawn from many separate occasions. So every concept could be described as a compendium of information relating to several different experiences. For example, a concept could contain information about how a single object could be recognised from several different points of view. So if memory is reconstructed from material like that, it follows that the reconstructed memory will contain much more detailed information than was contained in the original memory. We could say that the memory is augmented.

Momentary Consciousness

01.16
The next step that is required, is a small evolutionary accident so that the memory reconstruction process is targeted not at old stored memories, but at the on-going short-term memory. What the mechanism would be then be doing would be augmenting the system's current experience with additional information gained from previous experiences. We could say that it would then be "understanding" its current experience in a way that would allow it to anticipate future developments. I call that process an "interpretation" of events. It is also what we might call a "momentary" form of consciousness. The system "knows" what is happening and what to expect next. But that "knowledge" is thrown away almost as soon as it is formed.

Process and Consciousness

01.17

And that introduces a new idea which many people find difficult to comprehend. It is in fact, a crucial aspect of my explanation. The relationship between the doing of the interpretation process and the experience of consciousness, is not one of cause and effect. That is, the process does not "create" a conscious experience. Nor does it "generate" it, or "give rise" to it. Phrases of that kind imply a causal relationship. Which in turn implies that there is a way some kind of external intervention could break that causal relationship. That is not what I mean.

What I do mean is that the interpretation procedure and the experience of consciousness are one single phenomenon which we can look at in two different ways. We can take an inside view which reveals the internal mechanism and we can take an outside view which refers only to the observable external consequences of the mechanism.

There is a potential here for some confusion. An outside view is a reference to an internal mechanism. It is a way of talking about an internal mechanism. It is a description of the internal mechanism in terms of the observable consequences that the mechanism causes. There is, therefore, a supposed or implied causal connection between the internal mechanism and those observable external consequences. But there is no causal connection between the internal mechanism (as it is described by an explicit inside view - version 1) and the other version (version 2) of the internal mechanism as it is described by an outside view in terms of those observable external consequences. The two versions of the internal mechanism are the same thing.

To suppose otherwise is to make the hidden assumption that there are two different phenomena and that the second one (the experience of consciousness), is an indivisible entity which can only be felt by a human psyche and can never be analysed or explained.

This is a crucial issue and it is one on which my explanation hinges. I will return to it several times throughout this book.

Language and Intuition

01.18

The language we use to discuss these things is crucial. The meaning we attribute to the words and phrases we normally use are based on our intuitive understanding of the world. Intuition seems to be adequate in normal circumstances, but it becomes problematic when we are trying to look inwards at ourselves. It follows that we must be very careful about the words and phrases we use in these circumstances because they too are liable to force upon us a false impression of what is really going on.

Full consciousness

01.19

To be fully conscious in the way humans are, the mechanism needs to be able to remember the experience of consciousness. It needs to understand itself, and other creatures like itself, and be able to anticipate the behaviour these will exhibit. To do that it must have a concept of the thing which drives their behaviour - the concept of MIND and (for itself) of SELFMIND.

Once again the data compression algorithm will provide the means to do that. My suggestion is that the concept of MIND (for other creatures) will be formed by observation of body language signals - eye-pointing, hand gestures, tones of voice and the like. These, when processed to find what features they have in common, will produce various types or classifications of actions.

With respect to itself, the mechanism, unable to observe its own body-language signals with the same ease, will need to rely on internal indications of intention and use these to form the concept of SELFMIND and the behaviour it causes.

The phase-layer of language

01.20

That does not complete my description of the mechanism. There is an additional part, which is concerned with the use of language. But that is not essential for my explanation of consciousness so I will leave an exposition of that part until later.

Conclusion

01.21

My explanation of consciousness is a bit complicated. I admit that. To understand my idea at a gut-level you have to imagine yourself being a procedure, a procedure which is doing that convoluted multi-role performance. That is not easy. But I think it is a great deal more plausible than the several other ideas, which are knocking about, and which do not actually explain anything. These other ideas require one to accept unexplained inexplicable things as an explanation. How implausible is that?

Most of those who hold these alternative views, and write on the topic, devote a significant part of their texts trying to convince us that it is impossible to explain consciousness.

My explanation, in contrast, does not require us to suppose that there is any non-material ethereal entity floating about in the brain and where it can (in some unknown way) exchange information with the physical brain without actually being a part of it.

My explanation does not require us to suppose the existence of any hitherto unknown properties of quantum mechanics.

My explanation does not need to leap across an explanatory gap, or to solve an impossibly hard problem.

Lastly, and most certainly, my explanation does not make use of anything supernatural.

Fleshing out the details of that performance, and explaining how the brain might have got to be able to do these things, by evolution, and without divine intervention, is a story I will tell in this book.

Like every other component of our anatomy and physiology, the brain evolved. Evolution leaves its stamp on what it produces. The evolutionary part of my story is important because it draws attention to the fact that we when we are talking about the brain, we are not talking about a single finished product, which has a single way of working. We are talking about a composite thing made up of bits and pieces, each of which is the product of a particular phase of its evolutionary story, and in the particular circumstances which prevailed at various times past. Within this composite mechanism, all those components still operate as they once did and, in a sense, they fight each other for supremacy.

Inside and Outside Views

01.22

Some readers will find all this hard to accept because their intuition will be telling them that my explanation must be wrong. I say to them - when your brain is doing the consciousness procedure thing, it is also doing that intuition thing.

Intuition is just a collection of guesses that the brain makes about itself. That intuition procedure informs itself (i.e. it tells you) that you are in two parts - a physical mechanism part and something else which is much more mysterious, that cannot quite be explained. It tells you that the mind has an ethereal non-physical part that floats about alongside your physical brain exchanging information with the physical part, and has all kinds of emotional urgings, without actually being a part of your physical brain. Your intuition has to tell you that because, if it did not, if it tried to include the ethereal part within the physical mechanism, it would not be able to do its job properly. It would run straight into that computational impasse called "infinite recursion" and into the inaccessible explanations of behaviour which are lost in the vastness of evolution.

So relax. Your intuition may be telling you a story that is wrong and even totally misleading, but it is not inferior to anyone else's intuition. It is, in fact, doing the same thing as everyone else's intuition. It's just doing, as I shall explain in this book, what all intuitions must do - including mine.

FIG 01.22 INSIDE and OUTSIDE views of a procedure

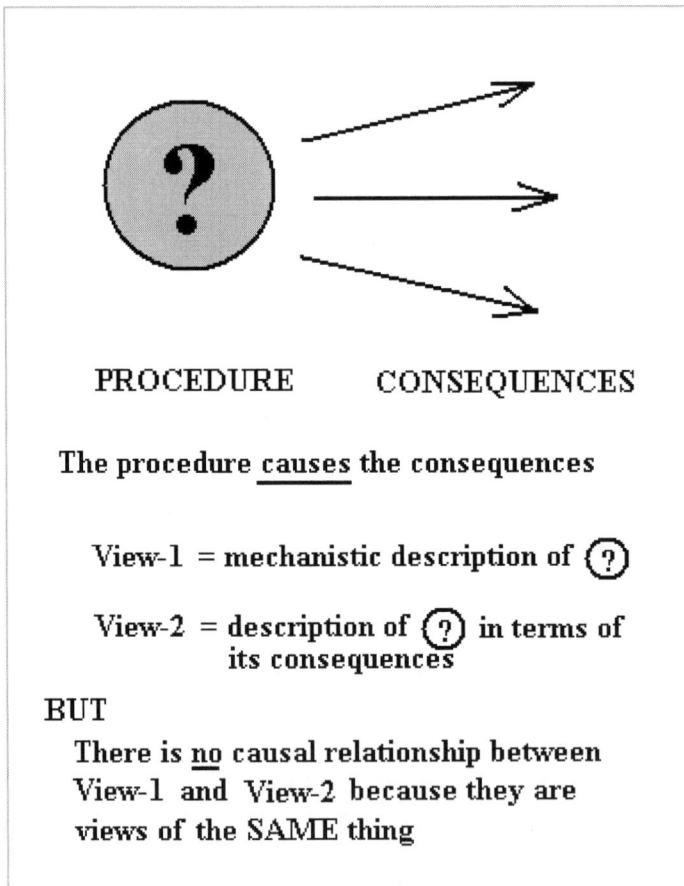

PROCEDURE   CONSEQUENCES

The procedure <u>causes</u> the consequences

View-1 = mechanistic description of (?)

View-2 = description of (?) in terms of
            its consequences

BUT

There is <u>no</u> causal relationship between
View-1 and View-2 because they are
views of the SAME thing

CHAPTER 2

A brief description of the structure of the system and an outline of how it got to be that way.

Evolution

02.01

Normally, evolution is an extremely slow process. It is also a process that is profligate with the resources at its disposal. It creates zillions of trial specimens, and it slaughters the vast majority of them.

Over the generations species usually become better at living than they were previously, within the particular environment where they live. But there is no fixed standard that defines what mutations are "good" and which are "bad". Goodness and badness are environment dependent. As a result, and since the environment varies a lot, the evolution of a species is pushed and pulled about in many different directions. Very often a species may become extinct. Over the years most species have become extinct.

Those who reject evolution usually do not appreciate just how slow the process is and how lacking it is in any kind of pre-ordained direction. It is not heading towards any particular end-point. It goes in whichever direction is available to it for survival, and that means that it goes in a great many different directions at the same time. But because the environment tends to offer various types of living space, these spaces tend to be filled by organisms which evolve/solve the problems of staying alive in ways that are similar. In Britain a badger grubs about in the dark, on the forest floor, looking for worms. In New Zealand a Kiwi, a flightless bird, which must once have been capable of flight, grubs about in the dark, on the forest floor, looking for worms. It's a successful lifestyle.

To call evolution a "random" process, does not quite capture the essence of it. It is random only in respect of the DNA changes.

But that randomness is mediated by the partly non-random mechanism of survival.

One particular life-style, which fits quite a lot of different situations, particularly situations which change rapidly - too rapidly, that is, to give time for evolution to evolve an anatomical solution to new problems, is not to be stronger, not to have longer legs, not to have longer necks than other creatures, or not to have better eye-sight, it is just to be smarter than other creatures - more able than others to predict what is going to happen next. It's that life-style and the evolutionary path to it - to a conscious understanding of a changing world - that I want to explore in this book.

Pseudo-evolution.

02.02

Pseudo-evolution is an artificial process, which mimics the most important characteristics of a real evolutionary process while avoiding the huge expenditure in resources, the enormous lengths of time required and its lack of predictable direction of progress. For pseudo-evolution we can legitimately speak of "improvements" and "progress" because there is a pre-defined and intended end-point. It is an end-point chosen by ourselves and chosen deliberately to coincide with the point (accidentally) reached by one particular pathway (in this case our own) as it was followed by real evolution (so far as we are able to tell).

The crucial feature of real evolution which pseudo-evolution must adopt, is that developments must occur in small steps and each step must be accompanied by some identifiable survival advantage. Evolution can tolerate neutral steps, which confer no particular advantage so long as these are not associated with some significant disadvantage. But it cannot do that for long and it cannot accumulate several unhelpful modifications, none of which have any associated advantage and then find later (and miraculously) that those different modifications can be combined to form some new and dramatic improvement. That doesn't happen. In the meantime, all these new modifications would need to be fed and carried about. They need to pay their way. Eventually the extra complexity, which non-useful modifications would bring, become a burden and hence a disadvantage.

Note: Evolution is not quite that simple. During times of plentiful food and low numbers of predators, the diversification of species can take place more readily because mutations which have no particular advantage can survive more easily than they can during more normal times when there is a fierce competition for survival. But the simplified version will serve us well enough.

Even with the blind ends and alternative pathways eliminated, the pseudo-evolutionary pathway we need to follow is still quite complicated. For a long part of the journey it doesn't look as if we are heading in any particular direction. But that is only an appearance. Every component of the system I will describe has an immediate advantage to justify its inclusion, and a role to play in the configuration of the intended end-point - a mechanism that performs conscious understanding.

Evolution and the problem of complexity.

02.03

Complexity is not a problem for evolution. It can produce structures and mechanisms of almost unlimited complexity, provided -

(1) There is a structure or mechanism, which is already very complex, which already exists, and from which a new and slightly more complex configuration can evolve in one small step.

(2) That small step provides the evolving system with some marginal survival advantage over its contemporaries. It does not need to be a great advantage - just one that gives it an edge over its rivals. That way the changed system can (probably) get a little bit more food than its rivals or gets the pick of the best mates.

Evolution plays a very important part in the story I have to tell about consciousness. The brain would not be the way it is if it had not been produced by evolution.

A hypothetical brain mechanism in Five Phase-layers

The mechanism which I will describe has five phase-layers. These phase-layers do not correspond to any actual physical structures within a real biological brain. I am uses the term "phase-layer" to avoid confusion with the structure layers present in the brain and the term "layer" as it used in neuroscience. My phase-layers are intended only to make the presentation of the system a little easier. The phase-layers evolve one at a time and each brings with it some particular function (and some particular survival advantage).

Phase-layer-1 comes first and for a while (a very long while) it had to survive on its own without the assistance of the others. For that reason it had to be self-sufficient. The evolution of any given phase-layer does not stop when other higher phase-layers put in an appearance. Changes, which previously would not have brought any particular advantage, might well do so when those higher phase-layers are operating.

It is also the case that the structural features, which evolve within phase-layer-1, will be features, which the other phase-layers will find useful.

A further and very important point - The prior existence of phase-layer-1 is the context into which the other phase-layers emerge. Those other phase-layers are not in direct contact with the environment. They are in contact with phase-layer-1. So, for them, phase-layer-1 is the environment within which they must survive.

Phase-layer-2, which comes next, is able to take advantage of features in phase-layer-1 - and perhaps put them to new uses. That is the way the whole system develops. Each additional phase-layer is able to access the structures and features, which already exist in the phase-layers below it.

Phase-layer-1 handles all the input and output with the external environment. If any higher phase-layer, having analysed the data available to it, determines some advisable course of action, it cannot put that action into effect without the assistance of the phase-layers below it. The upper phase-layers are not in control of the whole system. They can make only recommendations for action. As a result, there will always be contention between the actions preferred by those upper phase-layers and the actions which phase-layer-1 has been pre-programmed to take by its enormously long period of evolution.

Fig 02.04 - The five phase-layers

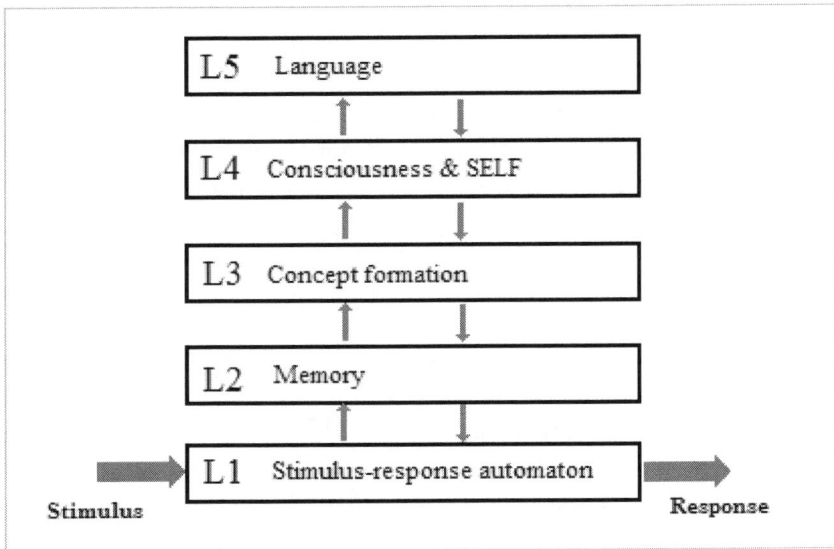

```
┌──────────────────────────────────────────────────────┐
│        ┌──────────────────────────────────────┐       │
│        │  L5    Language                       │       │
│        └──────────────────────────────────────┘       │
│               ↑        ↓                               │
│        ┌──────────────────────────────────────┐       │
│        │  L4    Consciousness & SELF           │       │
│        └──────────────────────────────────────┘       │
│               ↑        ↓                               │
│        ┌──────────────────────────────────────┐       │
│        │  L3    Concept formation              │       │
│        └──────────────────────────────────────┘       │
│               ↑        ↓                               │
│        ┌──────────────────────────────────────┐       │
│        │  L2    Memory                         │       │
│        └──────────────────────────────────────┘       │
│               ↑        ↓                               │
│  ⇒     ┌──────────────────────────────────────┐  ⇒   │
│        │  L1    Stimulus-response automaton    │       │
│        └──────────────────────────────────────┘       │
│  Stimulus                              Response        │
└──────────────────────────────────────────────────────┘
```

My hypothetical model of the brain is not like a well designed machine. It is more like a rather haphazard factory which has been in operation for a long time. The workers on the shop-floor operate in the way they have done since the company was founded. Above them are some new recently acquired departments, which have different roles to play. People from those upper departments, sometimes wander down to the shop-floor, pick up some information there, go back to their own desks and a bit later they come back to the shop-floor and say -

"We recommend that you don't do that. We think you should try this new way instead."

But note this. Those new recommended ways cannot do other than use the same tools and the same techniques that the shop-floor workers have always used. Those recommendations, moreover, are

29

sometimes ignored. The diagram illustrates the five phase-layers and the main contribution which each makes to the system as a whole.

The phase-layers one-by-one

Phase-layer-1

02.05

Phase-layer-1 gets information from the environment (which includes the conditions within its own body or frame). It reads all input signals and controls all actions - like the muscular movements of limbs.

Phase-layer-2

02.06

Phase-layer-2 provides two memory systems. The first is an ephemeral record of the succession of conditions of phase-layer-1. Note that – not conditions within the observed environment, the conditions of phase-layer-1. The second memory consists of selected entries from within the ephemeral memory.

Phase-layer-3

02.07

Phase-layer-3 deals with the memory systems in phase-layer-2. It reduces the space needed for these memory stores by removing from them chunks of material which are repetitive and then stores these repeating chunks elsewhere. To recover memories when required, it is able to slot these chunks back into their original locations. Note that – it is these chunks which will evolve into concepts.

Since the chunks have been derived from several previous occasions when similar events have occurred, each is, in effect, a compendium of previous experience. It requires only a minor modification to the system for these chunks then to be used to augment the ephemeral memory and provide a running commentary on events (which will include predictions about future events). Note that too – it is that process of memory reconstruction which will evolve to become the mechanism which the brain uses to construct a mental representation of events. A brain which is able to do that, is able to deal with its environment a little better than before.

Phase-layer-4

The advent of MIND

02.08

Phase-layer-4 carries this process of chunk formation a stage further. It enlarges the compression chunks with additional material extracted from the longer-lasting memory to produce its store of "concepts". Further compression of the chunks already formed, produces more general versions of individual exemplars to form (i) group concepts (generalised physical entities), (ii) causal connections (generalised pairs of conditions where the first to occur is a reliable predictor of the second) and (iii) abstract concepts (generalised events – each of which is a sequence of momentary conditions).

A significant aspect of this is the generalisation of observations of animate behaviour (eye movements, facial expressions and other forms of body language). These, when generalised, become a concept corresponding to the causal precursor of behaviour. This concept can be called a "MIND". So this chunk forming compression process creates a concept which can be used to predict future behaviour. The concept MIND therefore does not correspond to anything observed. It is a mental abstraction formed from things observed.

SELFMIND

02.09

In addition to this MIND concept, there will be another, which I will call the SELFMIND. A person cannot observe his or her own body-language with quite the same ease as he or she can be witness to the body-language of others. The formation of this SELFMIND must therefore be focused on other observable aspects of the environment. These predictors of SELF behaviour will be provided by sensory signals from internal organs. This SELFMIND concept becomes, for the brain, a representation of SELF and a repository for the memory of the on-going interpretation of events. This means that this SELF can acquire a history of its own experience and behaviour. This kind of information is an essential part of self-knowledge. A brain that can do all that, understands itself better than before. It can make more accurate guesses about what it is likely to do.

With the introduction of a SELFMIND concept the system has all the ingredients needed to be fully conscious.

Phase-layer-5

02.10

Phase-layer-5 introduces a mechanism for the use of language. By introducing language *after* the advent of concepts (and consciousness) I have reversed the conventional order of things.

Many philosophers and linguists have argued that language is an essential precursor to the development of concepts. I agree with that. But I also point out that that is true only in the case of *some* concepts, particularly *abstract* concepts. I think that language is essential for that, to ensure that our abstract concepts correspond to those of other people. That is important, because language is primarily about communication and there can be no convenient communication unless our concepts correspond to a considerable extent.

However, if we insist that language must be present first, we are in effect saying that other species, which are unable to use language in the same way we do, cannot be conscious.

I find that implausible. In recent years, animal psychologists have demonstrated that various non-human species have many of the abilities we associate with consciousness - empathy for others, a sense of right and wrong. It has also been shown that, in the right context, and with the provision of a suitable means of communication, many non-human species do have the ability to use language in a simple way. This suggests that they do, in fact, possess whatever are the essential precursors of that language ability. I claim that the essential precursor for language is the ability to form and utilise concepts.

I will develop these arguments later.

The rest of this book

02.11

In the chapters, which follow, I will describe each of these phase-layers in more detail. For each phase-layer I shall describe a hypothetical pseudo-evolutionary pathway in order to show that such a pathway exists. My suggested pathway is not necessarily the pathway that human evolution did in fact follow. But by showing that a possible pathway exists I hope to pre-empt any claims that evolution of the brain's ability to be conscious, is impossible.

My description will begin at a very simple level and grow steadily more complex. At several points I will pause and consider awkward details that appear to present the system with a problem which is difficult to solve.

How, for example, could the system develop a clock mechanism? When a system is at an early stage of its development, and has no intellectual abilities at all, how would it deal with the situation created if two different perceptions of the external world present themselves and demand different and quite contradictory responses, at the same time. How could the system decide which response should take precedence?

In each case, having considered how the system could survive in these difficult circumstances, we will see that there is in fact a mechanism which could solve the problem and which could have evolved from some pre-existing facility. At a later stage of the system's evolution, we will often find that these additional features are exactly what the system needs to enable it do some other, more complex thing.

Lucky? A miracle perhaps? I do not think so. The explanation for those apparently lucky twists and turns is simply this. If those facilities had not already existed, the system, as a whole, would not have evolved in the way it did. Some other characteristic would have emerged based on some other ability that did exist.

Water finds its own route downhill. It is not a miracle that at every juncture, there is some new direction in which it can go next. For every one of those new directions and new places to go, there must always be some place where it has already been, which is very close to where it will go next, and exactly where it needs to be to get there. That would be magical only if the next place was an *intended* destination. If you start off thinking that the destination is *intended*, getting there will always seem to be miraculous.

CHAPTER 3

Phase-layer-1

Laying the foundations of conscious. This chapter contains a good deal of technical detail concerning phase-layer-1 and could be skipped at a first reading.

The beginning

03.01

... Well ... perhaps not quite the beginning. No one knows exactly how life actually began, but the nature of that beginning is no longer a mystery. The basic ingredients are known - a molecule of DNA, or more probably of RNA which can more readily reproduce itself, a ribosome to do the production of proteins, some means to provide energy, and some means, like a cell membrane, to hold them all together and in the right locations relative to each other.

All the ingredients required have actually been constructed artificially and they have also been put together in a test-tube. The result is a form of life that has never previously existed [Venter 2012].

What is not known is how, in the history of the universe, these ingredients were constructed, brought together in the right order and brought into the right environment so that they could start operating together. But there is no shortage of plausible ideas about how all that happened.

The Pseudo-Euglena

03.02

Our starting point will be close to that beginning. Euglena is a small speck of pond life - a single-celled flagellate. It has a flagellum which is a long whip-like process which it twirls like a propeller to drive itself through the water. A real euglena is rather more complicated than I can deal with easily, so I shall invent a substitute - a pseudo-euglena.

The light sensitive spot reacts to incident sunlight. If the light is too strong the flagellum twirls and the organism sinks down in the water to where the light is less strong. If the light is not strong enough, the flagellum twirls and the organism rises to where the light is stronger. As a result the organism tends to stay where the oxygen levels are high, where the food is abundant and the sunlight, like Goldilock's porridge, is just right.

FIG 03.02 (1) Euglena

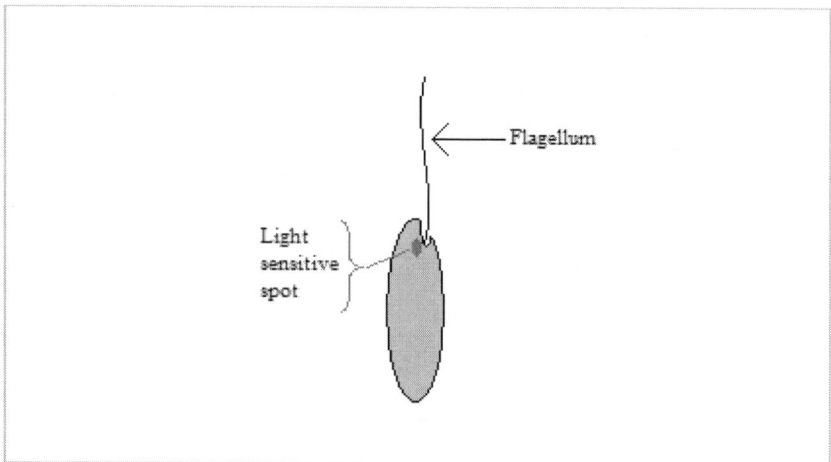

Any competent gadget enthusiast could knock up a mechanical pseudo-euglena to match that specification. All that is needed is a suitably buoyed plastic box, a small electric motor, a bi-directional propeller, a battery, a light sensitive diode and a trivial bit of electronics. We can take the physical hardware, (propeller etc.) for granted. For the purposes of this discussion we are interested only in the electronic control system.

What is needed at this simple level of mimicry, are three types of unit plus the signals that pass between them.

(1) The sensor unit can be simulated with a light sensitive diode.

(2) The detection unit is like a small computer. It has its own way of reading input signals and its own stored program which tells it how to analyse these signals. It also has some kind of switch mechanism which, when it is able to recognise or detect its pre-defined pattern of input signals, will switch on an output signal.

(3) The action unit. can be simulated by a servo-motor which responds to an input signal and will then rotate in which ever direction will reduce that input signal to zero.

Fig 03.02 (2) - basic units

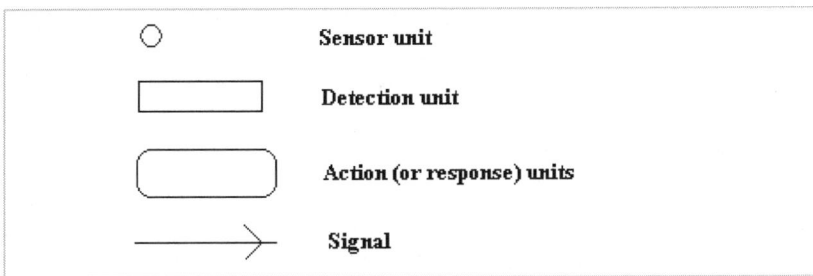

○	**Sensor unit**
▭	**Detection unit**
⬭	**Action (or response) units**
⟶	**Signal**

03.03

With these units we can simulate the control system of our pseudo-euglena in this way -

Fig 03.03 - pseudo-euglena

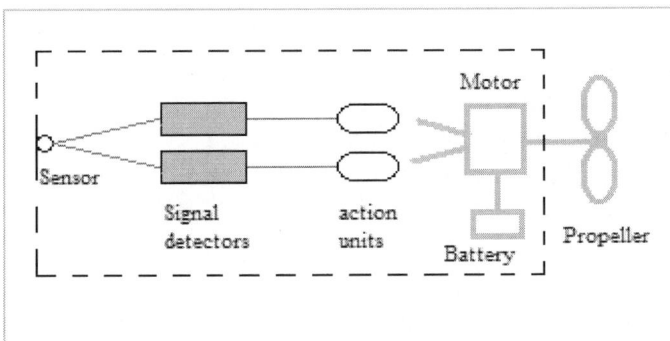

Note: I could, at this point, have raised the topic of perceptrons and various kinds of neural networks which have been developed and which bear some resemblance to the structure I envisage. But I have no wish to get embroiled in a detailed discussion of that, with all the attendant problems of the need for backward propagation etc. The idea that each detection unit has the power of a small computer cuts out a digression of that kind. We know that such devices can be constructed.

The evolution of phase-layer-1.

03.04

That is our starting point. We know that an organism like that can survive provided it can do a few more things like reproducing itself, absorbing nutrition and oxygen, expelling waste material and controlling the passage of water through its outer membrane.

So the next thing we must consider is how it can evolve in small steps and with each step bringing its own immediate advantage. The qualification "immediate" is important. Evolution carries no baggage labelled "Not wanted on the voyage".

03.05

A first step is to increase the number of the units. A single sensor unit can become a great many sensor units. The system will then have arrays of sensor units. And these arrays can develop in different locations.

Consider the evolution of an eye structure. All it needs is the development of an array at the bottom of a small socket or pit in the surface (gaining some directionality). The pit can then be covered by a transparent skin (to exclude dust). And that can develop into a lens (to focus an image on the retina). One step at a time. Each step with its own advantage leading up to a major composite advantage. Richard Dawkins has given us a much more detailed description of how an eye structure could evolve in gradual steps [Dawkins 1986].

03.06

Sensor units can also diversify and become sensitive to different aspects of the environment. Some will be sensitive to touch, to chemicals (taste and smell), to vibrations in the air (hearing), and so on. Some will be sensitive to, say, the concentration of glucose in the blood (or some similar analogue in a mechanical device, like battery strength). Some will become sensitive to the position of limb-joints, or to gravity (the balance mechanism in the ear).

Functional equivalence

03.07

The key to understanding the evolution of the phase-layer-1 system is the detection unit. This unit does not coincide with any single structural unit of a real biological brain. If it has any counterpart at all, it corresponds to a whole group of neurones intimately interconnected by synapses, and which, as a group, carry out some identifiable task.

Note: In biological brains, it is the synapses, which can be modified by past history and external influences, like the infusion of transmitter substances. So the synapses are what we might call the main active component in this mechanism. It might be more appropriate, therefore, to describe a unit of this kind as a group of synapses intimately interconnected by neurones and their axons and dendrites.

The diagram illustrates the idea. Here we see a unit of the kind described (a collection of brain stuff). This unit receives signals from the left and delivers at least one output signal to the right. Generating that output signal (or signals) upon receipt of some specified pattern of input signals, is the collective function of the unit.

Below that, in the same diagram, we see a single artificial detector unit which does exactly the same thing. The internal operations of the two types of unit may be completely different but the external behaviour is identical. The brain-stuff unit is "programmed" by having its components connected in a particular and very complex way.

The artificial equivalent is able to do the same thing because it has an internal program (i.e. a computer program) which tells it how to process the signals. It inputs equivalent signals and it outputs an equivalent signal under exactly the same conditions and circumstances. The two structures, the group of biological cells and gaps, and the artificial detector unit, can then be described as being "functionally equivalent".

Fig 03.07 functional equivalence

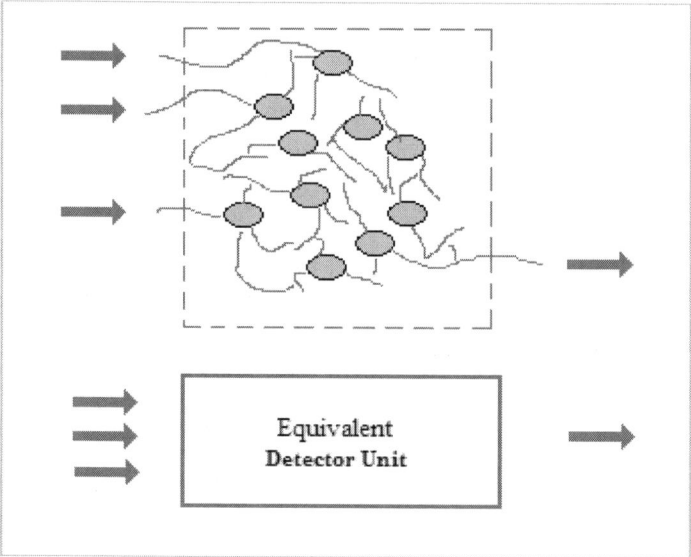

Line detection

03.08

Detection units can multiply and diversify. An important development would be the ability to combine with each other to detect more complex patterns of signals. Once the system has developed some kind of eye structure it will have multiple signals to be analysed. Instead of a sea of dots, these can now be treated as clusters of dots. Each cluster can be analysed by a single detector unit and then several clusters can be analysed as a cluster of clusters. In this way a set of interconnected detection units can detect quite complicated patterns of signals.

The diagram shows an array of sensor units on which has been projected the pattern of a white line surrounded by a dark background. The next picture shows how a set of interconnected detection units could detect the presence of that white line.

Fig 03.08(1) - Line detection

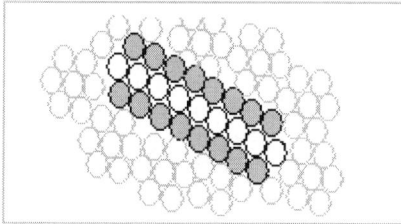

Fig 03.08(2) Detecting a line

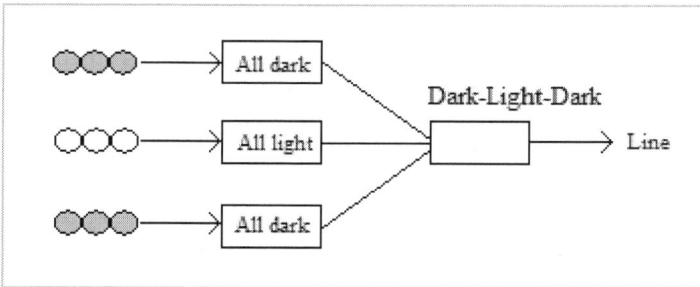

Action units

03.09

Action units can also multiply and diversify to provide a more complex set of responses with which the system can react to that increasing range of recognisable patterns within the environment.

The detection units are connected to the action units and can therefore trigger automatic responses whenever a particular pattern is detected.

Phase-layer-1 fully developed

03.10

Fig 03.10 Phase-layer-1

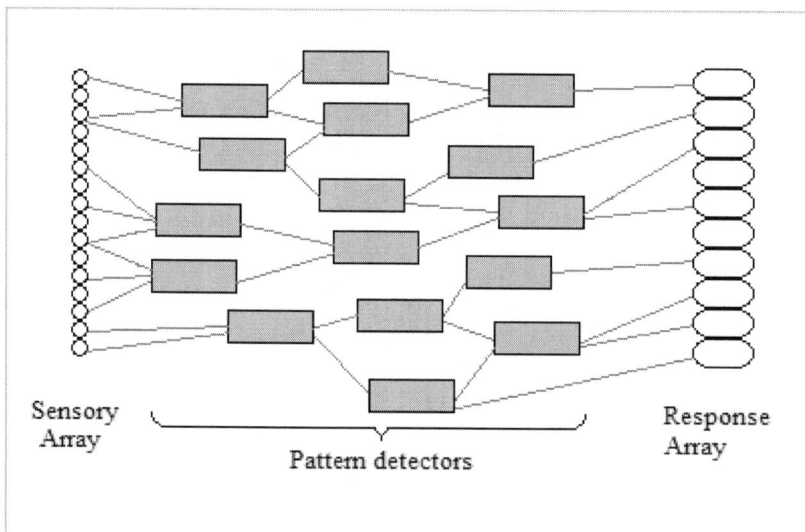

Sensory Array

Pattern detectors

Response Array

The result of these evolutionary developments, is a phase-layer-1 system with a great many more detection units. The diagram shows only one array of sensors and one array of action units with a scattered number of detection units between those two arrays. The true numbers involved are enormous. We should think in terms of billions of units.

The arrangement shown, and the one hinted at, has a superficial similarity to biological structures known to neuroscience - what Riensenhuber and Poggio have called the "standard model" of part of the mammalian brain [Reisenhuber and Poggio 2003]. The sensor units, detection units and action units, are not intended to have any direct physical resemblance to real brain components. These are notional units intended only to allow an exploration of the functional capabilities required to achieve the main objective. A pseudo-creature like that could seek the light, or seek darkness, seek food and seek to reproduce. Few people, however, would say that such a system, or the equivalent biological creature, was conscious. I certainly would not.

Subsumption architecture

03.11

Within the structure of phase-layer-1 there are various sub-systems each of which takes a form which can be represented in this way -

Stimulus ----> (detection) ----> Response

These individual sub-systems operate in an opportunistic way. In effect, each constantly scans the signals being received, for a particular pattern (its own individual pattern). When that pattern is detected the sub-system triggers its own individual response without regard to what other parts of the system may be trying to do at that moment. In computer science this arrangement is known as "subsumption architecture". It has certain advantages over a mechanism which has centralised control.

In the biological world we can see examples of the same principle at work in the behaviour of a flock of starlings or a shoal of fish. The behaviour of the flock may appear to be under some kind of centralised control but it is actually driven by each individual component of the flock or shoal obeying its own internal rules of behaviour.

The same principle applies to the various phase-layers within this system as a whole. Each phase-layer operates in the same opportunistic way as it contributes to the performance of the whole system.

It is difficult to see how any form of centralised control could evolve gradually. It is yet another of those chicken-and-egg problems. Without a mechanism to be controlled, a control system could not evolve gradually. However, without a centralised control system to organise it, a closely integrated mechanism could not evolve. It is also difficult to see how marginal survival advantages could be associated with parallel, step-by-step evolution of both. That would require a long sequence of lucky coincidences.

Subsumption architecture solves that awkward problem. Initially the sub-systems evolve independently of one another. Later, once a number of sub-systems are already operating, new systems can appear which take opportunistic advantage of particular conditions that those existing sub-systems occasionally produce. The complete system grows in the way that a number of isolated villages can evolve into a city. In the early stages, the villages develop alone. They are self-sufficient. To get a complete city, a traffic control system, or a town plan, is not required. For a long time after the city is formed the villages continue to operate in a semi-stand-alone mode as isolated communities each with its own commercial centre, its own tradesmen and its own focal point of community life.

The principle of subsumption architecture was brought to public attention by Rodney Brooks and his co-workers in the 1990s [Brooks 1990]. They constructed a number of robotic devices which demonstrated how effective that architecture could be. One of the devices they built had six legs. Each leg was controlled by its own subsystem. It could walk forwards or backwards. The device had a camera eye which could detect walls and similar obstructions. When there was no obstruction the device walked forwards. If there was an obstruction it went into reverse, turned to one side, and tried again. The camera eye could also recognise cylindrical objects. The device also had a grab-hand. When the robot device was released it behaved like a larcenous insect. It wandered around the laboratory and stole soda-cans off the research worker's desks.

Brooks published several papers on the topic but one, called "Elephants don't play chess" was given that title as a sarcastic response to anticipated objections posed by sceptical academics. Invariably he was asked at departmental seminars - *"But can it play chess?"* Within the field of artificial intelligence, chess had achieved almost mythical status as a key indicator of high intelligence. Brooks was reminding them that there are many indisputably intelligent organisms, which do not have that ability. If we could construct a robotic system which had the intelligence of an elephant, we would be doing extremely well.

Subsumption architecture makes evolution easier. Any change made to a tightly integrated system would usually result in the system failing to operate - not just failing to operate correctly, but failing to operate at all. Mutations which failed to be associated with an identifiable survival advantage would therefore be eliminated, immediately. And that would eliminate a lot of useful components. For a system with subsumption architecture, however, a new sub-system can be introduced, and even if it brings with it no identifiable advantage, the existing sub-systems will still operate. The burden of an extra sub-system, which contributes little to an improved performance, or does so only very occasionally, will eventually tell against the system's survival. But it can carry on for a while and perhaps give rise to other mutations which are more successful. Subsumption architecture provides an evolving system with some degree of robustness.

More features

03.12

Phase-layer-1 introduces a number of additional features. Each of these will be associated with an immediate identifiable survival advantage. We will find, however, that as the system develops further, and more phase-layers are added, that these extra features are essential to the functions carried out by those extra phase-layers.

A Clock

03.13

Any complex system, which contains circuitry featuring delayed negative feedback, is prone to go into sustained oscillations. Control system engineers often find difficulty in preventing unwanted oscillations. The most obvious example of that is the ear-piercing whine of a public address system which occurs if the microphone picks up the sound from the loud-speakers after a very short time-delay.

Any regular train of pulses can be interpreted and used, as the ticking of a clock. It is not difficult therefore to imagine how the phase-layer-1 system could develop a clock mechanism.

The phase-layer-1 clock segments time into very short intervals (measured in milliseconds). All signals which arrive at a single detection unit within a single time interval (or a single clock-tick) are treated as being simultaneous. So the whole system is forced into lock-step and henceforth we can identify separate time intervals using the symbolism

$$T1 < T2 < T3 < \ldots$$

This, by standardising a common time-frame for the disparate sub-systems, can be regarded as a belated form of centralised control - like insisting on all the village clocks being synchronised.

It is also possible to envisage a set of detection units that are triggered by those clock-ticks in such a way that the units are stimulated cyclically, rather like the read-out on a digital clock, to provide a sequence of unique patterns. If these patterns were incorporated into the general condition of phase-layer-1, the result would be that each phase-layer-1 condition would carry its own unique digital time-stamp.

Priority levels

03.14

What would happen if two separate patterns of signals arrived at two separate detection units, and if these two signal patterns stimulated two separate and contradictory responses? An obvious example of such an event would be the simultaneous appearance of a tasty morsel of food and a predator. To eat or to flee? Which should take precedence?

The way evolution solves this problem is, in effect, to allow one half of the population to choose eating and the other half to choose fleeing. The half which survives more often than the other will produce most of the next generation. As a result, the surviving population will have an instinctive pre-disposition to make a successful choice. We could say that they have got their priorities sort out.

We can simulate that for our evolving pseudo-organism by assigning priority levels to every sub-system. When there is a clash, the one with the highest priority level takes precedence. Getting it right for a vast number of units without allowing evolution to sort it out for us, and then waiting for an extremely long time, would be a challenge.

A further embellishment might allow the strength of signals to vary the priority levels of the responses they trigger. If starvation looms and the predator is a long way away, why not try to snatch a quick snack?

Instantaneous memory

03.15

The detection of change or of movement is very important for survival.

To be able to do that, the SRA (or Stimulus-Response Automaton) needs to be able to store the condition of a detector unit for a minimum of one clock-tick. It is then able to detect a new condition of that detection unit in the next clock-tick moment. In the diagram, the original input goes to unit-1. At the next clock-tick unit-1 transfers its own condition to unit-2 and then reads the next input.

Fig 03.15 detecting change

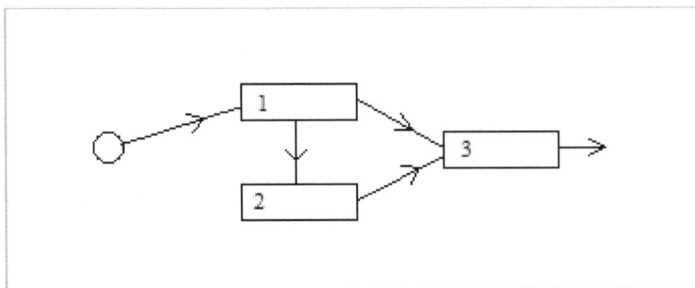

Unit-3 detects a difference between unit-1 and unit-2. Unit-2 constitutes a primitive form of memory, which we can call "instantaneous memory". To detect movement the system needs to be able to detect the disappearance of a signal from one sensor unit and the appearance of another at an adjacent sensor unit.

Goals and Anti-goals

03.16
Within phase-layer-1 a subsystem could (and probably would) evolve which is able to store the identity of the action unit which is currently active and is therefore able, at the next tick of the clock, to repeat that action when a new particular condition is identified. That means that there will be certain conditions which the system tends to repeat, or to seek. This condition will be termed a "*goal*" condition. The converse, an "*anti-goal*" condition, will trigger some erratic action, a jump or twitch for example, or a sudden freezing of activity, which may alter conditions. These forms of behaviour will again be arbitrary, but again natural selection will favour those, which have a tendency to give a survival advantage.

Motivation (Cause and effect)

03.17

I think that some readers may have difficulty accepting my explanation of goal and ant-goal conditions within this phase-layer-1 stimulus-response automaton, because it appears to reverse the normal order of causation. Normally we would say that a system tries to repeat a goal condition *because* that condition is a GOAL condition. Symbolically we might write -

GOAL => repeat(ACTION)   (where => means "causes")

What I have done in this book, however, is to declare that when an action is repeated, the condition it produces is called a "GOAL", and for that reason. So we can write -

Repeated (ACTION) => naming(GOAL)

In other words, the terms we use for our own behaviour (and eventually the concepts we form about them) are dictated by instinctive behaviour, not the other way round. Many readers will find that strange and counter-intuitive. The issue is crucial, however, for an understanding of my explanation of consciousness. Without that reversal of perceived causal connection there never can be a satisfactory explanation of what our needs, desires and other motivations really are, and where they come from. If we insist on a GOAL state being the causal precursor of action, we set ourselves an impossible task - explaining what a GOAL state is and what causes it.

That argument, about the causal ordering of goals, anti-goals and the actions that result, may sound a bit like the James-Lange Theory. These two philosophers individually proposed the idea that the emotions we feel are caused by the actions we take, rather than some internal condition of the brain, which precedes those actions. Please note that I am not saying that we feel emotions as a result of the actions after these have been taken. What I am saying is that the emotions we feel *are the same thing as* the *conscious anticipation* of those actions. The point is, we can anticipate that we are going to be compelled to take those actions (unless we do something consciously to prevent that), but we do *not* know why that is the case. The reason, of course, is not held locally within the brain itself. It arises as a result of innumerable incidents that occurred in the evolutionary history of our current species. There is no way that the brain (whether conscious or unconscious) can be directly and/or intuitively aware of that evolutionary history.

The limitations of phase-layer-1

03.18

Human civilisation has lasted only about 10 thousand years - a very short period of time in terms of evolution. According to my proposed mechanism, the structure of phase-layer-1 was laid down during the long period before the dawn of civilisation. Evolution has not had sufficient time to develop any kind of automatic response to the artefacts created by humans during that short period of civilisation. The mechanism of phase-layer-1 is totally dependent upon the slow process of evolution to develop the ability to recognise and respond appropriately to various ancient features of the environment. For example, to the shapes of creatures of various kinds, and sounds - like animal cries, falling water, wind, thunder storms, the breaking of twigs and scents - particularly scents. But phase-layer-1 cannot evolve quickly enough to deal with artefacts of modern life, the features of our social conditions - like crockery, new weapons, printed alphabetic characters, buildings, motor cars and the like. To develop the ability to recognise and respond appropriately to things of that kind, requires an extra kind of mechanism which will be provided by higher phase-layers in the system. It requires the ability to learn from experience.

The ability to learn from experience depends upon the ability to recognise sub-features which have existed within the primitive world context. If this had not been the case the acquisition of those higher skills would have been impossible.

Note: Alphabetic characters are a special case. They have been invented by ourselves, and they have been designed so that they can be recognised. It is no accident therefore that we happen to have the feature recognition abilities which make that possible.

The disadvantage of having no memory

03.19

When phase-layer-1 identifies some pattern of signals in the environment which are associated with a particular kind of response, it can take that response immediately and will continue to do so for as long as that pattern remains. But if the pattern which triggers the response disappears, the response must stop. That is not always a good thing to do (for survival) if an approaching predator takes cover temporarily.

For the same reason phase-layer-1 cannot develop complicated forms of response, and cannot learn from experience. It is compelled to use a standardised form of response. It cannot vary the response associated with a given trigger stimulus. It must instead wait on the slow and cumbersome trial-and-error mechanism of genetic mutation which can occur only at intervals, driven by the cycle of the generations.

Recognition of signal patterns

03.20

As a stimulus-response automaton the mechanism of phase-layer-1 has no need to understand the signal patterns which it is able to recognise. All it needs to do is to connect each occurrence of one of those recognised patterns with an appropriate response.

The things, that is, the features that it is able to identify, are "*understood*" (note the cautionary quotation marks) only in terms of the actions they trigger. The system does not know what an eagle is, or a worm. It does not have these concepts. But it can identify the difference in how they smell, the pattern of their different shapes, and the noises they make. The smell, the noise and the shape they have, may be considered to be nothing more than different stimuli. It is only later, when the mechanism with various higher phase-layers and more sophisticated abilities, that it is able to collect these stimuli together, to form concepts and to recognise them as separate features of a single entity.

I want to show that the ability to recognise features can evolve from the simple structures I have already described. For that explanation I will use visual shapes as the main example. That is because these are the things that are easiest to illustrate on two-dimensional paper.

Shapes

03.21

For some creatures (or for a functionally equivalent pseudo-creature) there are some visual shapes, which carry great significance.

Fig 03.21 bird, spider and eye

I am thinking of the black silhouette of a bird of prey high in the sky, or the leggy shape of a spider. For humans the shape of a human eye carries great importance for the ability to make social contact. It has been demonstrated that normal infants, from a very early age, are prone to focus their own eyes on the presence of a human eye within their field of vision [Carey 1980].

We need a few examples. All of the shapes in the diagram are dark shapes on a relatively uncluttered contrasting background, without shadows. In real life, that kind of helpful simplicity might not occur often, but it will occur sometimes and we have to start somewhere. So that is where we will start and hope to progress to shapes observed in more complex difficult contexts.

03.22

Various mathematical techniques have been devised for such purposes (radial basis functions, fast Fourier analysis etc.). These have been successfully applied in practical devices.

It is not clear, however, how these advanced and sometimes obscure mathematical techniques could evolve in small steps from existing structures and mechanisms. It does not seem likely that there could be some survival advantage to be gained from the possession of half of a complex algorithm. To remain faithful to the principles of pseudo-evolution, we need to go in the opposite direction. We need to start with some simple facility and then try to see how by making small additions (each of which has some identifiable advantage of its own) we could gradually construct a mechanism which is the functional equivalent of one of those complex algorithms.

The strip approach

03.23

If the phase-layer-1 system has the ability to detect short line segments, and is able to compare these for the degree of darkness each has, then it could evolve the ability to detect the external boundaries of a shape and then to divide it into a number of strips - as shown in the diagram.

Using the variable strength signal facility the degree of blackness of each strip can be compared, to produce a sequence of comparisons which characterises the way the mass of the shape is distributed.

That is only a first step however. The same measure (of distribution of mass) can be calculated at several orientations. These measures taken together characterise any shape uniquely.

Fig 03.23 (1) - recognition of shapes by strips

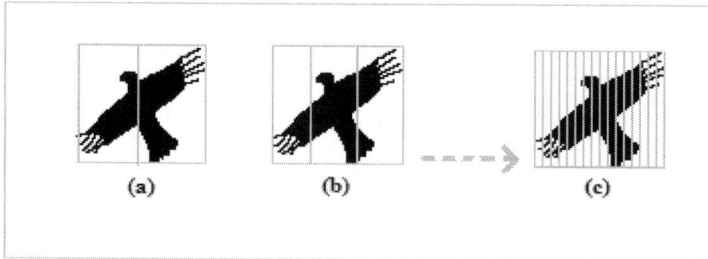

(a)　　　　(b)　　　　(c)

To demonstrate to myself, that that is the case I wrote a program which analysed and compared several shapes in this way (see Appendix). Because it deals only with the distribution of mass, the size and orientation of the shape is of no consequence. I used a 5-strip method and rotations of 22.5 degrees (16 orientations). The standard shapes used are shown in the next diagram. The results obtained for one test run are also shown. I also calculated the size and darkness of each strip, and produced the comparison ratios, by simple arithmetic computation. That is the easiest way when dealing with a computer. What I envisage, however, is that my evolving pseudo-organism could be able to produce analogous results using the relative measures - this one darker than that one. Both lighter than that other one.

Shape sensitivity can be progressively improved by gradually increasing the number of strips and by rotating by smaller and small angles. That means that this shape recognition procedure can be progressively improved by evolution.

The technique also has this advantage - when the same process was applied to a second shape which was not identical but was similar to one already processed, the parameters obtained were numerically similar. The similarity was measured by taking an aggregate of the discrepancies. If we had some unknown shape and a set of standard shapes for which the parameter values were known, the system could identify which of the standard shapes the new unknown one most closely resembled. If those standard shapes were, for example, a square, a triangle and a circle, the system could identify a new arbitrary shape as being "squarish" or "sort of round".

Fig 03.23 (2) - reference shapes

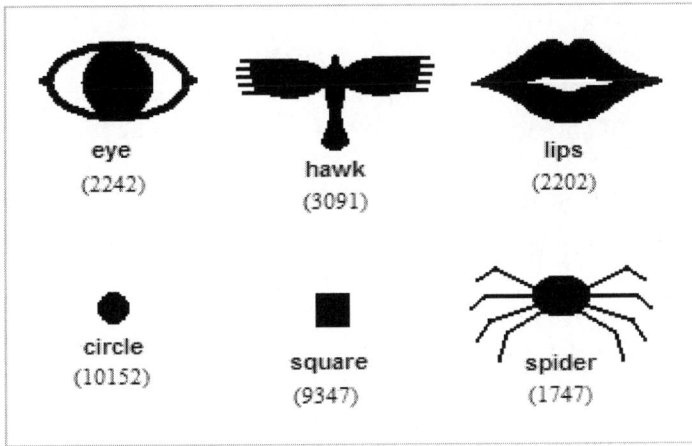

eye
(2242)

hawk
(3091)

lips
(2202)

circle
(10152)

square
(9347)

spider
(1747)

Fig 03.23 (3) - The bug

BUG

To test the procedure I compared the reference set with this shape, which I call "the bug". Note that the bug has six legs unlike the spider that has eight, and that it is much smaller than the spider shape.

The numbers shown in the previous diagram are the numerical discrepancies found between the bug analysis and each of the reference set. The discrepancy between the bug and the spider shape is 1747 which is the smallest discrepancy found. The bug was therefore identified as being "spider-like".

03.24

I offer the strip measurement technique, not as a practical method of shape recognition, but as evidence that a technique based on the use of detector units can be used in a variety of ways for feature recognition. By thinking about how the detector unit could be used to solve various recognition problems we can explore the characteristics which detector units must have.

It is of interest to note that there is a practical mathematical method which is often used in these circumstances. It is called the method of Fast Fourier Analysis. It depends on a very similar idea of subdividing the distribution of mass into smaller and smaller components.

The strip technique does not work if any part of the shape is occluded by some other object or is obscured in some other way. To deal with these complications the system requires some other technique. Partial outline tracing, by an adaptation of edge-tracing would appear to offer some chance of success.

Edge tracing

03.25

The recognition of objects often does not make possible the matching of exact patterns.

Note that any given cell might make a contribution to several line segment detectors (with different orientations).

One application of this technique is the recognition of a snake. Each observation of a snake will typically be characterised by smooth curving coils, but it is very unlikely that the way the coils lie will be an exact match for some other observation of another, or even the same snake. What we need to recognise therefore is the kind of shape it has - to classify it as consisting of smooth coils.

Coils of rope have the same basic characteristic. To do that we need to be able to trace the edge of the shape and to characterise that shape. In the next diagram we see part of a coil.

Fig 03.25(1) curved line in segments

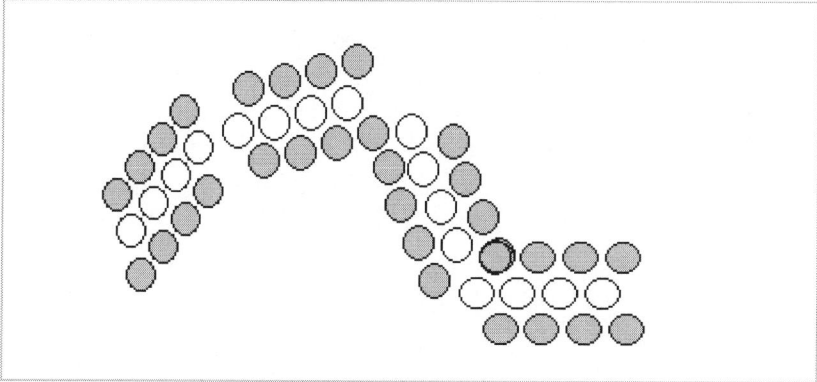

Imposed on that coiled line we also see a series of short line segments, each of the same length, each starting where the previous one stopped and each departing from that point at a particular angle which is not the same as the angle of the previous segment in the series.

Fig 03.25(2) - a coil as a sequence of line segments

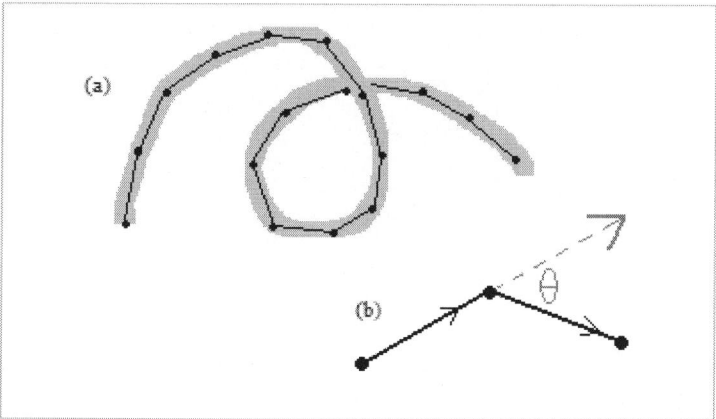

In the same diagram we see enlarged, the relationship and angles between two adjacent segments. Note the angle theta (θ) between the two segments.

Any line made up of segments of that kind can be characterised or classified according to the nature and succession of these difference angles. If they are all identical then we are looking at a circle. If they are approximately the same then we are looking at a "rounded" line of coils. If they gradually decrease and then reverse the direction of deflection, we are looking at serpentine waves. If they are all equal to zero then we are looking at a straight line. If the angles between the segments are erratic then we are looking at a spiky line. A saw-edge has regular reversals of direction.

These techniques have an interesting consequence. In order to do edge tracing effectively, the system must wait on the results of one part of the process before it can begin the next. That means it must adopt, in this instance, a linear approach rather than the massively parallel processing of which we know it is capable.

Fig 03.25(3) hidden cat

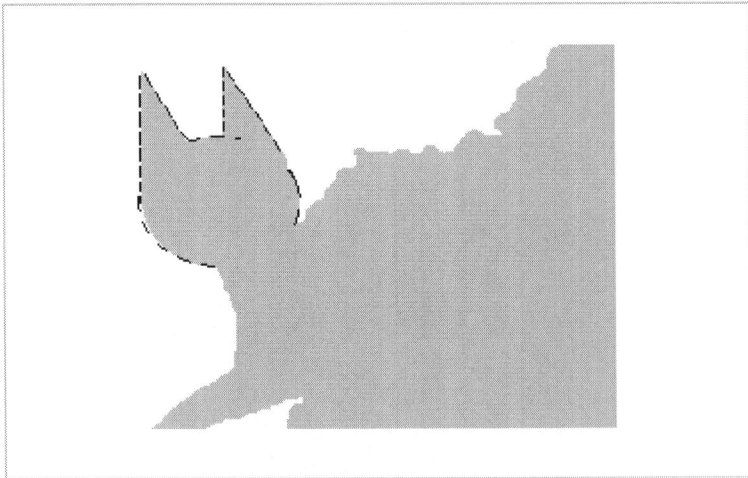

The next diagram shows another example of the application of the edge-tracing technique used for the identification of a partly obscured shape. Most people will recognise the shape shown as a cat emerging from behind a rock (or some such thing).

The cat has a relatively smooth outline while the rock is rough and jagged. The cat's head carries two distinctive partial shapes - the roundness of the head and the two sharply pointed ears. All of these characteristics could be identified by edge-tracing.

Again, I do not envisage that any arithmetic would be required. If the system had some standard angles - a right angle for example and one of forty five degrees, the sequence of line segment angles could be expressed in terms relative to these standards (and to each other).

Areas, gradients and regional boundaries

03.26

Fig 03.26 - gradient and edge

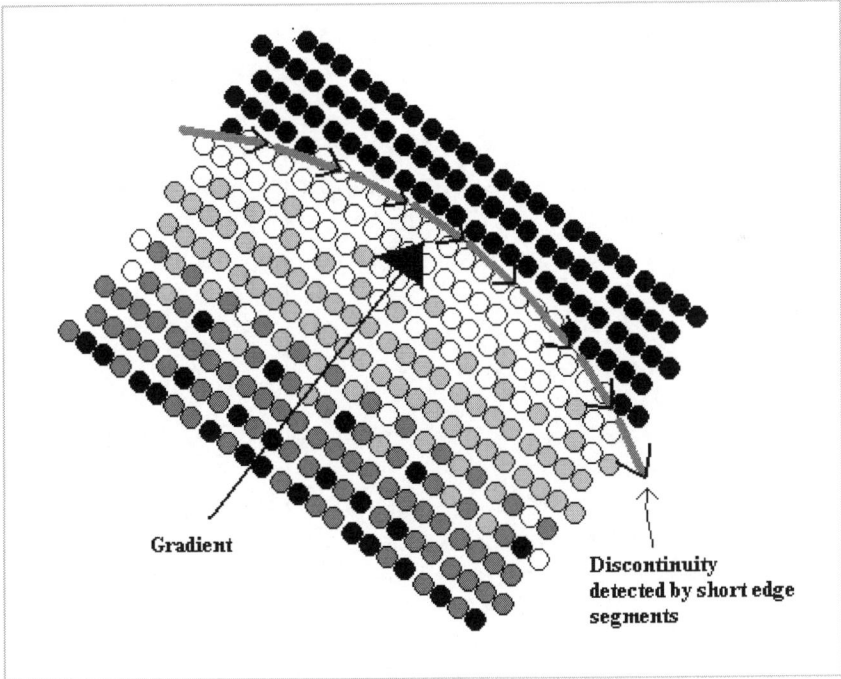

Gradient

Discontinuity
detected by short edge
segments

These capabilities are not quite sufficient for all purposes. The ability to recognise a gradient, and in what direction that gradient runs, can also be developed using the short-line detection facility. The density of two adjacent short lines can be measured and expressed as relative density. The relative density gradient can then be expressed for adjacent groups. The diagram illustrates the principle.

Selection by detection units

03.27

The significance of this, so far artificial the stimulus-response automaton (or SRA) is concerned (and ultimately as far as our artificial consciousness system is concerned) lies in what it tells us about the capabilities of the detection units. To trace a line, they need to be able to read signal-input from a small segment of the total input available, and then to progress to another segment which starts at the end point of the previous segment. Another part of the detection unit will then be able to express the comparison angle between the two by outputting a signal which has a magnitude proportionate to that angle. A general characteristic of the whole line can then be expressed in terms of the smoothness or spikiness of the sequence of the changes in direction. We know that a computer could be programmed to do all of that.

Subsumption and phase-layer-1

03.28

As mentioned earlier, the structure of the phase-layer-1 mechanism is an example of subsumption architecture. Each subsystem (detection unit + action unit) responds in its own individual way to its own pre-defined stimulus. Each action unit responds in its own individual way to a trigger signal from a detection unit.

Additional and more complicated forms of behaviour are then added later in the form of cross connections between detection units and between action units. The response produced by a detection unit to a given stimulus can become the input to another detection unit rather than a direct trigger to an action unit. These additional characteristics are added in a piecemeal way and are not as the result of some form of purposeful intellectual control.

Action units

03.29

The ability to recognise various features of the environment is of little use unless there is an associated ability to respond in some useful way. Obviously, if you are a small creature which would be a tasty morsel for a buzzard or an eagle, the appearance of that black shape in the sky would be the trigger for one of a variety of escape procedures - freeze motionless or dive into a burrow for example.

In the early stages of evolution the type of response would be very simple. But as the system evolves more complex responses will develop so that we could say the SRA is able to choreograph a response consisting of several movements some of which will be repeated several times.

Fig 03.29 - Jointed limb

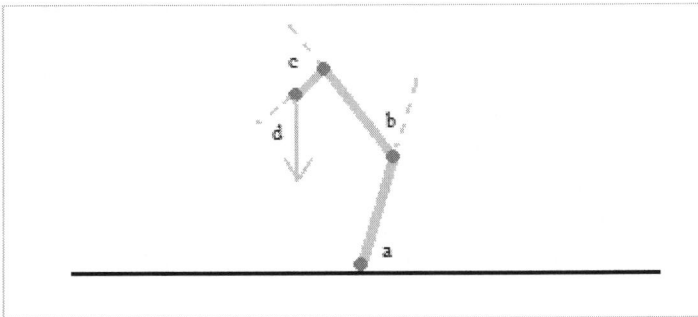

We should also note that the list of possible responses includes the release of transmitter substances, which can diffuse within the brain and affect a great many synapse junctions.

However, the most obvious component of any physical action response is a muscle contraction stimulated by a nerve signal. But the movement of a limb would normally require several different muscle contractions which are introduced in a programmed sequence.

The diagram shows a simplified limb with four joints including a shoulder joint. The arrowhead represents the tip of an extended finger. For ease of presentation on a printed page I have restricted the limb to move only in a two dimensional space. The location of the tip of the arrowhead can be specified by giving the values of the four angles (a, b, c, d). If the limb could move in a three dimensional space we would need more angles and these would include rotational angles. But the basic principles of position-by-angle can be illustrated with this restricted version. The most important principle is that a given unique location of the finger-tip can be specified by a great many different angle settings. Not only that. The trajectory through which the limb must move to reach a specified point will depend upon the time-sequence in which each joint is moved to reach its specified angle.

The joint-angle method, however, has one great advantage over other methods. If you want to move your hand to touch something or to pick it up, the joint-angle method allows you to calculate all of the intermediate positions of the joints (elbows, wrists, etc) so that you can select a trajectory which will achieve your objective without putting some one else's eye out with your elbow in the process. One of the problems associated with the programming of industrial robot arms, is the problem of how a robot can mount, say, a piece of metal in the chuck of a lathe without the robot arm getting its own fingers caught in the jaws of that machine.

Clearly we need sensors (internal sensor arrays) which will provide data on the positions of the relevant angles. However, when you shut your eyes and try to touch a specified point on your own body it quickly becomes clear that your ability to do that without visual guidance is only approximate. You can usually succeed, but without great confidence. Position by dead reckoning based on angle specification alone, is not precise.

If this was just a question of computer programming and the control of a robotic arm, the problem would be relatively simple - a straight forward calculation involving angles and trigonometry. But it is more than that. The human appreciation of distances in three dimensional space is surely not a matter of trigonometry. We do not have sensory equipment which is equivalent to protractors and rulers. All we have are limbs, tactile sensations, vision, muscles contractions, and relative, not absolute measurements of position and joint-angle So precise limb positioning must use visual or tactile feedback techniques.

That comes later, however. In this, the early stages of its evolutionary development, our phase-layer-1 pseudo-creature requires only pre-programmed actions for routine activities - walking, jumping, snatching, grasping. And it does these things in the "subsumption way" - that is, with each leg or arm doing its own thing, in its own way, without reference to what other limbs or bits of the system may be doing at the same time.

The sequences of action required for these can be defined by genetic inheritance for they do not need to be capable of subtle variation. The ability to learn from experience and to modify these routines accordingly, comes at a later stage and we shall deal with them when we discuss the higher levels. For the present the SRA can react to stimuli with the pre-programmed responses, which enabled past generations to survive and reproduce.

Neural plasticity

03.30

The characteristics of phase-layer-1 - the signal patterns which its detection units are primed to recognise - were established over a very long period of evolution. But environmental conditions change, sometimes very slowly, and sometimes quite dramatically - as when an earthquake plunges an area of dry land under the sea (or vice versa). Also creatures move from one geographical area to another where they encounter new conditions, new vegetation, new climatic conditions. If you (and your ancestors) lived in an extensive flood plain you may have to spend your whole life seeing predominantly only horizontal lines and without ever seeing a long vertical line of any kind. However, if evolution did not equip you with the ability to see vertical lines, you would never be able to operate successfully in any other environment (such as a forest). Creatures like that would be at a disadvantage because if the flood plain was inundated and you were forced to move to the forest, you and your descendants, would not survive for long.

Evolution operates at too slow a speed to keep pace with some of these changes and if the creature concerned is to adapt successfully to these new conditions, (and our pseudo-creature which will try to mimic these abilities) it must have some other shorter-term way of adapting itself.

Characteristics inherited from past generations cannot be changed by the experience of a single individual. One way an individual can affect the future genetic characteristics of the species is to survive and reproduce or to die and fail to reproduce (see NOTE below).

But there is another, more subtle mechanism of adaptation which must be put into effect by each and every individual. It works this way. Each individual can be "over-endowed" with detection units which can recognise all kinds of signal patterns - many more than is strictly required for any given single environment. It is then up to each individual to throw away what is not needed. If that is the case then when a creatures moves to a new environment it may be disadvantaged initially, but offspring born to these displaced individuals will be able to hold on to what was previously a redundant characteristic.

"Use it or lose it", is the catch phrase for this way of adapting to new circumstances. It has been established that that is indeed how we humans (and some other mammalian species) operate. During a short period following birth, a creature will loose the ability to recognise particular features unless they are utilised. For example, kittens raised in a special enclosure from which all horizontal lines had been eliminated, lost the ability to see horizontal lines [Blakemore and Cooper 1970]. It is a mechanism known as "Neural Plasticity". Humans raised in countries where the natural mother tongue does not contain certain forms of aspirated sounds, lose the ability to hear those sounds - one reason why it is difficult for some Europeans to learn certain Eastern languages.

To mimic this effect all we need is for the artificial system to be subjected to a period of maturation, during which a count is kept of the number of times each detection unit is able to identify its specified signal pattern. At the end of that period of maturation, the unused detection units are purged from the system.

This idea might well be put to use by someone trying to construct a mechanism of the kind I describe. Detection units could then be manufactured en mass with an automatic assignment of specifications. This would avoid the need to construct each individually. Redundant detection units with specifications which are never used could then be purged.

NOTE: recent work in genetic science indicates that some genes are able to "activate" or "switch-on" other genes. It seems that a state of "switched-on-ness" can be passed from one generation to others. This is not the same as the inheritance of acquired characteristics but it has a superficial resemblance to that.

Selectivity, feedback, inhibition and interrupts

03.31

A further word on the properties which phase-layer-1 must develop. Phase-layer-1 is a stimulus-response automaton. But it cannot possibly provide a response for every possible combination of stimuli. As the number of stimuli increases, the rapid increase in the number of possible combinations would overwhelm it.

However, subsumption architecture helps to limit the numbers involved by being selective. Each subsystem concentrates selectively on a very limited pattern of signals. This selectivity means that most combinations will be ignored.

Later, as the system evolves, more subsystems will be added and some of those will be able to inhibit the activity of others. In effect this mechanism will be able to tell the system -

"When this stimulus occurs, ignore that one."

There would also be a need for a similar inhibition of the action units. This would be the equivalent of the statement in a computer program which is called a "DO-UNTIL" loop. In effect it would tell an action unit to perform a particular action until some new stimulus occurred - then stop.

Action units should be able to provide feedback on their level of activity, so that the detection units can recognise and choreograph a sequence of actions. Thus a system which is constructed and depends entirely upon in physical components and their interconnections, can operate as though under the control of a software program.

The inhibition facility, could, if applied on a sufficiently large number of detection units, operate like a general interrupt.

CHAPTER 4

Comments on Phase-layer-1.

In this chapter I introduce the idea of inside and outside views - two different ways of looking at and describing a single mechanism. This idea is fundamental to my explanation. Not understanding that idea is also the most common reason for a failure to grasp the validity of my explanation.

The stimulus-response automaton (or SRA)

04.01

Phase-layer-1 is a stimulus-response automaton. It does not "know" what each recognised pattern signifies. It just recognises a pattern and acts as it has been programmed by evolution to respond to that particular pattern.

The phase-layer-1 mechanism, when it is acting alone - that is, when it is acting in isolation from the other phase-layers (which is what it must have done before the other phase-layers evolved), corresponds to what most people think is the way a robot must operate. It is a dumb machine. It does a few apparently "clever" things and it gets by in a relatively satisfactory way. The species survives - or enough of them do. Usually they reproduce in large numbers which compensates for a very high mortality rate.

A creature, or mechanism like that, will also sometimes, or even quite often, do what we would regard as "stupid" things. It cannot understand the context within which it is operating. It lives, as it were, only in the here and now. It has no memory of the past, no insight into the future, and no concept of how things are related to one another.

Awareness

What we can say, however, about this phase-layer-1 system, with its multiple sensor arrays and the many complex responses of which it can become capable, is that it is "*aware*" of the world around it. Used in that way, and in this context, the word "*aware*" does not explicitly imply any special internal property of the mechanism. It is used purely as a description of the system's internal mechanism only indirectly by making reference to its overt behaviour.

A problem arises if we use the word in another way - one which we regard as saying something about what is going on inside. Think about how we can speak of a person being "suspicious", "cowardly", "courageous", "annoying" – and so on. Maybe we think we are describing something of the internal character of that person but what we are actually describing is how that person behaves, or the effect that behaviour has on ourselves.

No one can actually tell us precisely what the word "aware", used in that way, implies about the internal circumstances - apart, that is, from some vague hand-waving notion of a kind of internal knowledge of what is going on outside.

When it is used in *my* way, however, the word is useful. As we increase the range of external conditions, which the mechanism can recognise, and to which it can respond, we can say that the system is becoming "*more aware*". Used that way awareness is not an all-or-none commodity. Awareness can evolve in stages. It is compatible with evolution.

We can keep adding extra abilities until, at a higher level (phase-layer-3 to be precise), we will be able to say that the system is "conscious". That means that awareness is a kind of simple primitive precursor form of consciousness. Used in that way, both words, "awareness" and "consciousness", are terms which apply only to the behaviour of a system, as it is seen from the outside.

As we increase the complexity of the external behaviour, we can also watch the increasing complexity of the internal mechanism, which is needed to bring that about. We can do that because it is ourselves who are making these internal changes.

We can use a different set of terms to describe what is going on inside. These inside terms will tell us nothing at all about the corresponding changes that are happening on the outside.

That provides us with "*inside*" and "*outside*" views of an operational system. That idea is crucial to my explanation of consciousness. By keeping those two types of description of the system apart and not allowing ourselves to muddle them up, we can avoid a great deal of confusion which has bedevilled the debate about consciousness. Confusion has reigned for a long time. It has trapped some very bright people. It continues to do so.

Leibnitz

04.03

Over three hundred years ago, the mathematician, philosopher and genius Gottfried Wilhelm Leibnitz made an oft-quoted remark to the effect that -

"If the brain was expanded to the size of a mill so that we could walk about inside, we would see only wheels and pulleys and the like. We would not see anything that looked like a thought."

Leibnitz was wrong. Yes, of course, we would indeed see wheels and pulleys, but not *only* those things. We would also see these physical components working together. That is what a thought is - a working together of the physical parts of the brain in a particular way. Leibnitz's mistake is caused by thinking that consciousness and thinking are *things* and not even considering the possibility that they might be only the outside view of *procedures*. We can understand Leibnitz's mistake. He did not live with the example of computers. We do have that example, so we should be able to avoid making the same mistake.

Waterston

In 1845 John James Waterston submitted a paper to the Royal Society of London for publication in its journal "Philosophical Transactions". What Waterston's paper proposed was that the kinetic movement of molecules of a gas and the temperature of the same body of gas, are actually the same thing. Two views - but only one phenomenon. He did not use the terms "inside" and "outside" views, but that was the central idea in his paper. He correctly identified what we now call the equi-partition of energy. "Temperature" is the outside view. "Kinetic energy" is the "inside" view. When you are inside you cannot see the outside view. When you are outside you cannot see the internal mechanism. What we should not do is to get these views muddled up.

We should not ask -

"But how can a molecule feel hot?"

Waterston's paper was rejected as "rubbish" by the President of the Society. In the years that followed, work carried out separately by Rudolf Clausius, James Clerk Maxwell and Ludwig Boltzmann established that same theory as a part of accepted science. Boltzmann's name was given to the most important mathematical coefficient in the mathematical theory of the subject. Nearly half a century later, in 1893, Waterson's paper was rediscovered among the Society's documents.

04.05

I anticipate that some will claim that by suggesting that *"awareness"* and *"consciousness"* are merely the *"outside view"* counterparts of internal mechanisms, I have done a kind of verbal trick - that I have somehow "explained-away" awareness and consciousness as imaginary entities. However, imagination is a brain mechanism too. If we say that something is just imaginary, we have not rid ourselves of the need to produce an explanation of how that works.

Anyway, that would be a misinterpretation of my thesis. I am not suggesting that awareness and consciousness do not exist. I do not suggest that any more than Waterston suggested that temperature did not exist. He did not explain temperature *away*. He just explained it.

The phenomenalists, epi-phenomenalists or whatever they want to call themselves, that is, the people I call the "supernaturalists", are people who describe an entity as being "conscious" and hint that that means that there something else, some internal extra supernatural counterpart, which gives rise to the overt behaviour of a conscious person, and yet at the same time they signally fail to tell us what that supernatural explanation is - they are the ones who are "explaining-away" (into a non-material nothingness) the existence of consciousness.

To my mind, the supernatural can never be an explanation of anything. It is an admission of failure to explain.

Unsupervised feature learning

04.06

The approach to the visual recognition of visual scenes, which I have described in chapter 3, is an example of what is called "unsupervised feature learning". I have avoided discussion of any techniques that involve complex mathematics - partly for my own sake but also for the sake of readers who are similarly unfamiliar with mathematical notation. Any reader who is interested in these ideas will find a very interesting (video) seminar on the topic by Andrew Ng [Ng 2013]. Ng is the director of the Stanford Artificial Intelligence Laboratory and an Associate Professor, Computer Science Dept. Stanford University. In his seminar he illustrates his presentation with examples drawn from the field of vision research and also from audio research. For both, the approach he describes is highly successful. He also extends his talk to include the issue of natural language processing. While he claims some encouraging results in that very different field, he also admits difficulties.

The ideas I have offered in chapter 3 concerning the "strip approach" and the gradual improvement and increasing complexity of feature recognition structures based on a very simple line-recognition structure, has similarities with the techniques Ng describes. Interestingly, I have anticipated the difficulty which would affect any attempt to extend the same ideas into the field of natural language processing and have suggested a different approach (see later).

Acquisition of learned detection units.

04.07

Evolution, as I have remarked, is usually a very slow process. It was assumed, in the previous chapter, that all the detection units described, evolved in the normal way by natural selection. For that reason all the units were constrained to be able to recognise objects, shapes etc, which have been present in the environment for a very long period of time and which have significance for a given organism's survival. For natural selection to operate, however, features selected must have some impact on the way an organism behaves or the way other organisms behave with respect to that target organism. So we are not just concerned with, for example, a mouse having an ability to recognise the silhouette shape of a bird of prey. Also of significance is the way the mouse responds to that recognition event.

However, in modern times there are many features of the environment which have been added to the environment recently. Natural selection cannot always have an effect on the gene pool quickly enough to meet the demands of these new arrivals and so there has to be an additional mechanism which enables an organism to acquire new recognition abilities. The method of acquisition must be either by direct personal experience, or by instruction by older more experienced individuals.

We shall see later that my proposed model provides several extra mechanisms which do that. If an organism is to be able to learn by personal experience it must be able to remember and analyse that personal experience. If it is to benefit from the experience of other individuals it must able to observe their behaviour and to empathise with their unfortunate experiences, it must have an inherited propensity to mimic observed behaviour, and it must acquire the ability to learn by communication with others. Most importantly for the human species, that means the ability to communicate with language.

CHAPTER 5

PHASE-LAYER-2

Remembering the past.

In this chapter I discuss a number of technical details of phase-layer-2 but I also discuss the way information is transferred from one phase-layer to another. This is an important consideration and reflects the way evolution leaves its stamp on the system's structure.

Phase-layer-1 is the source of information for Phase-layer-2

05.01

Phase-layer-2 provides the system with two kinds of memory. We have already seen that phase-layer-1 has a brief one clock-tick kind of memory. If the system can develop the ability to store the condition of a detector unit for one tick of the clock, then there is nothing that could prevent it storing that condition for two, three or a great many ticks of the clock. It could also do that for a great many detection units at the same time. If we can describe phase-layer-1 as a mechanism which enables the system to survive in the here and now, then phase-layer-2 is a mechanism which, on behalf of the system harvests phase-layer-1 for information about the past.

I have illustrated the various phase-layers of the system in diagrams as physically separate. In reality, however, these functional identities are much more likely to be physically intermingled.

Note this, however - if phase-layer-2 provides the system with a memory by retaining the condition of the detection and action units in phase-layer-1, then it cannot also be storing the memory of a pattern of what we could call "raw data" as it occurred in the environment. What it is storing is an *interpretation* of that raw data - a selective interpretation created by phase-layer-1. Thinking that the brain stores raw sensory data is a common mistake. I offer an alternative view.

The "matrix form" or STATE format of remembered data

05.02

If phase-layer-1 consists of a very large number of units (detection units and action units), each one, at each moment in time, will have a condition that is characterised by the signal it emits. Each may send its output signal to several different destinations, at the same time, but there will be only one output signal going to all those destinations - a single message, per unit at any one instant. Each sensor unit has a type or mode - visual, tactile etc. and a location within the sensory array of which it is a constituent. When the conditions of several detection units are stored in memory each output signal will be reduced to a single datum point.

Fig 05.02 - The "matrix" form of data

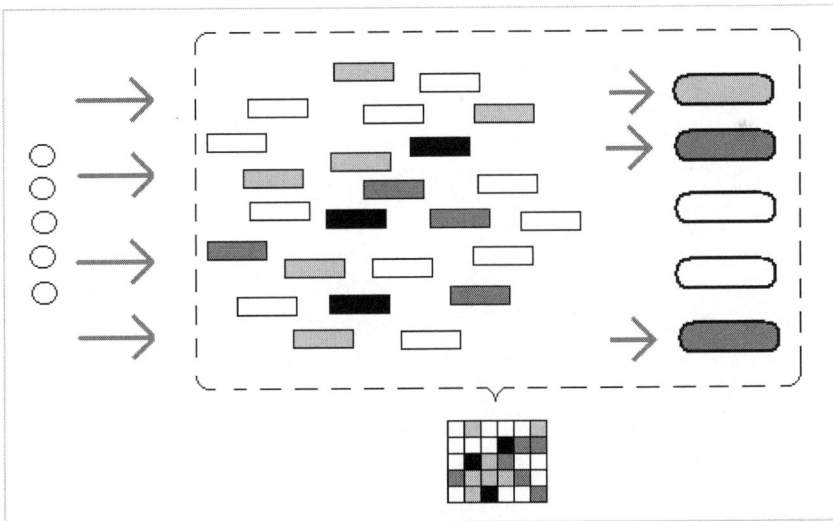

The diagram illustrates the idea schematically. It shows some sensor units feeding into a collection of 25 detection units. These supply signals to five action units - 30 units in all. There are several other data, which need to be added to that. There is, for example, the clock reading - a set of unique patterns generated in sequence as the clock ticks. Since these do not repeat themselves, each record of the phase-layer-1 condition is unique. The record also needs to show the strength of response by each phase-layer-1 unit.

In the diagram, the various conditions of detection units and action units are indicated by different shades of grey. These data, <u>excluding</u> the sensor units but <u>including</u> the action units, can be represented by a 5 x 6 matrix and a matrix like that is shown below.

No significance is attached to the matrix format shown here. Each element is an isolated datum. The collection of data could have been shown as a linear vector or a set. If there are N individual units to be recorded, there will be N^2 potential connections between them. To ensure that the volume of data stored is a minimum we need to avoid a combinatorial explosion of that kind. The mechanism could possibly reduce the data volume by selecting only important data for storage. "Importance" in this context might be determined by the position at which the unit stands within the network hierarchy - far from the initial sensory input units and close to the output action units (including the action units themselves). Different people will be likely to differ in this respect - see section 09.24 on eidetic memory.

This matrix is a very condensed form of information. In computer technology, in a graphic image, each pixel is represented by a group of "bits". These contain information about such things as colour and intensity. What I am suggesting is that within my hypothetical system there will be many more items of information which must be captured by the matrix representation. But the matrix is still a condensed collection of apparently meaningless pixels. Within phase-layer-2 these pixels cannot signify anything by themselves. They merely record. In order to make the system capable of initiating any kind of action, the information - the pixels held in that form - must be transferred back into the phase-layer-1, to the network of detection units - and in that way into a direct connect with the action units.

It is in this arbitrary matrix of dots format that I envisage phase-layer-2 being able to store a memory of the past conditions of phase-layer-1. Data by itself has no significance. Significance is thrust upon it by whatever procedure tries to read and process it.

The multi-dimensional matrix

05.03

The matrix form, as it is illustrated here, makes the point that the store of information, read and recorded by phase-layer-2, is initially meaningless and arbitrary. It is just dots or pixels located in a space of information.

The analogy I have in mind when I think about the information made available by phase-layer-1, is of a rather boring official inspection process in which the inspector does no more than tick boxes in a form which correspond to features observed. What he later makes available to his superiors, is just the collection of ticks in boxes.

Fig 05.03(1) The "Fuzzball" - a multi-dimensional matrix

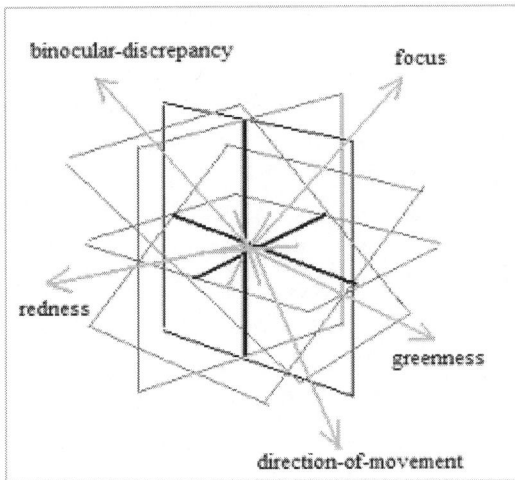

To mean anything, they have to be processed in order to make a connection between the ticked boxes and action that needs to be taken as a consequence. Note, however, that phase-layer-1 also does have boxes which correspond to the actions which evolution has programmed into its responses. So in a sense phase-layer-1 is telling phase-layer-2 what significance it attaches to each tick.

Henceforth, in the fully evolved multi-phase-layer system, the information which the system must process consists of nothing but those forms and the boxes with and without ticks. It is divorced from the external environment. Any action it takes must consist of nothing more than a few ticks in a few additional boxes which is then passed down to phase-layer-1 for action to be taken.

The analogy is reasonable except for one point. In this system there are no "superiors". Every subsystem does its own thing in its own way, and tries to achieve some kind of compromise with other parts of the system.

It is not easy to illustrate a multi-dimensional object on a two-dimensional page. I've done my best in the diagram. The result, as can be seen, is what I would call "*a fuzzball*".

For simplicity I will continue to show the matrix form of data as a 2D matrix. Please remember, however, that it is actually a multi-dimensional object in which every dimension is represented by a connection to an appropriate set of detection units.

The fuzzball matrix format has another interesting characteristic. It may appear meaningless, but it is clear that if there is some mechanism within the brain that is able to use the information provided by the matrix, that matrix format must contain all of the information needed to enable that to happen.

Consider the presence of colour within a visual image. Within the part of the matrix, which is concerned with visual experience, there must be some reference to the three dimensions of colour (red, green and blue). These correspond to the three maxima for three types of light sensitive cell. If every pixel is associated with a location within the visual scene (so much up and down, so much left to right) so we must also consider each pixel as having a location on these colour axes (so much red, so much green, so much blue). These data are present as just another set of boxes with ticks in them. Each tick is another dimension. Colour introduces three dimensions. Priority another. Time is a dimension as is direction of movement. Shape introduces several more dimensions with axes pointing towards "roundness", "squareness" and many more. There may be no upper limit to the number of dimensions which could be included for particular species (including bats - see later).

Gestalt psychologists have noted that our visual perception seems pre-disposed to group together all aspects of a scene which move in unison. If you look at a sea of random dots and then you see that a collection of these dots suddenly starts to move in a common direction, then even if those moving dots are distributed all over the scene, apparently at random, then they will be perceived as being part of a single entity.

Fig 05.03 (2) One of the dimensions. Directionality of movement.

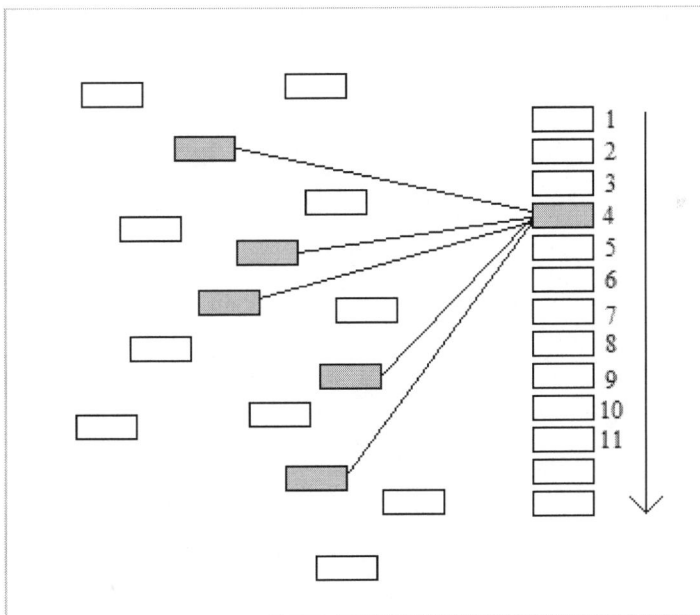

The conclusion I draw from that, is that the detection units, which are associated with the movement of those randomly scattered dots, are all located at the same position on a "direction" dimension. The various detection units which detect that common movement, must be linked to a single unit associated with that direction. In the diagram I have arranged the common direction units in a single column to emphasise that they constitute a single directional "axis", but there is no need for them to have any specific physical location.

The point I am making with this meander into the issue of direction and colour, is that the matrix format can be multi-dimensional in terms of the information it carries - in contrast to a visual image which is limited to two dimensions.

Short term memory - the TRACE

05.04

Phase-layer-2 provides two forms of memory.

Fig 05.04 - formation of the trace

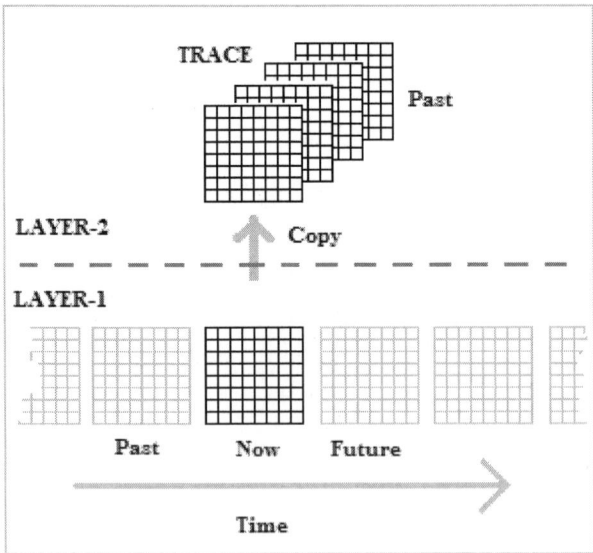

The first of these is a short-term or ephemeral memory, which consists of successive values of the phase-layer-1 condition. As each clock-tick occurs, the existing condition of phase-layer-1 is recorded in that matrix form.

Each matrix is a "state" of phase-layer-1 So let us write that in this way -

(S1, S2, S3, S4, S5, ...)

Where each S is an instantaneous "state" representing the condition of phase-layer-1 at a particular moment in time. Let's call that sequence "The TRACE".

When the length of the sequence reaches some arbitrary point, it starts to overwrite itself. Each matrix (or state of phase-layer-1) therefore has a duration within the short-term memory of several clock-ticks. To abide by the rules of pseudo-evolution we need then to ask - what survival benefit would such an arrangement provide?

Consider the behaviour of an organism which is programmed to respond with some form of escape behaviour when it recognises a particular pattern of signals within the environment.

That pattern could be the silhouette of predator. Escape behaviour would then be triggered, but would cease if the visual pattern of the predator disappeared from view. That might not be a good strategy if the predator has merely stepped behind a tree. It would be safer if the escape behaviour kept going for a while. And that is exactly what a short-term memory could achieve by keeping available the perception of that predator's presence.

An arrangement like that would also enable the organism to develop more complex types of escape behaviour. Not just running, or hiding perhaps, but running and then hiding. The implication of that is important. The content of the trace must be accessible to the mechanisms of phase-layer-1. In effect, the TRACE is inserted back into phase-layer-1.

The phase-layer-2 response

05.05

If the data content of the trace is accessible to phase-layer-1, then phase-layer-2 is able to influence the action taken by phase-layer-1, provided the priority level associated with the trace data is higher than any condition within phase-layer-1 itself. That is, it must be able to generate some kind of interrupt or alarm signal within phase-layer-1. That cannot be guaranteed however. The trace must, as it were, take its chances with the data currently held in phase-layer-1. But since the condition of phase-layer-1 is constantly being copied into the trace with every tick of the clock, it is the trace, which will become the ring- master of this particular circus.

Interrupt messages

05.06

We need to consider how an interrupt message facility could develop. We have already seen that a form of interrupt mechanism is an essential part of the phase-layer-1 mechanism in relation to the detection of movement and change. The system of variable priority levels also plays an essential part. When a change occurs, the detection unit, which is programmed to recognise that change, must send a high priority signal to others. That signal must suspend or suppress the priority of on-going actions. A large number of detection units must therefore be primed to suppress themselves when a signal of that kind is detected.

Is that feasible? Is there a marginal survival advantage associated with such a mechanism? I think there must be. It would be advantageous if the system had some means to abort actions after they had been started if some new development occurs. The individual is chasing a meal and a large predator appears.

Longer-term memory.

05.07

There are obvious advantages to be gained by extending the duration of the short-term memory. However, an indiscriminate memory of events, which is more than short-term, also carries very onerous overheads.

The sheer volume of information which would require storage would be huge and most of it would be repetitive and mundane. As it becomes larger and larger the chances of that memory having within it conflicting high priority signals becomes greater and the ability of each to attract the attention of phase-layer-1 becomes diminished. Searching the memory trace for events of a particular kind becomes more and more laborious as the length of memory increases. Some compromise is required which will limit the duration of the memory trace to some optimum value of, perhaps, a few minutes.

Fig 05.07 (1) - selective memory

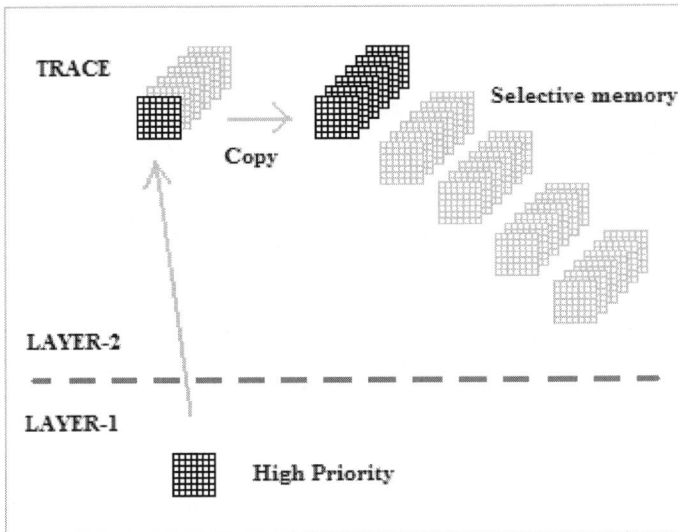

A solution to that problem is to select only the most important items and to store these for a longer period of time. However, since the system is still a long way short of having anything we could describe as an intellect, it has no way of identifying what is important - other than by relying on the priority levels attached to these items by phase-layer-1.

Fig 05.07(2) prediction of high priority state

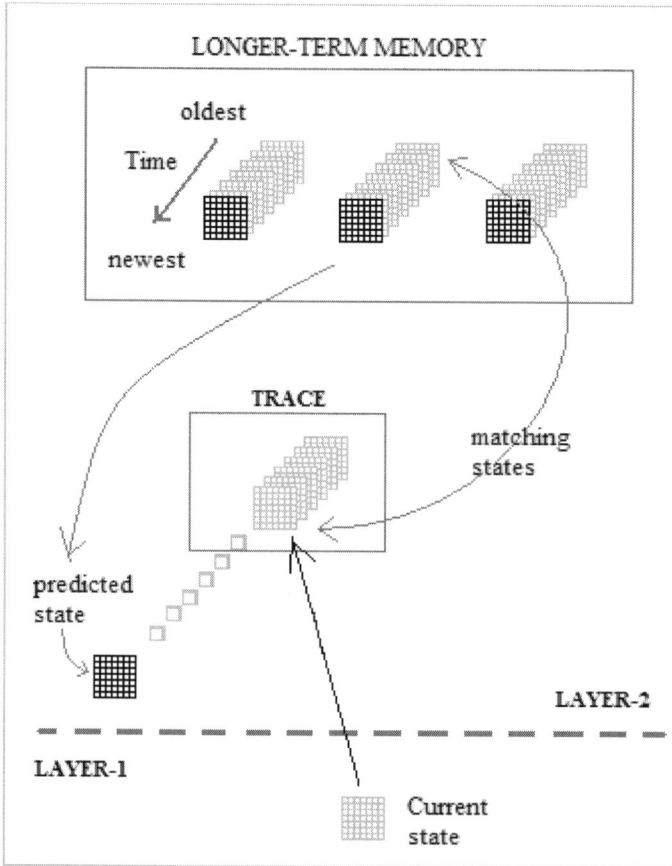

Phase-layer-1, it will be recalled, derived these priority levels by a process of trial and error during its long evolutionary development. Once again we see that it is that period of evolution which sets the basic criteria for the survival of the mechanisms, and it is these basic criteria which limit and give the rest of the system a launching platform for its subsequent development.

So the selection of information to be stored in longer-term memory, is based on the occurrence of high priority items stored in the short-term memory. That is illustrated in the diagram.

That procedure can be carried out without the aid of any complicated intellectual abilities and it will result in the storage of a collection of traces, or sequences, each giving information about an approaching high priority condition, such as a goal or anti-goal.

Note that. Each of the entries in the longer-term memory consists of a trace which has a high priority event at one end - the most recent end.

(S1,S2,S3,S4, ...Sn*)

where time advances from S1 to Sn and * indicates a high priority condition.

It follows that if the system is able to recognise the re-occurrence of S1, or better still the sequence S1,S2,S3, then it can anticipate that Sn* will occur in a short time. The diagram illustrates.

The efficacy of this mechanism depends upon history repeating itself and on the ability of the system to match states (or parts of states) in a way that allows for some tolerance of discrepancies. The technique allows prediction no further into the future than the time duration of the trace memory. It is clearly not a very accurate method of prediction, but it is better than no prediction at all. The system consisting of phase-layer-1, on its own, lived only in the present. We can now see that the system consisting of phase-layer-1 and phase-layer-2 together, is able to live in the past, the present and the future, but only to the extent determined by the duration of the trace (in both directions).

When a prediction is made, the stored sequence in longer-term memory provides the system with a script to be followed - if the predicted state is a goal state. What the phase-layer-2 mechanism must do is to make the data in the selected sequence, like the current trace itself, available to determine the behaviour of phase-layer-1.

Avoiding anti-goals.

05.08

If the predicted state is not a goal but an anti-goal, that raises an interesting problem. In these circumstances, the prescribed sequence of actions provides only a list of actions which should NOT be taken. These will increase in urgency as the high priority anti-goal approaches, but they do not indicate what should be done instead. The best that might be possible in the short term is to adopt some kind of immediate "startle" reaction. This may be an action with no obvious objective - a jerk, a jump, or some such thing. That may, on some occasions, change circumstances sufficiently to avoid the predicted progression to an anti-goal.

That opens up a further possibility. If those new conditions, created by the startle reaction, can be matched with conditions in some other sequence in the longer-term memory, the system may be able to find there a script to be followed to an alternative and much more desirable goal-state.

So if the system "wants" to avoid some "unpleasant" condition it could first throw in a random disturbance to change the environmental circumstances and then "choose" from a range of actions (based on a match with those new conditions) which will produce a more "favourable" outcome.

I have placed quotations round several words in the previous sentence to indicate that they should not be taken literally. There is no mechanism here, which could reasonably be described accurately as "wanting" or "disliking" or "choosing". But note how easy and tempting it is to slip into that loose form of description, using the terminology of "wanting" and "disliking".

This is the terminology for externally observed behaviour. It is succinct and it can act effectively as a substitute for a detailed and verbose description of the internal mechanism which produced that external behaviour. I have noted earlier that a detailed description of the internal mechanism is often inaccessible so these outside view descriptions may be all that is possible. It is a speech mannerism which we use frequently in every day parlance. It is what we call "figurative" language. If I say, "*That book is trying to fall off the arm of your chair*", you will be immediately aware of the circumstances without being fooled into thinking that the book has some kind of internal conscious motivation for its falling (or thinking that I think that).

And that form of language (and the mental representation which is associated with it) is crucial to my explanation of consciousness (in terms of inside and outside views).

Although this ability to predict and select a suitable course of action, is of limited accuracy, it does represent one important evolutionary step into the business of making predictions and of learning from experience.

Purging the longer-term memory.

05.09

Although the entries in the longer-term memory are selective and limited to those containing a high priority condition, it is still the case that the need to store more and more data will eventually overwhelm the mechanism's storage capacity. It is essential, therefore, that the mechanism should have some way to purge the longer-term memory of content which is relatively unimportant. Recall that the priority levels originally used to identify the importance of entries, were set by evolution over a very long period of time. Circumstances move on and it is possible that conditions which were important a long time ago, no longer occur with such frequency.

One way to remove items of that kind would be to keep a count of the occasions on which each entry in longer-term memory was identified and used as a script for action. Those with a low frequency could then be removed.

This technique is reminiscent of (and may evolve from) the way the phase-layer-1 system can purge itself of redundant detection units (neurological plasticity).

Short-term memory

05.10

I stated at the outset that this book was concerned with a functional description of the brain and that I would try to avoid discussion of what is known about its physical structure. It is known, for example, from psychological tests, from the study of damaged brains and from scanning experiments, that the human brain does have a short-term memory, that that memory appears to be located in several different parts of the structure and that these separate parts have different functional capabilities. From the narrow perspective I have chosen, however, the physical separation and the localisation of these parts is not of significance. The ability of the brain to carry out the required functions is not affected by locality or distribution.

CHAPTER 6

Comments on Phase-layer-2 - and a useful analogy.

Konrad Lorenz

06.01

As I was writing the words above, about how the longer-term memory could provide a creature with a script for the actions it should perform to attain some desirable goal, I had a strong recollection of a text I had read a great many years before - Konrad Lorenz, "King Solomon's Ring". The following passage comes from Chapter 9, "The Taming of the Shrew".

Lorenz had constructed an observation chamber or artificial habitat where he could watch the behaviour of water-shrews.

"In a territory unknown to it, the water-shrew will never run fast except under pressure of extreme fear, and then it will run blindly along bumping into objects and usually getting caught in a blind alley. But unless the little animal is severely frightened, it moves, in strange surroundings, only step by step, whiskering right and left all the time and following a path that is anything but straight. Its course is determined by a hundred fortuitous factors when it walks that way for the first time. But after a few repetitions, it is evident that the shrew recognises the locality in which it finds itself and that it repeats, with the utmost exactitude, the movements which it performed the previous time. At the same time it was noticeable that the animal moves along much faster whenever it is repeating what it has already learned. When placed on a path which it has already traversed a few times, the shrew starts on its way slowly, carefully whiskering. Suddenly it finds known bearings, and now rushes forward a short distance, repeating exactly every step and turn which it executed on the last occasion. Then, when it comes to a spot where it ceases to know the way by heart, it is reduced to whiskering again and to feeling its way step by step. Soon another burst of speed follows and the

same thing is repeated, bursts of speed alternating with slow progress. .... Once the shrew is well settled in its path-habits it is as strictly bound to them as a railway engine to its tracks and is unable to deviate from them by even a few centimetres. If it diverges from its path by so much as an inch, it is forced to stop abruptly, and laboriously regain its bearings. The same behaviour can be caused experimentally by changing some small detail in the customary path of the animal. ... [The shrews] were accustomed to jump on and off the stones which lay in their path. If I moved the stones out of the runway, placing both together in the middle of the table, the shrews would jump right up into the air in the place the stone should have been; they came down with a jarring bump, were obviously disconcerted and started whiskering cautiously right and left, just as they behaved in an unknown environment. And then they did a most interesting thing: they went back the way they had come, carefully feeling their way until they had again got their bearings. Then, facing round again, they tried again with a rush and a jump and crashed down exactly as they had done a few seconds before. Only then did they seem to realise that the first fall had not been its own fault but was due to a change in the wonted pathway and now they proceeded to explore the alteration, cautiously sniffing and be whiskering the place where the stone ought to have been. This method of going back to the start and trying again always reminded me of a small boy who, in reciting a poem, gets stuck and begins again at an earlier verse."

[Lorenz 1952]

06.02

A shrew is a mammal. When that asteroid slammed into the Gulf of Mexico at Chicxulube and, as is widely believed, wiped out the dinosaurs, it was a small shrew-like mammal that was thought to have survived the conditions which followed, and which gave rise to the evolution of mammals - including humans.

A shrew is probably conscious and will certainly be capable of more sophisticated behaviour than that which Lorenz's account seems to suggest. The point about subsumption architecture, however, is that a collection of different mechanisms, some primitive, some more sophisticated, can operate together, each operating in the way it normally does and each doing what it does best. My hypothetical phase-layered model is entirely compatible with the idea of a shrew sometimes operating in a conscious exploratory "whiskering" mode and sometimes in "script mode" exactly as Lorenz described. By "script mode" I mean following specified actions - as it were in auto-pilot. This would leave the higher parts of the brain to concentrate on a smaller number of specialised tasks until an interrupt signal draws its focus of attention on to the cause of that interrupt.

The Knitting Pattern analogy

06.03

At this phase-layer-2 point of the system's evolution the system is still some way from reaching the stage of conscious experience. Yet the format of information storage, at this stage, has an important bearing on that topic. For many people intuition seems to suggest that we are able to recover from memory some kind of internal graphic image of our experiences. These intuitions are clearly influenced by the importance that sighted people attribute to vision, but it cannot be sustained when one considers the conscious experience of people who have been born blind. Nevertheless the notion of an internal graphic image format for both current and remembered experience remains a dominant intuition.

I do not dismiss these intuitions as imaginary or of no importance. I think that even if I do not accept them as a literal fact, I do think that any valid explanation of consciousness must also be able to explain why we have those intuitions. So I am anxious to ensure that at this early stage in the evolution of my proposed system, the information relating to those intuitions is not thrown away.

The "*fuzzball*", as I have termed it, has a great deal of information and one aspect of that information will be an indication of the source from which any particular part of the information was derived. We can think of that as being like tying a label on the data content of the fuzzball - this bit from vision, that from the ears, ... and so on.

An analogy might help to clarify. There are two ways in which information about a knitted woollen garment might be given to a person. One way is to hand over a photograph of the finished pullover or whatever. The second way is to hand over a set of knitting pattern instructions. To a person who is an experienced knitter, the second method is probably more informative. I suggest that the condensed format in which information about experiences is stored in the brain, is more like a knitting pattern than a graphic image. A knitting pattern contains the information that would enable an experienced knitter to knit herself an understanding of the garment. So the stored memory of an experience would not, as it were, show an action replay of the original experience, as a set of graphic images. It would inform the person trying to recall the memory how to reconstruct that experience.

Constructing procedures

06.04

Because the terminology we often use (when we discuss brain functions), comes from computer technology, that terminology tends to exert an undue influence on our thinking. Thus, when we talk about computers, we often make a distinction between hardware and software - and there is, undoubtedly, a clear physical difference, in any given context. And that is true even although we know that each of these can be re-cast as the other. Software can be realised as hardware and vice versa. That is the basic idea which underpins the idea of a Universal Turing Machine.

But although we know that, we still tend to think in terms of that distinction between hardware and software. But in the brain, in physical terms, there really is no such distinction. Everything inside a brain is just a complicated and interconnected collection of brain-stuff. Some collections can act as static representations and other collections can do things. So if we are content with the idea of the brain constructing a representation of something experienced in the so called "real world" (and putting that construction in working storage) and of creating memory storage records (in long-term memory), why should we not also be happy with the idea that it could construct a method of doing things - by creating just another set of interconnected brain-stuff? That is - why can it also not construct programs? And then use them to do (or to construct) other things?

The knitting pattern analogy is a central and important part of my proposal. I am aware, however, that it is just an analogy and that, as it stands, it lacks detail about how it could actually operate. I think about these things as arising from the memory-reconstruction procedure - slotting concepts into appropriate locations within a stored memory.

The diagrams I have drawn of the structure of phase-layer-1, show the collection of detection units feeding signals to the action units which then pass signals to the muscles to control the limbs. But some of the signals of the action units can feed backwards into the collection of detection units and trigger some actions there. We could get a re-organisation of stored records. And we could get a momentary construction of procedures. These procedures when they operate could be anywhere within working-memory. So if we are looking with brain-scanning equipment to find the neural correlates of these actions, we might find that we are looking for chimera. In view of the fact that "trying to find the neural correlate of consciousness" is a very active topic of research, it seems to me that that consideration may be of importance.

It could be, for example, that searching for the physical location where consciousness takes place within the brain, is rather like trying to find the location where snowflakes settle, when there are great many of them, distributed widely, and they are settling on to the surface of a warm ocean.

I shall return to that idea later when I have developed the system to the point where it can legitimately be described as being conscious.

The ability to construct procedures and place these in working memory for enactment, opens up the possibility of ephemeral procedures being created, as it were, on the hoof, as the mechanism is engaged in understanding events. I shall tackle the issue of understanding language at a later time (Chapter 11) but we can note here that one important and potentially puzzling aspect of language understanding is the way we deal so effectively with ambiguity. For example, if we are discussing a game of snooker, a statement such as "he's going for the rest" will immediately, and seemingly automatically, be interpreted as a reference to the player reaching for the thing a snooker player might use to support the cue, for a stroke which lies beyond arm's reach. The idea that the player might be about to depart for a short period of repose, seldom occurs. The explanation we are often offered is that the context "potentiates" or "pre-disposes" us to that interpretation. What I have never seen, however, is any attempted description of a mechanism which could put that pre-disposition into effect.

I can offer an explanation. If the system is able to create ephemeral procedures "on the hoof" and hold them, briefly, at the ready, in working memory, we can see why context dependent interpretation would work so effectively. In effect these would be additional structures, acting as additional detection units – which have been acquired by learning from past experience.

CHAPTER 7

Packing more information into the memory and the consequence of that - the beginning of conscious thinking.

Phase-layer-3: Introducing concepts

07.01

A blind man might progress to the edge of a cliff in a series of small steps. The fatal step, the one which takes him over the edge, need be no larger than any of the others, but the consequences could hardly be more dramatic. Something similar happens when my proposed evolving system takes the next step towards consciousness. Small step. Huge consequences. In this case, however, the change is life-preserving and life-enhancing rather than fatal. The system starts to form concepts and with concepts it can start to understand where it is, and what it is doing.

Thinking with Concepts

07.02

"Without concepts, there would be no thoughts. Concepts are the basic timber of our mental lives."   [Prinz 2002]

"When we recognise something, we find an exact match or a good partial match between a pattern of sensory data and some kind of stored record of identical or similar entries that we have seen in the past. Finding a match does not in itself achieve IC [Information Compression]. *But if we decide to memorise the newly-recognised entity in terms of stored patterns, we are in effect merging the new sensory data with the previously-stored patterns and thus compressing the new data.*

Imagine how inconvenient it would be if we could not memorise things in this kind of way. Every momentary perception of a given person would create a completely new memory record despite the fact that a person's appearance and other attributes normally remain largely unchanged from one moment to another. Apart from producing huge amounts of redundancy in our memories, this failure to merge our perceptions of a given person into a single concept would make it very difficult to do simple things like remembering whether or not that person likes sugar in their tea or remembering to send them a card on their birthday."

[Wolff 2001]

Yes ... but what are concepts and where do they come from?

A small quibble with the first quotation - I would have said, "*... without concepts there would be no <u>conscious</u> thoughts*". In previous chapters of this book I described ways in which I think a brain can do quite a lot of unconscious thinking (and the taking of action) without the use of any concepts at all.

And a reservation regarding the second quotation. Wolff writes "*...if we decide to memorise the newly-recognised entity ...*" I question if "*decide*" is the right word in that context. A conscious decision does not need to be involved. As I shall explain here, the acquisition of a concept is an important component of conscious decision making, but it is not necessarily itself the subject of a conscious decision. It happens. We may or may not be conscious of that happening. Our brains have a genetic pre-disposition for the formation of concepts. It is not something we can decide not to do.

Concepts and "understanding"

07.03

When we look at the world around us (and taste, and smell and touch and hear it) our eyes, tongues, noses, finger tips and ears, are assailed by a jumbled mass of different signals.

Well ... No.

Actually, that is not quite the right way to describe the situation. That form of words attributes too much of the initiative to the environment itself. The environment does not know that we are here, watching it do all the stuff that it does.

It is the mechanisms of our perceptions that take the initiative. They it is, which create these input signals. Those mechanisms of perception detect (we could say they "*grab*") the information that is available in the external world and generate signals. For example, the various wavelengths of electromagnetic radiation which impinge on our eyes, the vibrations in the air which strike our ears, and such like, these are not signals. They are just features within the environment. They would have occurred anyway if we were not here to see them. They have no intrinsic significance. Those electromagnetic waves are not coloured. The colours we experience come from us. We make them. Our eyes, ears etc, capture these various features and turn them into signals with some kind of significance - for us.

Like all the other sensory arrays, the retina of the eye sends signals to the rest of the brain, and the brain gathers those signals together, organises them into groups, and chops them up into what we regard as meaningful chunks. It is phase-layer-1 that does the initial part of that stuff. Phase-layer-1 brings the raw data in, identifies the signal patterns it is programmed to identify, attaches to those patterns all that extra information about the colour spectrum, direction of movement, shape recognition, proximity to standard shapes and, most importantly, actions which should be taken in response.

"*Send to the brain*" is another dubious form of words. It is more appropriate to consider eyes, ears, touch-sensitive finger tips etc. as outlying extensions of the brain, which are in contact with the environment - like the branch offices of a global corporation.

07.04

Once all that stuff has been done, by phase-layer-1 and recorded by phase-layer-2, phase-layer-3 can start to take things a bit further. It can add still more information that relates to lots of previous occasions when similar things happened. It can chop the information up into concepts.

A concept is a meaningful chunk of signals, which has lots of connections to other meaningful chunks. Being meaningful means that it has an effect on how we behave. We (and any other conscious creature) can take several of those chunks and/or concepts, put them together in a particular way and build an understanding of the world around us. That way we work out what is happening. It is like building a dynamic representation of events.

The completion of the picture tells a story about what is happening, what has already happened and what is likely to happen next. In terms of my analogy with knitting pattern instructions, each of us knits an understanding of our own environment and our own experience.

Momentary consciousness and full consciousness

07.05

To have a conscious understanding of some aspect of the world the system must -

(1) Recognise and identify an entity or event when it encounters it.

(2) Predict what is likely to happen next - after that recognisable thing has been encountered.

That, I think, is sufficient for a limited form of consciousness, what we may call "instantaneous" or "momentary" consciousness. The system understands what is happening and what it is doing. It can make limited predictions of future events. But it cannot retain a memory of those events in terms of its own understanding. That is, it has no concept of SELF as an entity which is having those experiences. For full consciousness it requires further abilities.

(3) It must develop the concept of SELF.

(4) It must retain a memory of the events which this SELF has experienced.

(5) Based on these abilities it must be able to predict how this SELF is likely to react to those predicted events (i.e. will it like or hate the predicted condition?)

Phase-layer-3 does the first two items on that list. To get the full works, however, the system needs phase-layer-4. We'll get to that shortly.

The Jigsaw analogy

07.06

To understand what is happening and what it itself is doing, the system must construct an interpretation of events as they happen. Building an interpretation is like building a jigsaw picture using concepts as the pieces which are to be fitted together. Note that it is the construction procedure itself, the act of construction, which constitutes an understanding - not its finished and static end-product. Note too that the significance of an experience, that is, the consequences which flow from it are built-in during the construction process as it is happening. Those predictions come as part of the concepts which are the constructional units - the building-bricks used in the construction process. The consequences are not something which must be calculated separately and at a later time using a separate procedure.

A single concept provides the system with an understanding of just one snippet of the world - and does it in a very general way, disconnected from everything else. To make that understanding correspond to an actual occasion or incident the system must construct an understanding of the whole environment, the context of the entity or event, the relationships between entities, the roles they play in the events described, all this as these events are being experienced. To do that the system needs several concepts and these must fit together in a way that is unambiguous.

The picture must have internal consistency, Those pieces should fit snugly together. But there must also be a degree of flexibility - as though the pieces were made of rubber so that a fit can be contrived. Avoiding the contradiction, that that implies, is problematic.

How does it get started?

07.07

But there is a snag. The formation of concepts has to start somewhere. First there are no concepts. And then there is one concept - the very first concept to be formed.

What use is that? You cannot build a jigsaw picture using just one jigsaw piece. As I have insisted all along, with this pseudo-evolution story, every step along the pathway must be associated with at least one identifiable survival advantage. So where is the advantage associated with one jigsaw piece? If there isn't one, the evolution process would need to go in some other direction.

The answer is this - The system must start forming concepts for some other reason. It has to form concepts without knowing that they are concepts or that they are going to be useful at a later time. The advantage that it gets by doing this will therefore seem to have nothing at all to do with concepts or how to use them.

Data Compression

07.08

Most of us are familiar with the idea of data compression. When we transmit text or graphic images to friends, or download files of recorded music via the Internet, we use file formats like .ZIP, .JPG, .GIF and .MP3. Each of these file formats corresponds to a different data-compression algorithm. They share a common strategy. The original file of "raw" data is scanned, chunks of data which repeat several times within the file, are identified. These chunks, wherever they occur, are extracted and one copy of the chunk is stored elsewhere. A much smaller chunk of data, which can be termed a "tag" or a "bookmark", is then inserted into the file at the several points from which the original chunk was extracted. Each tag contains information about where the single copy of the original chunk has been stored.

When there is a need to recover the original data, the original chunk is found and copied and that copy is then inserted back into the location from where it was extracted. This takes time, and so the price that must be paid for the advantage offered by data compression, is the extra time taken to recover the data in its original form. Whether that price is worth paying depends upon the nature of the data, how often it needs to be recovered, and on the detailed operation of the compression algorithm. Some algorithms sacrifice accuracy of recovery for the sake of faster recovery, or a greater degree of compression. In a graphic image of a landscape, for example, we may find that a pale blue sky of subtly varying shades of blue, might lose those subtle differences and become one unbroken field of a single shade - or a patchwork of three or four shades. An algorithm of that kind, which loses some of the original data, is known as a "lossy" form of compression.

The crucial aspects of this compression process, from the point of view of concept formation, are two-fold.

(1) The process produces a collection of repetitive "chunks" of data (without there needing to be any intellectual intervention required to identify which chunks should be selected).

(2) The process offers an immediate advantage - a reduction of memory store size, which allows more memory to be stored in a given size of brain. Even at the very start of the process, when compression has dealt with only a single repeating chunk, a significant reduction in memory size would be achieved. Each additional chunk discovered and extracted increases the survival advantage. So the requirement of pseudo-evolution that each step should be associated with an immediate advantage, is met in full.

Compression chunks

07.09

Initially the compression chunks have no intrinsic significance. Even at this stage, however, we can see that there are three different types of compression chunk.

(1) There are chunks which are totally confined to a single state within the memory trace.

(2) There are chunks which spread over two states.

(3) And, there are chunks which spread over many states.

One-state chunks

07.10

The identification of a one-state chunk, in which all the associated characteristic features are observable at the same time, will be associated with what we often call "a physical object" - a "thing" in other words. When you observe a physical object, like a chair, you observe its colour, its shape, its location and its size. And you observe all of these things simultaneously. When you leave the room (or if the chair leaves the room), all of these properties disappear at the same time. If that is the case then the patterns of signals associated with each of those properties must be present within a single state of the current TRACE.

Fig 07.10 - One-state chunks

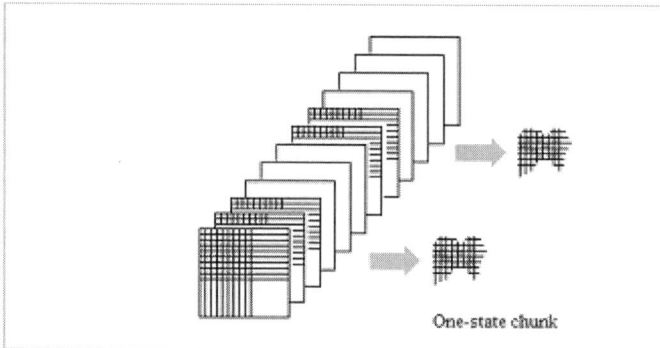

One-state chunk

When that trace is copied to the longer-lasting memory, they will all be part of a single state within an entry of that longer-lasting memory store (and possibly more than one entry). Since the object will be experienced for more than an instant, a state containing all of these features will recur several times.

The characteristics associated with an object are usually presented in different ways. Orientation, location, different ambient lighting and distance, can all affect the appearance of an object. Distance changes the volume and quality of sound as well. The compression algorithm needs to be tolerant of small differences.

Two-state chunks

07.11

When two states (which are not identical or matching) occur repeatedly, as a pair, in such a way that when the first occurs we can be sure that the second will occur shortly, then there has to be some kind of link between them.

Fig 07.11 - Two-state chunks

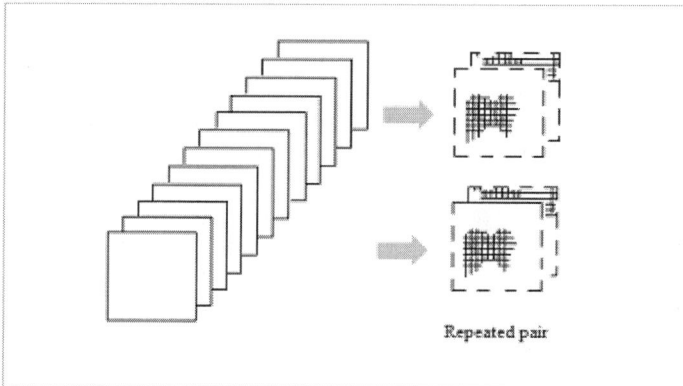

Repeated pair

The link between them, however, is never actually observed. Nevertheless, if we find that we can rely on the first being an accurate predictor of the second, we will suspect that the link is there. We give that link a name. We say that the first is "causing" the second to occur.

The identification of a linked pair of that kind helps the brain to anticipate future events and by doing that it helps the brain to "understand" what it is observing. That is what I mean by "understanding" - knowing how the world "works". What I am suggesting, therefore, is that the identification of paired states of that kind is what provides us with the concept of causation.

Multi-state chunks

07.12

Multi-state chunks can also be formed. These will be difficult to identify. But the difficulty in the recognition of a larger size of chunk is eased if one-state chunks and two-state chunks have already been recognised and replaced by bookmarks.

We need to ask what in real life would correspond to a multi-state chunk of that kind.

Fig 07.12 - Multi-state chunks

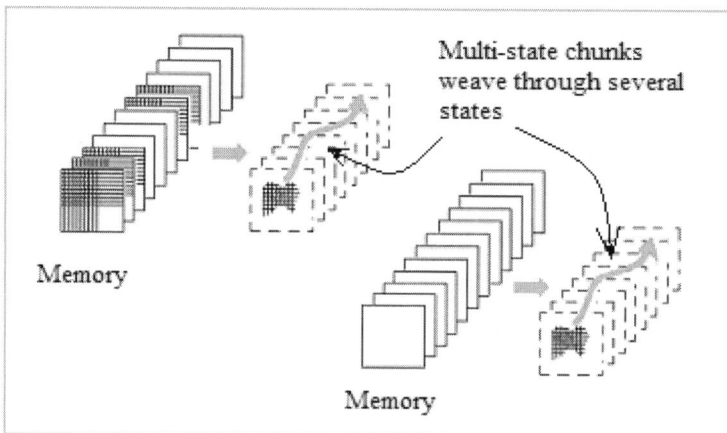

A multi-state chunk is, in effect, a script which relates (or instructs) how a procedure is carried out. It identifies physical components. It describes the characteristics of these components and how these arrangements affect or cause other events to occur. To make use of a concept of that kind it is necessary that the particular components involved should be identified and slotted into position. This piecing together, is rather like casting actors into the roles defined in a short play. The play describes the plot.

Assigning actors (and physical components) to the various roles enables the action to be performed and thus understood.

We have to be careful about the use of the word "understand". What I am trying to do here is to describe the mechanism of understanding. So I cannot use the word "understand" as if it is a component within that description. In a hot liquid the movement of the molecules is the internal mechanism of the phenomenon we call temperature. The individual molecules do not feel hot. In a similar way the procedure of fitting together of concepts to construct a representation of events is the mechanism of understanding. So the concepts, as they are put together to form a representation of experience, they themselves do not understand anything. There is no ghostly presence nearby to understand anything. It is that process of fitting together that is the mechanism of understanding. In terms of my analogy, the mechanism in our brain knits our understanding of our experience. Understanding is not looking at, still less wearing the finished garment. Understanding is the knitting of it - all that stuff with clicking needles and industrious movement of the elbows.

Matching (Tolerating differences)

07.13

A compression algorithm can be applied to any set of data. All it does is look for repeating items. But what constitutes a repeating item depends upon what criteria are used to determine a "match".

Consider a standard deck of cards and the game called "snap". To win that game you must be the first to recognise and respond to any pair of cards which are "identical". But it is a fact that every card in a standard deck is unique. The 7 of Clubs is not identical to the 7 of Hearts. Yet for the purposes of the game we deem them to be identical.

In some other game we might decide to ignore the number values and treat every card of the same suit as being identical. Likewise we can decide that face-cards are considered to be identical. It depends upon the rules of each game, and we decide what these rules are. We can also change the rules as we go along.

We could also simply ignore what is written or printed on the cards and decide that the only thing of importance is the fact that a card is a piece of cardboard with printing on one side and a pattern on the other. In that case the concept we would acquire by looking for chunks which match that description would simply be the concept CARD.

The total collection of chunk-groupings will then tend to adopt the structure of a hierarchy - as shown in the diagram. But the hierarchy will not be perfect. Within this structure there will be many complexities. If the structure is like a house with many floor levels, then there will be within the structure many mezzanine floors and sub-mezzanines between the mezzanines.

Fig 07.13 A property hierarchy of Cards

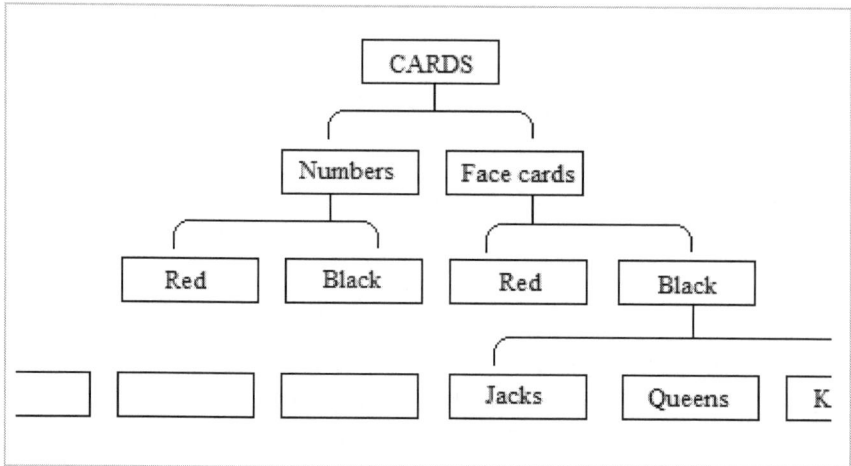

In computer science a structure like that is called an "inheritance hierarchy". The idea of inheritance, refers to the way the properties of any particular item within the structure are shared with its super-ordinate node within the structure and its own properties are passed down to its subordinate nodes.

In this context however, where we are talking about evolution, the term "inheritance" could be ambiguous and so it is best to call this structure a "property hierarchy".

The concept DOG

07.14
Playing cards do not illustrate the problems which arise when physical objects are animate and can alter their own appearance.

Fig 07.14 - dog concept with physical components

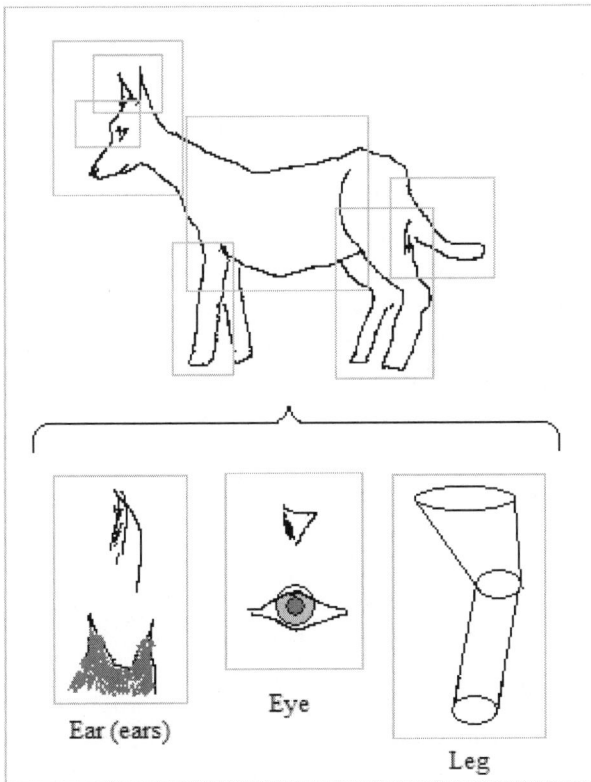

A complex animate object like a dog, is made up of several sub-objects. A tail, a head, a leg, a pointed ear, these are all objects in their own right, as well as being the sub-objects of a dog. Before a dog-chunk is identified, these sub-objects will have been identified and replaced by tags. So the chunk which corresponds to a dog will consist of data within which the sub-objects have been replaced by tags. It is easier to match an ear-tag with another ear-tag, than to match subtly different ears-shapes which are observed when a dog changes its position.

The figure is a schematic illustration of the progression from isolated sub-objects to a composite object.

The physical components of a dog could first be identified as individual items. At that point the world is a confusing jumble. At that point too, the data compression procedure is doing nothing more than extracting arbitrary repeating chunks which have no obvious significance. The memory store is compressed and there is no need for any other justification.

However, once these have been identified and replaced by tags, another application of the compression algorithm, which needs to match only the replacement tags and does not need to work through the subtle variations in shape etc. could note that all of these individual items frequently occur together (in a single state) as a dog walks into the visual scene and then walks away again.

This will produce a new composite chunk which can then be extracted and tagged. The collection of items illustrated in the lower part of the diagram, becomes the composite item illustrated in the upper part. This new thing is the concept of a particular dog called "Fido", say.

Enhancing a one-state chunk

07.15

The point I am trying to make with this example, is that the mechanism can creep up on the sophisticated form we call concepts. Compression chunks can be enhanced to become concepts by repeated applications of the compression algorithm.

What is stored internally is not a visual image. It is a collection of information which informs the brain what it is looking at.

The detailed version of the EAR is associated with a PAIR OF EARS. The information that these things tend to occur in pairs is a significant part of what we know about ears. The same would be true about EYES. Hairiness would be another characteristic, which would be included in the package of information about each component of a DOG. A visual image is only one part of the source from which all of this information is derived. Some of it would come from tactile experience. Some of it from sounds and smells.

When Calvin Coolidge was on a visit to a farm, one of his aides remarked that the sheep nearby appeared to have been sheared. Coolidge is reputed to have replied *"Sure looks like it from this side."* Why does that seem odd? Perhaps it is because we all know that when we look at a sheep, the information to which we have access, in fact, includes all of the sheep - not just a one-sided view.

Enhancing two-state chunks

07.16

Strictly speaking, the pair of states do not need to be chronologically adjacent. They could be separated in time with other states occurring in between. In those circumstances, however, the pair will be much harder to identify as a repeating pair. The adjacent pairs will be among the first repeating chunks to be recognised. Non-adjacent pairs will come along at a later stage.

The identification of two-state chunks will be made easier if the physical objects present in the observable environment have all been replaced by tags.

Consider these examples -

(1) A moving ball strikes a second; the second ball moves away.
(2) A moving object strikes a surface; a noise is heard.
(3) An object is released; it falls.
(4) The image of an object gets larger; a noise gets louder.

Consider the situation that arises if all the physical objects and identifiable events in these accounts are replaced by tags and then the compression algorithm is re-applied. What we get is -

(A) Something happens;
(B) Something else happens.

The individual variations which are associated with each individual part of a two-state chunk, are ignored, and we are left with an empty shell consisting of a pair of states (without internal details). This occurs with such regularity that we can write -

(A) therefore expect (B)

Alternatively

(A) causes (B)

This, I suggest, is the origin of the concept "causes". The implications of that suggestion are many and significant.

David Hume and Causation

07.17

Almost three hundred years ago the philosopher David Hume drew our attention to the fact that no one has ever seen what he called a "*necessary connection*" between a causal precursor and the effect it produces [Hume 1739/40]. All that we do see is that one event follows another. Statisticians often point out that a statistical correlation does not necessarily indicate a causal connection. That should give us pause before we jump to the conclusion that a statistical correlation is all a causal connection really is. But there is more to it than that. This is a statistical correlation which is virtually perfect. The conclusion that (A) causes (B) can be reached legitimately from that observation of statistical correlation if in addition we have evidence that without

110

(A) (B) does not occur. That is, that we can prevent the occurrence of (B) by preventing the occurrence of (A).

An implication that follows from these ideas, is that "causation" is not necessarily a feature of the universe around us. It is really a basic feature of our psychology. It is the mental model we use to enable ourselves to predict events within the environment. In this respect it is similar to colours, which are a product of our minds, but which we tend to project into the environment and regard as coming from it, and not from ourselves.

The mental creation of causal-links is a survival strategy which belongs to the way we look at the universe. They are the bridges we build in our minds, to carry ourselves across the gaps in our understanding of events. From our perspective any change to the environment requires a causal precursor. That is a given of our psychology. If there is no obvious candidate, we invent one. "Forces", like gravity and magnetism, are inventions of our own, designed to allow us to predict observed events. We convince ourselves that we have got it right, if predictions based on those assumptions are supported by observation. So are gravity and magnetism real? To answer that question perhaps what we need is a pragmatic definition of the word "real".

The universe does not need to know the laws of physics, or solve differential equations in order to know what it should do next. But _we_ need to know the laws of physics and be able to solve those equations if _we_ want to anticipate the next thing the universe will do.

Causation, I suggest, should be regarded as a useful mental device which helps us to understand our environment - rather as a magnetic compass (usually) helps us to find our way about the world. But we should not be unduly surprised when we find that, in certain circumstances, that device fails to operate as expected. In experiments in quantum mechanics, time and causation can appear to run backwards. Or do they? If we regard causation and time as fixed properties of nature these observations are astonishing. But if we realise that causation and time are features of our own psychology that astonishment dissolves. Whether we use the concept of causation, or the mathematical notation of consistent histories, is unimportant. Both are merely tools which enable us to predict future observations in particular circumstances. The two methods have equal status and equal merit so long as they provide accurate predictions. The Earth does not need to consult a magnetic compass to know what way to point its axis and we should not be unduly surprised when our magnetic compass fails to work as expected when we reach one of the magnetic poles.

Enhancing multi-state chunks

07.18

A multi-state chunk, is a large and complicated structure. It can be regarded as a chronological chain of one-state and two-state chunks. If these more easily recognised components are identified and replaced by tags, the task of identifying a multi-state chunk is much easier. So the easy ones will come first - moving, rolling, bouncing, standing still. Later, the chunks will be expanded to include walking, shouting, talking, transferring from hand to hand. And still later - a lot later - will come activities such as purchasing, shopping and house construction.

Selection criteria

07.19

It is sometimes hard for ourselves, in the light of our ability to recognise various physical objects in the form of concepts, to transport ourselves back to an earlier stage in the acquisition of concepts, and to see these things as just arbitrary chunks. But that is how it must be in the early stages. These chunks, moreover, are not chunks of sensory data coming from the environment. They are chunks of data coming from the phase-layer-1 stimulus-response automaton. For that reason they include more than data originating in the external environment. They must also include the data coming from the triggered action responses.

The implication of that is significant. The data which phase-layer-1 provides not only consists of data (the conditions of its detection units), it is data which has been interpreted in terms of the actions which these data trigger. If these action responses are included in the memory records then they too can be used by the selection process. So if several different things all trigger a similar response, they can be gathered up and used to form a single compression chunk.

This is a system, which must lift itself off the ground by its own bootstraps without the assistance of the kind of knowledge which we (who have already travelled by this pathway) now have.

The meaning and significance of data are defined by the consequences that are defined by a process that reads and acts upon that data.

Enhancement by repetition of the compression procedure.

07.20

Consider, for example, the concept CHAIR. Chairs come in all shapes and sizes. Since a chair is an artefact of modern life, phase-layer-1 will not have been able to evolve a shape detection mechanism for chairs. But chairs will still be a part of our experience and so the pattern of data associated with the experience of a chair will be present within the longer-lasting memory store and eventually be identified as a repeating chunk. But the shapes, the visual experience, not to mention the comfort experienced when we sit on an armchair, an upright chair, a three-legged stool, a piano stool, and so on, are all very different from one another. So these physical objects will become separate compression chunks. However, if these compression chunks are removed and replaced by tags, re-application of the compression algorithm, being able then to ignore the differences in the physical shapes of these things, but still be able to note the similarity in the use to which they are put by humans, will be able to extract the compression chunk which we might now label - "*things you sit on*". The observation of the act of sitting on something is not confined to a single state. So this chunk will need to be a multi-state chunk. Within that chunk the thing which is being sat upon will be undefined (but will contain a number of pointers to the various entities from which it was derived).

Priority as a criterion

07.21

At a later stage an additional criterion can be introduced - the degree of priority with which a chunk may be associated. A chunk of data which has been identified as being of very high priority will then be included in the set of chunks which are extracted and stored elsewhere even if that chunk does not repeat often or (if the priority is high enough) even if it does not repeat at all. But that comes later. For the present, the only survival advantage which drives the evolution of these facilities is the advantage of saving memory space. It is only later, when the interpretation process begins to be performed, that the ability to predict becomes a factor and the prediction of high priority events becomes an important survival advantage. For the present, therefore, repetition is the only criterion involved in chunk selection.

Restoration of memory

07.22

The compression procedure brings with it, not only a collection of useful chunks, it also brings with it that memory reconstruction procedure. Recall how that is done. The tag which replaced an extracted chunk is consulted to discover where the extracted chunk is stored. The chunk is then recovered. More correctly, the stored chunk is copied. (The chunk may be needed on other occasions so the mechanism should not remove it from the store of chunks.) That copy version of the chunk is then inserted into its original location within the long lasting memory.

That requires the mechanism to be able to copy material from one location to another. The implication of that is that within the brain there are areas with unused storage locations where new structures can be created. It has often been suggested that a part of the brain is used as "working storage" [Baars 2013] and my proposal is in agreement with that.

Some forms of compression chunk are not strictly identical. When that happens, the tag or bookmark used to identify the extraction/insertion location, can be used to hold any items of data which are peculiar to that particular experience. As the chunk is restored to its proper location, those additional items of data can also be restored and any links between the original memory and the chunk, which were broken, can be reformed.

With that facility available, all that is needed to put those compression chunks or nascent concepts to work, is a small "accident". The memory reconstruction process must be applied to the TRACE. The trace does not automatically have tags, but there will be parts of it which hold material that coincides with particular compression chunks. If the system starts to "reconstruct" the TRACE, while it is still current, it will be adding to that current record of events, additional information which was gained on previous encounters with the events that gave rise to those chunks.

Interpretation of the TRACE

07.23

This process of memory reconstruction is exactly what is required to make use of the chunks in a new way. This is will be called the "interpretation process".

The figure shows the development of an interpretation structure applied to the trace. Each chunk of material in the TRACE which can be recognised as corresponding to some previously formed concept, is replaced by that concept.

The TRACE is short-lived. That means that while the interpretation process will enhance the system's understanding of events, it will be only a momentary enhancement. The system is given forewarning of important events in the very near future. It will "understand" physical objects in the sense of having information about what these objects are used for. That could be described as a form of conscious understanding. But it is not the full works, because the information is not retained for future use. Previously, I used the analogy of a jigsaw puzzle. I said that concepts are used like jigsaw pieces to construct a picture and that is a good analogy. But it is a picture which does not last.

Fig 07.23 Interpretation of the TRACE

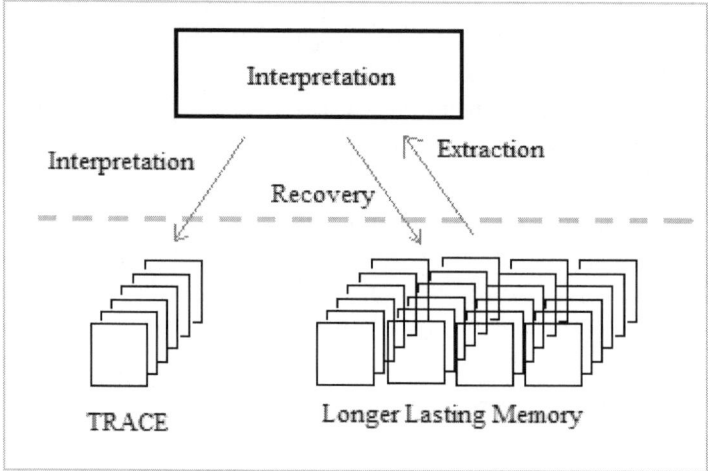

Even so, the picture is useful. If there is some event or condition which tends to be triggered by the appearance of a given physical object - a dog barks, a ball bounces, a falling object bangs when it hits the floor, a box is often opened to gain access to its contents - data relating to those frequently associated observations, will then be included in an expanded chunk. The system takes an important step forwards as it acquires the ability to make predictions.

We could call it "instantaneous consciousness" or perhaps "conscious awareness". The understanding of events, which it is able to form, is gone almost before it is formed.

Indexing and Dreaming

07.24

Because the TRACE is ephemeral, the interpretation process must be carried out at speed. To make that possible the system needs to be able to characterise each chunk in a way that will enable it to be found very rapidly. Each chunk must be indexed. That is, it must be examined for the presence of characteristic components and these must be recorded in association with information about the chunk's storage location. That is precisely what the tags in the compression process do. So we could regard the tags-forming procedure as a plausible evolutionary precursor for index formation.

Indexing is also a slow and laborious task, and if it is to be done efficiently, the system would need to inhibit the arrival of new experiences. In other words, the system needs to go to sleep, and to dream.

Dreaming, I suggest, is the background indexing procedure at work. Memory is scanned and reconstructed. Repeating chunks are identified. Index tags are prepared. Old memories and old chunks are recovered to confirm the content and its relevance to the new chunks. New concepts are formed by linking new chunks with old chunks. The storage locations of the new chunks/concepts are recorded with the tags and the updated tag is stored in an index.

A certain amount of this background activity can take place while the system is awake, by interleaving the background task with the current foreground tasks (i.e. the system can take mini-naps). Some species of animals, which, for safety's sake take little sleep, must do that quite a lot. But that is inadequate if background activity is significant (as it is in humans). If sleep is denied, the brain will then become unable to identify relevant concepts. It will become confused. A sleep-deprived brain would keep switching off in an effort to catch up with its background task.

Other work

07.25

The idea that data compression can be linked to the formation of concepts, has been around for some time [Rendell 1985]. However, most experimental work has been directed towards the development of practical systems which can be applied in specific contexts [Wolff 2001]. There have been few attempts to investigate data compression as a potential solution to the general question - How does a biological brain form concepts from sensory information? Such experimental work that there has been, has also been concerned mainly with the processing of "raw" data, that is, data produced by an optical retina, or similar (such as the output from a so-called connection machine). Often too, experimental systems introduce guidance (supplied by a knowledgeable human advisor), to enable an automatic system to identify what concepts are of significance to ourselves.

The mechanism being discussed here differs from these other approaches in that it proposes the application of data compression techniques (without any form of human guidance) to data which has its origin in the phase-layer-1 SRA, which includes data related to the active response the SRA has developed to each identifiable stimulus and which has been specially selected by having been identified as "high priority" by that SRA (see later).

This means that, in effect, not only that we are applying compression techniques to a highly condensed, and multi-dimensional form of information, but that we are taking advantage of a great many years of evolution and natural selection, as a substitute for the kind of human guidance used in other systems.

Reporting on his experiments with human concept formation, Jacob Feldman stated as his main result, that simple concepts are easier to learn than complex ones [Feldman 2003]. That may seem to be so obvious a conclusion that it scarcely merits comment, but it is in fact a very welcome indication that the method of concept formation seems to involve the identification of common features from a number of examples. This stands in contrast to the idea that concepts are categorised in terms of the extent to which each resembles various stored exemplars. Both methods may operate in parallel.

Flexibility of concept properties

07.26

When a concept is retrieved from the store and used to enhance the TRACE, it must be possible for the properties identified within the concept, to be modified. If the TRACE records the observation of a three-legged dog, the concept DOG would be fetched, and the standard issue of four legs modified to be three legs, before the concept is inserted into the TRACE. Note that the knowledge that a dog normally has four legs is an important piece of knowledge about dogs, so the standard issue should remain available within the augmented structure (with one leg explicitly deleted).

The convergence of a property hierarchy

07.27

Earlier I remarked that we should not suppose that this structure will be as neat as the one illustrated. The properties associated with each concept, and the way they are arranged, will depend upon the unpredictable experience of each individual person (or pseudo-creature). You encountered Fido and Spot. I encountered Rover and Pluto. So the bottom levels of my property hierarchy will be quite different from the bottom level of yours. But as we develop these hierarchies and progressively discard particular properties, that discrepancy will change. The two property hierarchies will converge at the top level. Perhaps Fido and Spot were black and Rover and Pluto were white. But when we have both developed our property hierarchies, we will find that at the top level, where all the individual properties associated with individual dogs are no longer there, the concepts we have are very nearly identical. My general idea of a dog is probably very like your general idea of a dog.

At this stage of its development the system has no words with which it can refer to any specific item. It has been reported, however, that some dogs are able to demonstrate that they have the concept DOG, by selecting, with a nudge of the nose, pictures of a variety of dogs which they have not seen previously [Range 2008]. Lack of language does not appear to hinder the formation of simple concepts.

Generalising events and actions

07.28

The same re-application of the compression algorithm can be carried out on multi-state chunks, with a relaxation of the criteria required to establish commonality, the result is a generalisation of the events involved. A particular visit to a supermarket, will be merged with all other visits to the same supermarket and the result will be the concept of shopping in that particular supermarket. The date, the weather, the items purchased and the means of transport used, will all be eliminated.

Only those aspects of the visit, which are common to all, will remain. That concept can at the next stage of compression be merged with other kinds of shopping expedition, to produce the generalised concept of shopping, a transaction in which money is exchanged for goods. Later still the concept of internet shopping can be introduced and merged. Buying a house is usually a complicated affair involving lawyers, mortgages and the signing of documents, but it has some of the general features of a purchase. From this will emerge the concept of ownership, and legal recognition of ownership. These are abstract concepts.

From this idea we can obtain a definition of an abstract term. It is the generalisation of a number of events and activities, shorn of all particular details and retaining only the important common core of these actions.

Note: these same principles can be applied to the formation of abstract mathematical concepts. In this case, however, there is nothing that corresponds to basic sensory experience. No one has ever seen a perfect circle or a perfectly straight line with zero thickness. No one has ever encountered a derivative except for the way we present these ideas as diagrammatic analogues. The formative procedure for these things may start with actual observations, but then the properties these things really have are modified or idealised.

Knitting Patterns again

07.29

Earlier, I offered an analogy between the format of memory storage and knitting instructions. Consider the computational burden which would be placed upon the system if during this indexing procedure, the indexed features of a graphic image had to be re-recognised and re-isolated before a new entry could be properly classified and stored with similar items. Consider too the difficulty we have in explaining how this process of searching for and combining snippets of graphic images could give rise to new images never previously experienced.

But note how easy and natural that explanation is, if memories are stored in a format which has similar characteristics to knitting instructions. If we take snippets from several instructions, paste them together and then try to knit the garment defined in that way, the result is likely to be somewhat grotesque and it is unlikely that anyone would want to wear it. But it is obvious that there would be a result of some kind.

Representation

07.30

The idea, that the brain is constantly building models and checking them for accuracy, raises a question. What format should we adopt to present these representations to ourselves?

The answer is that the format, which we use to communicate our ideas about representation to ourselves, is not of any great importance. Anything that gets the message across will do. We could invent graphical methods, or mathematical notations of various kinds. We could invent new formal computer languages with which to express models. The issue which is of importance, however, is that the format chosen should be able to express, or represent, all the forms of information required and that the processing procedures are able to extract the information they require in order to guide how the system responds.

Earlier, I offered a graphical format for representations. The basic unit was the "STATE".

Fig 07.30 (1) the representation of a state

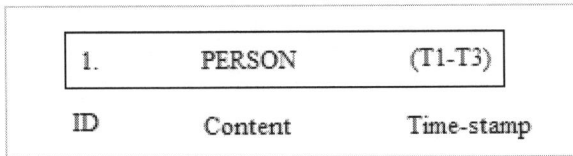

1.	PERSON	(T1-T3)
ID	Content	Time-stamp

The next diagram shows the relationship between the representation of a state in that graphical format, and the matrix form of data which can be obtained from the TRACE structure and from each entry within the Longer-Lasting Memory.

In the diagram, the state with ID No = 1 is shown as a rectangular box. The time-stamp indicates that it is a single-state chunk which extends through three adjacent matrices in the phase-layer-2 TRACE structure or an element within the Longer-Lasting Memory. That is, it is a representation of some physical entity, which entered the field of vision (or of touch or hearing or scent) and stayed there for more than a single moment.

For the representation of this, as a single box-shape with ID number and time-extension, no complex change of format is required. All we have here is a change of presentational format (or notation) on the printed page. The time-stamp indicates the period of time (and therefore the number of matrices) during which the entity persists within the field of experience. Time is just another of the dimensions that the brain adds to the fuzzball of information.

The point I am making here is that the box-shape representation of states, is not new information nor is it a different form of representation. time-stamp showing the time at which the object had that location.

Fig 07.30(2) Box-shapes representing STATES

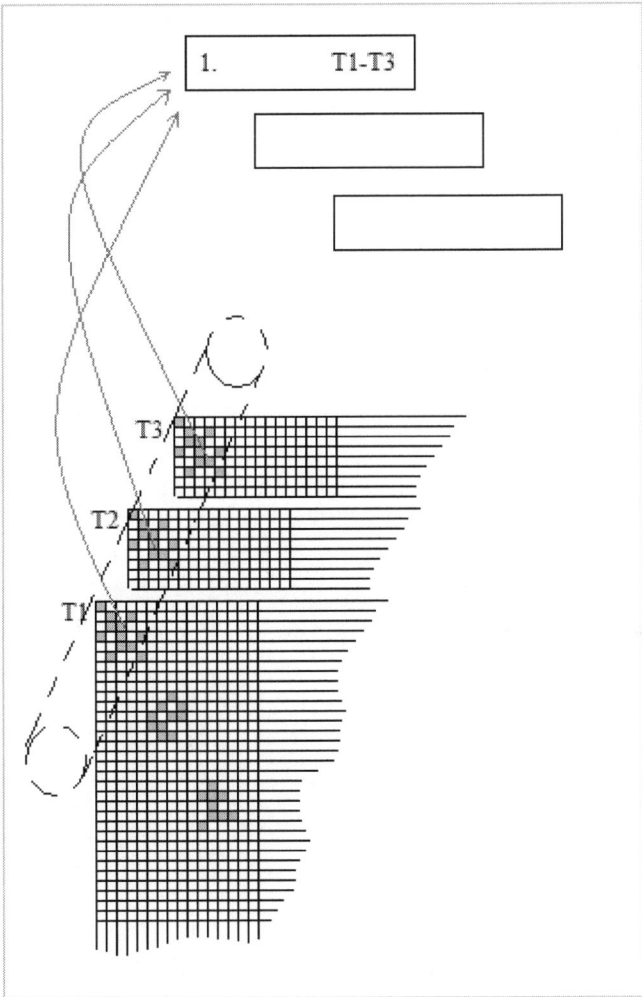

It is just a different notation for the presentation of the same information to ourselves. The diagram tries to show the relationship. There is a single object which persists through four different matrices with time-stamps T1, T2, T3 and T4. The object (OBJECT-X) is present at all of these times. That has been given the time-stamp T1-T4. However, the object has several different locations and each of these has an individual

Naive physics

07.31

Herman Bondi was a physicist, a Nobel Prize winner and, in the middle of the last century, a popular presenter of science programmes on TV.

He used to say that a typical person learns more physics in the first two years of life, than he or she will learn during the rest of that person's span. And that is true, Bondi used to add with a twinkle, even if that person goes on to become a professor of physics.

"Naive physics" is the term often used to describe the kind of knowledge acquired in those early years. Objects fall downwards. Objects weigh heavily in the hand. Water adopts the shape of its containing vessel. When two objects collide there is usually some kind of sound produced. That kind of thing. We are so accustomed to these observable features of our world we tend to forget that being able to recognise them as concepts, is a skill that needs to be learned..

What we do *not* need to learn, is how to observe and how to form concepts from those observations. The ability to do these things is part of the legacy we were bequeathed by evolution.

Fig 07.31 A single object with several locations

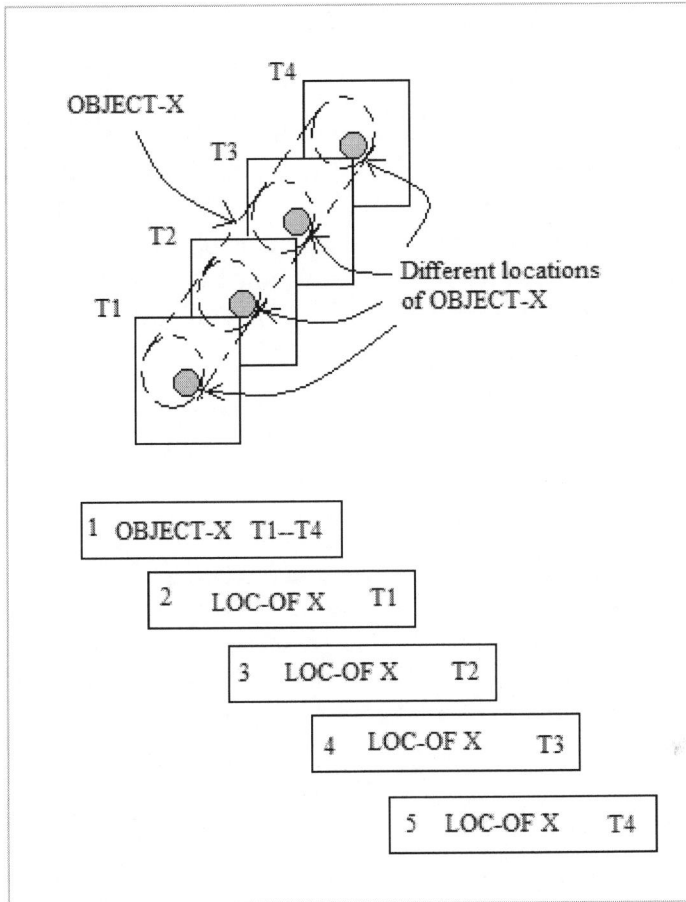

The representation of naive physics.

07.32

We need to find a way to incorporate the knowledge the system must have of the basic ways in which matter behaves. The compression algorithm can organise the representations of all kinds of physical object into a property hierarchy. The issue being addressed here is this - How do we represent the properties of the highest level in that property hierarchy? What are the basic properties of a PHYSICAL-OBJECT which are inherited by all the subordinate physical objects.

The representational structure shown in the next diagram is extremely clumsy. Perhaps there is a more elegant solution. But somewhere within the system there has to be an explicit representation of the learned fact, that if a physical object is not supported, it will fall, and go on falling until something intervenes to prevent it falling. To my mind the representation of SUPPORT must include within it a representation of FALL.

Fig 07.32 - Support/Fall

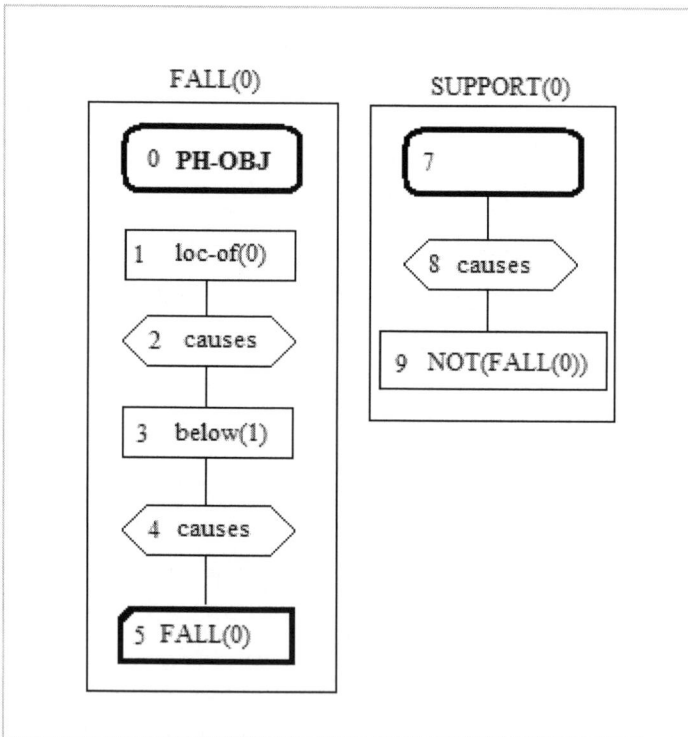

Note the re-use of the representation of FALL inside the representation of FALL. That technique is called "recursion" and it is clearly a recipe for disaster unless there is some way an external intervention can prevent it running on until the computational mechanism runs out of storage space.

Note also the use of the "causal-linkage". The location (state-1) causes the physical object to fall to a lower location (state-3), which then causes the physical object to fall further.

This avoids the use of explicit loops. The use of loops has problems of its own since we do not know in advance how many loops will be involved.

The idea is that this representation will be associated with the concept PHYSICAL-OBJECT (at the top of the property hierarchy) and that it will be inherited, as a standard or assumed property, by every physical object within the property hierarchy. The inclusion can be indicated by placing a reference to the FALL property. There is no need for all of this representation to be expanded every time a physical object is involved. The solution proposed for prevention of the parts explosion problem should be adopted. Keep these expanded representations, available, but not shown, until they are needed. Nevertheless, the property FALL is one of the basic properties of a physical object, and indeed is part of the definition of what the description "physical object" means.

There will be many other basic properties which will require representation in a similar way. I did not say this project would be simple.

NOTE: I am well aware that not all physical objects fall downwards. Some things like balloons float upwards and aeroplanes fly. However, it would not be impossible to amend my suggested representation and create different categories of object which behave in non-standard ways.

The limitations of phase-layer-3

07.33

Phase-layer-3 can understand its environment, in the sense that it can predict the likely outcome arising from the events it can observe. However, it has no memory of that understanding. It is conscious only in the immediate way that I have described as conscious awareness or instantaneous consciousness. It cannot predict the behaviour of other sentient creatures. It cannot predict its own reaction to future events. So it cannot extend its ability to predict to take into account its own behaviour and that of other animate species.

To make that extension possible it has to have some concept of a MIND that drives the behaviour of a living creature. It also needs a concept of SELFMIND with emotional drives which can be expressed as desires and dislikes. That notion of itself as a conscious entity with goals, enables it to avoid infinite recursion and also to dodge the problem of the evolutionary origins of its instinctive reactions to events.

CHAPTER 8

Comments on Phase-layer-3

Compressing Memory

08.01

Phase-layer-3 has a primary task and a secondary task. The secondary task evolves from the first.

The primary task is to reduce the brain-space needed by phase-layer-2 to store its memory records. The technique of data compression is well known and established. A store of data is scanned, repeating chunks of material are identified, these chunks are then removed and replaced by a tag or bookmark. One copy of the extracted compression chunk is stored elsewhere and each tag carries a pointer which indicates where that common chunk of material is stored.

08.02

To recover a memory record, when that is required, the tag is consulted, the stored chunk is copied and is then slotted back into the location from which it was removed.

To achieve still higher levels of compression the compression algorithms, of which there will be many different varieties using many different criteria for the identification of a match, will be re-applied to the original memory store and also to the store of compression chunks already formed. As more and more chunks are identified and replaced by tags, it becomes easier for the mechanism to identify a wider range of repetitive chunks by virtue of commonality of association or using a narrower range of common properties.

129

Types of chunk

08.03

In the early stages of this process, three types of chunk can be identified which correspond to physical entities, causal connections and time-extended events. Later, as the compression process widens its scope, these sharp distinctions will be come blurred. Many physical entities which have no overt similarity in their visual appearance, can then be grouped together because they are used to perform some common action (like opening a tin can).

Property hierarchy

08.04

The structure which results from this activity takes the form of a property hierarchy. This reduces the space required for storage because the properties which are associated with each individual exemplar, can be stored just once at a higher node in the hierarchy and be "inherited" from that higher node whenever that exemplar becomes the focus of attention. The mechanism of property inheritance is similar to the memory recovery process.

08.05

The secondary task, which evolves from the primary one, is the formation and use of concepts. A concept is a chunk of material to which has been added additional material relating to the context in which it occurs. Since each is formed from many different exemplars, which occurred in different circumstances, each concept (or extended chunk) will contain information, which relates to all of them. It follows that if a concept is used by the memory recovery procedure, it will bring with it that additional material that was derived from other exemplars. As a result the relevant memory trace will be enhanced.

Moreover, that additional material will include information to which we could apply the description - "*and what will happen next might be ...*". In this way, the process of reconstructing memories becomes memory enhancement and an enhancement to the powers of the mechanism to anticipate future events.

Note the use of the words "*might be*". This mechanism does not predict the future precisely. It opens up alternative potential futures. Until those events have actually occurred, however, they will retain that "*potential*" status. The status will change as events unfold.

08.06

It requires only a small adaptation (or mutational change) to the mechanism so that the memory recovery procedure is applied not only to the longer-term memory store in phase-layer-2 but routinely to the short-term memory, or TRACE memory store. Since the trace is a record of experience now and in the recent past, it follows that the process of inserting concepts into the record of new events, which are recognised as having happened in the past, means that the system has acquired the ability to explain those events to itself and to anticipate likely future events. It is this process of enhancement of current events that I have given the name "interpretation".

Although the immediate survival advantaged gained by chunk formation is related to the economy of brain-space and does not appear to have anything to do with the recognition of components within the environment, we can see in this ability to form these chunks the beginnings of another important facility – the ability to augment the collection of evolved detection units, with another collection of detection units that have been acquired by learning from experience. Herein lies our ability to identify artefacts of the modern world.

Note that it is not so much the finished product (the interpretation structure) which is most important about this process. It is the process itself - the active recognition of components and their use in the construction of the interpretation which can be described as the process of "*understanding*" the system's current experience.

Hidden duality

08.07

I think that that is a very important point. It acts as the propulsion unit of my whole proposal. Consciousness, indeed every brain function, is an activity. A mental state, or any static condition, cannot by itself achieve anything. The only thing it can do is to inform some active procedure which accesses it and then responds in some way. It is that response which is the function of the brain. If we think of that interpretation structure as consciousness itself, then we have to propose some additional activity which will access the structure and then behave accordingly. And if we do that then we have once again introduced another form of duality (a hidden duality) and transferred consciousness to an ill-defined second part of that duality. We will also have launched ourselves on an infinite regression to infinity by failing to recognise that ultimately understanding has to correspond to some kind of active process.

08.08

The interpretation process can be considered to be a form of primitive consciousness. As it carries out the process, the mechanism can be said to "understand" what it is experiencing. But there is no mechanism in phase-layer-3, which would enable the results of the interpretation process to be stored for future use. So this form of consciousness is momentary. The system acts. It understands what it is doing. And then it moves on to the next experience. To reach the level of full consciousness the facilities offered by phase-layer-4 are required.

Qualia

08.09

"Qualia" (singular "quale") is the term often used by supernaturalists to describe the subjective experience which we "see" or in some other way "experience" a collection of information about some scene or aspect of the external world. The existence of qualia is a contentious issue and seems to have become a sharp dividing line between those who hold a materialist view of consciousness and those who do not.

The non-materialists, epi-phenomenalists, or whatever collective term we want to use - Dietrich and Hardcastle (2004) called them "mysterians" because they all insist that consciousness is too mysterious to explain in any normal way - they all seem to regard qualia as a decisive issue - that is, one which tips the argument in their favour. Many (although not all) associate qualia with a visual experience. That is the impression, which we gain from an intuitive version of qualia. We know that that cannot be the case however. People who are born blind are still able to have similar vivid experiences based on hearing and touch. There cannot be anything corresponding to a visual image incorporated into these so-called qualia, any more than there can be textured surfaces which can be touched, odours which we can smell and taste or air vibrations which we can hear. Most people, when they reflect upon the issue, will concede that it is wrong to place a great deal of emphasis on vision. Nevertheless, for people who are sighted, it is the visual aspect of qualia, which impinges most forcibly.

Some try to get round the problem of being explicit, about what qualia are, by using a form of words suggested by Thomas Nagel [Nagel 1974]. They say that "*there is something that it is like*" to be a conscious person having a quale experience. I will deal with Nagel's arguments later, but for the present I note that that form of words does not actually tell us very much.

08.10

My explanation of qualia suggests that when the brain observes a scene, that observing or seeing or whatever, is done by phase-layers 1 and 2. But the scene (or whatever we want to call it) does not register directly at a conscious level in the phase-layers above. Moreover when it is seen (or touched, smelt or heard) at that lower unconscious level, there is, to use Nagel's famous phrase "*nothing that it is like*". There nothing we could call a "subjective experience". We could call it "an experience" in a general way, but those words do not imply anything significant. The visual signals arrive from the sensor units, the detection units identify the pattern, and an appropriate set of automatic action responses are triggered or potentiated. Just that. Phase-layer-1 does its appointed task. Phase-layer-2 records and stores the condition of phase-layer-1.

My explanation of qualia, is that at that higher conscious level, what the brain creates and stores (by the process of interpretation) is better described as an "understanding" of the events and circumstances experienced. When we remember the subjective experience of a quale, what we remember is the information which enables that understanding to be re-created.

Thus, if I walk towards a tree, my subjective experience is not a visual record of the tree. Rather it is an understanding of the tree such that I am able to classify it as a particular kind of tree. The mechanism can calculate or predict that if I continue to walk towards it without deviation, I will bump into it and perhaps hurt myself; that if a large predator suddenly appears), climbing into that tree might offer me a safe haven; that if it is cold I could cut the tree down and use the timber to build a log cabin or construct and light a fire. I know that a tree is a living thing, which has a limited life span and so on. That understanding is multi-dimensional and contains a wealth of information which is not (literally) observed at that time.

At the phase-layer-2 stage, the system has the data it has obtained from phase-layer-1. Earlier, I described that data as being like the information held by a form where various tick-boxes had been marked. At that stage the data is nothing more than an apparently arbitrary collection of datum points (or ticks in boxes). To determine what the data represent, the nature of each tick-box must be determined. To do that, the data must be referred or remitted back to phase-layer-1, which has the physical brain units needed to translate the data into actions (or into potential actions). Anticipation of those potentials and predicting the likely consequences of those actions, is what a conscious understanding provides.

Fig 08.10 Quale: confrontation with a tree

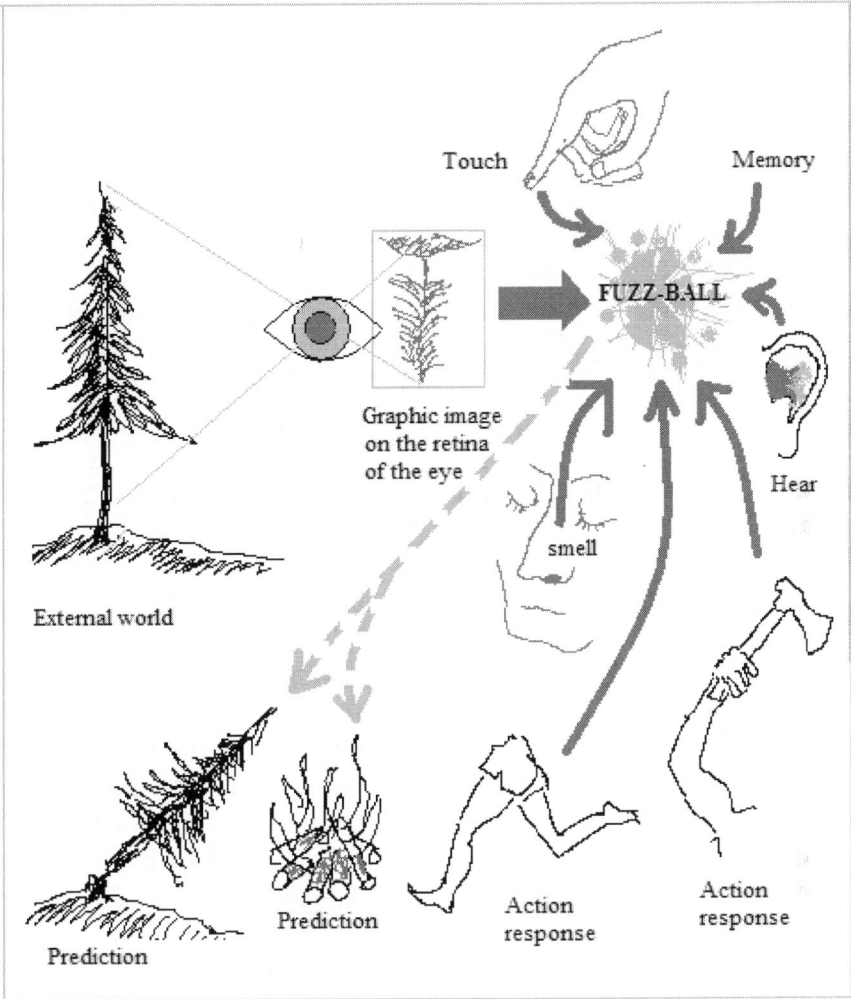

To those who protest and ask why it is that that subjective understanding of the experience is so like a visual experience I say this - How do you know what a visual experience is like? What do you have to compare it with? The electromagnetic radiation which impinges on your eyes has no colour. The only thing visual or coloured about the experience which is incurred by phase-layer-1 is the fact that it will record those signals as having a source which is identified as being particular light sensitive sensor cells (with particular optimum sensitivities in the colour spectrum). In effect, it says - that signal came from vision cell 1 zillion and seven counting from the top left corner". Phase-layer-1 labels those signals in that way. That is why your intuition will tell you that you are looking at the scene. It is that label which provides the colour. What does a label of that kind "look like"? What "*is it like*" to see a label of that kind? I think "seeing" is the wrong terminology. But it is the terminology which intuition presses upon us. This effect is often called "the doorbell effect". When the doorbell rings, it rings inside the house and yet we consider the effect as having had its origin outside the front door. Note that we can also identify time as another characteristic which has a local origin yet is regarded by intuition as having an external source.

Note: At this point the issue of colour is often raised. What is "red"? Why is it different from "green"? Is my red different from your red? And so on. The notion that colour is not, repeat not, a visual experience, but is something added by the brain to our understanding of a quale experience, blunts the force of these questions. The record of these experiences are labelled as have their source within the visual system – so they have to appear to be something seen. But they are not. See section 17.03 on synaesthesia. Colours must have some kind of visual character attached to them. The only logical requirement, however, is that they be different from other perceptions and have the extra dimensions such as a specific location which accompany any visual experience.

08.11

Phase-layer-3 harvests information from phase-layer-2 and uses the stuff it gets to create the concepts, which the mechanism needs to be able to interpret experiences.

In terms of that analogy of the stored information being like a knitting pattern instructions, we could put that another way. Phase-layer-3 re-groups and re-organises the data to create the wool that the mechanism needs to knit itself an understanding of its own experiences.

To say that *"there is something that it is like to have the experience of a quale"* means only that a person's brain is engaged in the procedure of interpretation. It is using structures formed from past experience to construct a representation of current events in terms of actions, implications and predictions of future events.

This interpretation if translated into words (which the system would be saying to itself), would be something like this -

"This is what is happening. This is what is being done. And this, on the basis of what happened previously, is what can be expected."

I have put those words into passive voice because at the phase-layer-3 stage the system has no concept of SELF. So we get *"This is what is being done"* rather than *"This is what I am doing"*.

What is definitely missing from that interpretation is *"And this is why I am doing it"*. For that additional form of interpretation, we must await the evolution of phase-layer-4.

Putting dreams together.

08.12

I have suggested that dreams are, for the most part, procedures by which concepts are indexed in terms of significant features and are stored in appropriate locations for easy retrieval. To identify those storage locations, old records must be accessed and re-scanned. The result would then be a very mixed bag of "snippets" of material passing through the interpretation process - but not being retained in memory. An outstanding feature of these dream experiences (when they are remembered for a short time) is how bizarre they are and so unrelated to physical possibility.

This observation offers additional support to the notion that old mental records are stored in a format which is akin to a knitting pattern, rather than more explicit graphic images.

If we cut up a set of photographs of different woollen garments and then stick them together in some arbitrary way, the result is unlikely to be recognisable. If, however, we were to cut up a set of different knitting patterns and then put these together in an arbitrary sequence, it is entirely possible that a skilled knitter might be able to knit something which corresponds to the instructions and which would be recognisable as a woollen object - not a garment perhaps and almost certainly not something which anyone would try to wear - it might, for example, have three sleeves and two neck-holes, but it would be a "thing" nevertheless.

The reason why parts of images cannot be readily combined is that they do not adapt to accommodate each other. Knitting instructions do adapt. Each partial instruction starts where its predecessor ended and that gives continuity to the whole.

Prinz's analysis of concepts

08.13

In his book "Furnishing The Mind" Jesse Prinz listed seven issues concerning concepts and for which any satisfactory theory must provide explanations [Prinz 2002].

(1) Scope - the theory must embrace all the different types of concept which humans are known to form.
(2) Reference/Intentionality - must explain the relationship between each concept and the things (perhaps in the real world) which the concepts appear to "stand for".
(3) Cognitive content - must identify the information content of a concept. That must also include some information about the context within which the concept is encountered.
(4) Acquisition -
    (a) how does an individual acquire a given concept?
    (b) how did natural selection potentiate the acquisition of
        concepts?
(5) Categorisation -
    (a) to what set does a given category refer?
    (b) what are the properties that define membership?
(6) Compositionality - how can concepts be put together to form new concepts?
(7) Publicity - how can concepts be shared by several people?

The account of which I have already given an outline provides explanations for all of these.

Scope

08.14

I have described how the extraction of compression chunks automatically correspond to physical objects, to causal-links and to scenarios; how gradual enhancement of these basic chunks can add extra information about contexts and repeated application of the compression algorithm will produce increasingly abstract forms of these concepts in the form of property hierarchies.

Reference

08.15

I have argued that a reference is in fact a reference to an internal mental structure of some kind. These are considered to be representations of supposedly external objects, but they are, in fact, internal. When the structure to which the reference is made, contains several components, the reference is to all of these components (perhaps ambiguously). Context will determine whether or not resolution of that ambiguity is important. If it is, then some additional means (like more conversation) must be used to achieve that resolution.

Cognitive content

08.16

I have argued that a concept is derived indirectly from personal experience - as that is interpreted by the phase-layer-1 mechanism. That interpretation includes information about the action taken by phase-layer-1 in response to particular patterns of incoming signals. In this way the conceptual representation of, say, a cup, will include the pattern of response which triggers the pinching action required to pick the object up.

Acquisition

08.17

I have shown that data compression is a plausible first step in the formation of concepts. It has the required marginal survival advantage associated with improved brain storage within a limited capacity. This makes it plausible as an evolutionary step in its own right, regardless of the advantage it can eventually provide when the compression chunks accumulate and are developed into concepts.

Categorisation

08.18

I have shown that repeated re-application of the compression algorithm with a gradual relaxation of the criteria which determine a match, can be the basis for categorisation (and abstraction).

Compositionality

08.19

I have discussed how the system can re-use concepts to construct an interpretation of current experience by combining concepts, and making use of the tags as points of attachment. I have also argued that this procedure is a plausible evolutionary development from the memory reconstruction process (after compression).

Publicity

08.20

I have argued that since (as we are obliged to think) there is a real external world, which is the same for all of us, and since (as I have suggested) the mechanisms of our formation and use of concepts is determined genetically, the concepts which we do form as a consequence of our individual experience, will tend to be very similar. They will not be identical however. And therefore each of us will have a unique view of the world and a similar but nevertheless unique way of chopping that world up, into conceptual "chunks" - or, at least, that would be the case if it were not for the ability to communicate using verbal and body-language. The simple act of pointing with a finger at an object as we name it, is one way we bring our (named) concepts into correspondence. From that simple beginning, however, more sophisticated ways of communicating, of which spoken language is the ultimate example, allow us to bring our concepts into correspondence. This is particularly important for abstract concepts since there is no way these can be identified by ostensive definition (i.e. by pointing).

Summary

08.21

The account I have provided here concerning the formation and use of concepts appears to meet in full the requirements listed by Prinz.

08.22

I anticipate that some readers will have difficulty accepting my suggestion that the performance of a procedure (whereby the structures I am calling "concepts" are slotted into the TRACE structure), and what we call the conscious understanding of current experience, are really just one and the same thing.

I have to confess too, that I had a long struggle with that notion myself. What I found was that the longer I thought about it, the more acceptable the idea seemed to be. What I found helpful to bear in mind was that what that pervasive intuition seemed to be screaming at me, was not valid. Conscious understanding is not a "thing". If we are not to keep on putting it aside for consideration later, we cannot for ever go on thinking about it as though it was a single indivisible phenomenon which can be detected only by the human psyche - as though that psyche was some kind of miraculous "consciousness Geiger-counter" of which the inner workings are beyond our understanding. I reject all that. There has to be some kind of internal mechanism that does the understanding. My answer to that is that it is the interpretation of the TRACE that is that mechanism. It knits that understanding. It knits the system's ability to relate and to predict.

CHAPTER 9

Phase-layer-4

Full consciousness.
The coming of the SELF, SELFMIND and understanding.

09.01

In previous chapters, the description of phase-layers 1, 2 and 3 brought the system to the stage where it was able to perform what I called "momentary" or "instantaneous" consciousness. It did that by enhancing the current TRACE by inserting concepts where there was a matching pattern of data in that TRACE. The TRACE, however, is ephemeral and so the extra information gained was lost very quickly.

In this chapter, I will describe how phase-layer-4 brings the system to "full consciousness". It does that by extending the formation of concepts to include the concepts of SELF and SELFMIND, by storing within the SELFMIND a long-lasting conceptual memory of past events, and its interpretation, or understanding, of these events. In that way it constructs an understanding of itself as an entity with continuity. More correctly, it stores the information from which an understanding can be constructed.

Knowing itself in that way, provides the system with an ability to anticipate its own behaviour, and therefore to be able to predict future circumstances with greater accuracy. The SELFMIND structure, however, does not coincide with, or refer to, anything directly observable in the external world.

09.02

Recall the nature of a concept. The concept DOG described earlier is a useful example. Most people have seen a dog. They have probably seen several individual dogs. But no one has ever seen an entity that corresponds to the concept DOG.

I use upper case characters deliberately. DOG is a theoretical thing. It is a mental construct. It exists only in the mind as an abstract compendium of lots of individual dogs. DOG was created by the compression procedure. It was not produced by some intellectual computation. The survival advantage that resulted from its evolution was a saving of brain-space, not some kind of fore knowledge of how useful concepts could be.

DOG has only those properties which every dog has. It has no properties which only one or a few dogs have. Within the property hierarchy of all things, DOG is subordinate to ANIMAL and ANIMAL is subordinate to PHYSICAL-OBJECT. So DOG will inherit (or acquire) all the properties which ANIMAL has and all the properties which PHYSICAL-OBJECT has. Organising the stuff that way saves a lot of space and yet all of the data can still be extracted from the concept store when it is required.

By knowing that DOG is subordinate to ANIMAL, the system can "know" that a DOG has a finite life-span - that it is born, that it grows and matures, and that, eventually, it will die, decay and become a skeleton.

I have put quotes round the word "know" to remind the reader that the word should not be taken too literally. It is another of those words that takes an outside view of behaviour but which, at the same time, seems to imply something significant about an associated internal mechanism. At this stage, however, that implication is becoming less nebulous, because we are steadily adding detail to the internal mechanism.

By knowing that it has all the properties of a PHYSICAL-OBJECT, the system can know that if a DOG is dropped, it will fall downwards and that if it falls and then hits the ground, it is likely that a sound will be heard. Knowing all that - being able to construct a representation of these things and these events and therefore being able to predict the consequences of certain events, is part of what I think "being conscious" means.

09.03

The development of that property hierarchy is a dynamic thing for a human child. The structure changes as a person matures. In the early stages it will be observed that if a dog - a real live individual dog - jumps and lands from a height, it will land with a thud. So too with a cat, and any other animal of a certain size. But during the re-organising of the hierarchy, as new compression chunks are enhanced, and new concepts are added, those common properties will migrate upwards until they stick at an important representative level for a whole group of things.

Big animals land with a thud. Large metal objects land with a clang. This hierarchy is a very messy ill-structured kind of thing. But it holds essential information. The property hierarchy is about as condensed a way of writing it down as is possible.

MIND

09.04

Observations of intelligent animate behaviour will produce observations like these -

(1) Grim face => unpleasant aggressive behaviour

(2) Shouting => unpleasant aggressive behaviour

(3) Hard staring eyes => unpleasant aggressive behaviour

(4) Shaking fist => unpleasant aggressive behaviour

Here the symbol "=>" means "expect to observe".

By "unpleasant behaviour" I mean some type of behaviour which would cause a person to be in an anti-goal state.

Now apply the data compression algorithm to all the forms of body-language which portend unpleasant aggressive behaviour.

(Grim face/shouting/hard staring eyes/shaking fist) = M.

I have chosen the term "M" to denote the compression chunk produced by that procedure. But what exactly is M? It is the mental construct which is derived from observations which are reliable predictors of unpleasant aggressive behaviour. In common parlance, M is another name for "angry mood". An angry mood, or any component part of it, is a reliable predictor of angry behaviour.

Just as DOG does not correspond to any observable item in the external world, so ANGER, similarly, does not correspond to an observable item. Both, however, are the result of data compression on items and snippets, which are observable.

Further observation of other forms of body-language will produce other indications of mood such as - HAPPY, AMUSED, ANXIOUS, ECSTATIC, etc. If the system then re-applies the data compression algorithm to these mood indicators it will get this -

(ANGRY, HAPPY, AMUSED .....etc.) ---> MIND

That result MIND, is the mental construct which acts as a reliable predictor of mood and hence of behaviour. Since the observable body-language which indicates any particular mood will usually occur before the behaviour it predicts, the existing mechanism for seeing a causal linkage will apply.

MIND => BEHAVIOUR (Mind "causes" behaviour)

Here "causes" is just another concept formed by collectivising the various occasions when expectation is induced.

Note that we have not invented any new structures or procedures to get to that point. Everything required was already in existence.

SELFMIND

09.05

And now, what of SELFMIND? The distinction I am making between MIND and SELFMIND is not normally recognised. However, if I am correct in suggesting the way in which the concept MIND is constructed, then there has to be an important difference between the formation of MIND and of SELFMIND.

A person cannot observe his or her own body-language as easily as he or she can observe the body-language of others. That is particularly true of body-language relating to the eyes.

There must be some alternative source of information which enables prediction, and is available to the mechanism.

Consider again the mechanism of phase-layer-1. The condition of phase-layer-1 having received information from external sensors, includes the activation status of the actions units, with which it is programmed to respond.

In the diagram I have tried to illustrate the idea that when we look at a scene, the information received starts its journey in the retina as something like a graphic image, but it is rapidly converted into a multi-dimensional object called, in an earlier chapter, a "*fuzzball*".

The condition of phase-layer-1 having received information from external sensors, includes the activation status of the actions units, with which it is programmed to respond.

In the diagram I have tried to illustrate the idea that when we look at a scene, the information received starts in the retina as something like a graphic image, but it is rapidly converted into a multi-dimensional object called, in an earlier chapter, a "*fuzzball*".

09.06

I return to the issue of qualia. The diagram sums up my argument in the previous chapter about what a quale experience really is. As suggested in the diagram, visual information is mixed with information from a great many other sources, including the action responses, which have been programmed by evolution into the phase-layer-1 mechanism. There are many other components to this understanding of the events, which do not appear in the diagram. There is the immediate past for example. Why are you running towards the tree? Were you running for some other reason or was the tree always your intended destination? These considerations and much more are part of your understanding of the circumstances in which you find yourself. The phenomenon that some people call a quale is a great deal more than a visual experience. The question is - at what stage in the proceedings does this happen. My answer is - this happens when the mechanism is performing the conscious augmentation of the TRACE.

I do not apologise for re-visiting the issue of qualia. It is fundamental to the confusion which surrounds the issue of consciousness. It is difficult to shake off the idea that when we pay attention to that fuzzball of information, that we are looking at a graphic image of some kind.

Why is that? If the basic data contained in that multi-dimensional structure comes from the set of phase-layer-1 detector units, and not directly from the sensitive cells of the retina, why does the information itself retain the apparent property of being visual in character?

The bits of information originally gained by the phase-layer-1 mechanism from vision, must retain the information it has about the source of that information. In effect, as I suggested earlier, phase-layer-1 must tie a label on to the relevant information which says "*this comes from vision*" and "*that comes from hearing*". Signals are just signals. In themselves, they are identical in all physical respects. If there is extra information to be tagged on, that must be expressed in terms of the interconnections between detection units. These extra connections constitute some of the extra dimensions in the fuzzball.

The implication of that is that when the system provides itself with an interpretation of events, it is telling itself that it, itself, is experiencing those events by vision or by hearing or by whatever form of sensory perception is appropriate. So when you think you are looking at a graphic image that is because the mechanism, that is your intuition, is telling you that is what is happening. The suggestion that our intuitive understanding of events may not be an accurate account, is one of the more disturbing things to emerge from my proposed explanation of consciousness.

In the first sentence of Chapter One, I wrote that consciousness was a procedure by means of which the system explains itself to itself. By constructing that long-lasting INTERPRETATION of its experience the system is, in effect, saying to itself - "*This is ME looking at this scene and this is what I am seeing.*"

I re-iterate, at that point the system is -

(1) The thing being represented.

(2) The thing doing the representation.

(3) (Including a representation of self-representation).

(4) The thing that is the user of the information provided.

And that curiously convoluted multi-role performance is my explanation of why being conscious is a "*subjective*" experience. A subjective active experience is a synthetic mental construct which is your understanding of your very personal experience.

09.08

Fig 09.08 The parallel INTERPRETATION structure

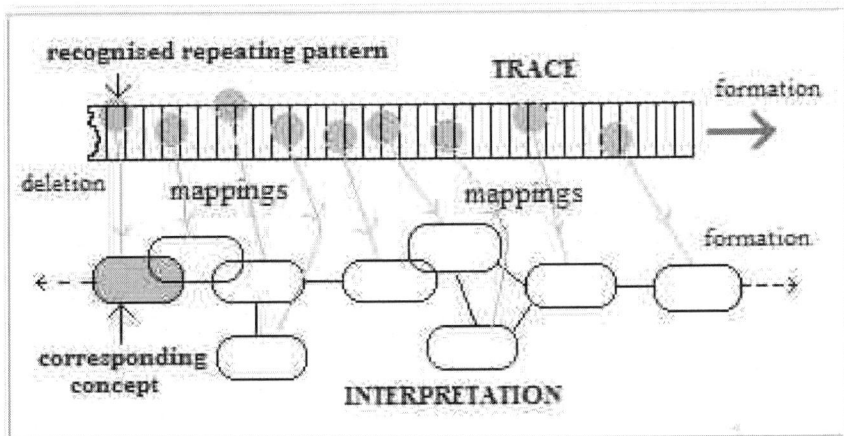

With the advent of a SELFMIND structure the system has acquired some structural location where it can deposit these very long lasting memories.

Furthermore, these long lasting memories will use concepts as the construction units. It would therefore be difficult for the system, when trying to recall old memories, to be able to distinguish between things which actually happened and things which were added to that memory as part of a general conceptual understanding of events (but not actually witnessed).

09.09

In writing this account I have frequently encountered difficulty in finding words and phrases which correctly express my meaning.

That is because the words and phrases we use in normal parlance reflect an erroneous view of circumstances which intuition presses upon us. I talk about the system "trying to recall old memories" as though the "system" has some kind of personality of its own and has some kind of supernatural mechanism by means of which it can understand its own memories. I do not want to give that impression but find a lack of suitable ways to express my true meaning.

What I want are ways to express the circumstance that by actively processing one part of its memory records, that process of "actively processing" is, itself, the internal mechanism of understanding.

SELF-Modelling

09.10

The system needs to know itself in order to be able to anticipate how it itself will react to predicted future events. But the predicted events cannot be accurately predicted if its own response to those predicted events cannot be anticipated. That is what is called in computer science - "*a deadly embrace*" - a situation that occurs when two procedures are each waiting on the other to do something - and so nothing happens. When that condition happens in a computer the normal way to respond is to switch off and re-boot the computer. Re-booting one's brain would be a neat trick.

The only way that I can think of by which a system could accurately predict its own response to a future event, is to construct a model of itself, feed that self-model with the hypothetical conditions of the predicted future event, run that as a simulation, and observe the outcome. That is the situation illustrated in part of the diagram (The problem).

Unfortunately, if the self-model is to be an accurate model of SELF, it will need to have another model of self, which it can run as a simulation of itself. And if that is the case, then that inner-inner self-model must have an inner-inner-inner self-model, and so on ad infinitum.

A solution is illustrated in the other part of the diagram. One part of the mechanism is shaded grey. That is the part which has been excluded in order to avoid infinite recursion. It follows that the same part (and a little bit more) will be shaded out of the calculation, within the inner self-model ... and so on until there is at least one inner-inner ... self-model which has no self-model within itself. At that point recursion stops.

Fig 9.10 - avoiding infinite recursion

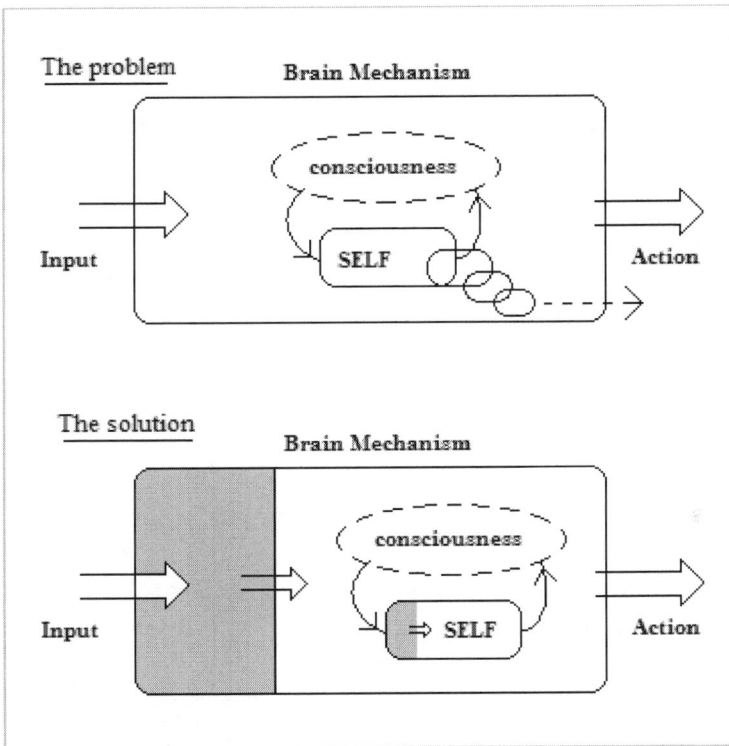

09.11

We may conclude that the concept of SELF cannot contain a complete and detailed representation of the whole of the brain mechanism. That concept, which is a constructional unit and is built-in to the understanding of an experience, must represent the SELF as having a mysterious inner part which delivers automatic reactions to common events. The condition of that inner SELF can be described only in terms of what is readily observed - the external consequences which it causes. That is, it can be represented by using only an outside view.

We have already encountered this situation when I discussed the difference between an inside view (the internal mechanism included) and the outside view (consequences only). In order to avoid infinite recursion the system must regard the model of itself (or part of the self-model) as a kind of alien mechanism which produces consequences but has no internal mechanism. The internal mechanism cannot be observed. The consequences can be observed. So it must assume that there is some internal mechanism but can describe that mechanism only in terms of consequences - that is, in terms of moods and emotional drives. These descriptions are exactly the same as it provides for itself in order to predict the behaviour of other people. But there is a difference. This "other person" is itself.

The concept of SELFMIND

09.12

To construct an interpretation of its on-going experience, the system must put together the relevant concept structures. The concept structure which represents SELF is like all the other concepts which represent physical objects. It has all the physical components of a human body, it has a location in the hierarchical structure of group objects (somewhere among the animals), and like all the concepts which represent people, it includes a component - a concept in its own right - which represents the MIND of that person. But this one is the SELFMIND concept and within it the system must try to represent what is going on inside. And that, according to the argument presented in the section above, is exactly what it cannot do without finding itself confronting the problem of infinite recursion. There is, as I have pointed out above, a way of avoiding that which involves judicious elimination of certain aspects of the SELFMIND and replacing it with a greatly simplified version which represents it as having no internal mechanism but only the external consequences of that unknown internal mechanism.

But there is also a much bigger problem which would cause difficulties even if the infinite recursion problem did not exist. It's this - the foundation phase-layer of the system, phase-layer-1, is the phase-layer which provides the system with its basic GOALS and ANTI-GOALS. It is true that the system can, by interpretation and conceptual analysis, identify certain SUB-GOALS for itself, conditions which represent intermediate staging points towards one or more of the basic GOALS. But the basic GOALS remain as phase-layer-1 defined them to be.

Why? That is the kernel of this extra problem. The explanation of how the phase-layer-1 stimulus-response automaton acquired those particular GOALS is not available anywhere within the system itself. That explanation is distributed over the whole of the brain's evolutionary history, and that is a mechanism which just cannot be simulated. It is stuffed full of zillions of minor accidents which occurred and killed off individual organisms which had other GOALS and other ways of reacting to stimuli. And because these events are largely determined by environmental circumstances, which are themselves accidental, even if we could simulate the process there would be no guarantee that the outcome would be the same.

So there is just no way the system can calculate the GOAL choices that are made by phase-layer-1. By being conscious, however, the system can sometimes anticipate those automatic or instinctive reactions and substitute another form of behaviour. But that is not always possible or certain to be successful.

The best that can be achieved is a compromise. It can represent phase-layer-1 (and phase-layer-2 which is also part of the unconscious mechanism) as a mysterious alien with its own way of doing things, its own pre-dispositions, dictated by some unknown internal mechanism - more or less as we do for other people. That requires that we characterise that inner alien self in terms of emotional moods.

We assume it has its internal mechanism. But we do not know what it is. So we look for clues which will guide our predictions about what it will do next. The concept of SELF contains the concept of SELFMIND, and that SELFMIND is represented as having moods, which pre-dispose it to take certain actions in certain conditions. These correspond to the GOAL and ANT-GOAL conditions. Which are components of the representations or certain events.

Is there a precedent for this? Is there some concept which is known and accepted - which does not actually exist, but which is still a useful component in a representation and yields useful and practical predictions?

Yes there is. The square root of minus one (denoted by "i") is a concept commonly used by physicists and mathematicians to solve a wide variety of quadratic equations and to calculate the behaviour of electromagnetic events and gadgets. Yet there is no such thing as "i". We can never find a piece of string that is "i" units long. Nevertheless it is an extraordinarily useful concept.

I suggest that the notion of mental moods is the same - non-existent but extremely useful for predicting future experience. The concept of "mood" is also one which, despite its lack of a counterpart in reality, but because of its useful character, readily enters the lexicon of our intuition.

The Intuition of Duality

09.13

This then, is the strategy which must be adopted by the system as it forms the concept SELFMIND. This is what the mechanism of intuition must tell itself - that the SELF is an internal mechanism with a hidden internal mechanism which, for reasons unknown, has its own goals and anti-goals. These are interpreted (and explained) as inexplicable emotional drives. Some of these goals come from the most primitive regions of the mechanism and will be related to short-term personal gratification. Others will derive from regions of the mechanism which have a grasp of longer-term consequences and may therefore be related to the finding of favour within society.

No wonder we get the impression that we are really a duality.

Moral Decisions

09.14

Moral decisions are choices made consciously for a reason. But, as Voltaire so neatly identified, the brain mechanism will not necessarily be aware at a conscious level - of the reason why these reasons exist.

The dilemmas, which are faced by every person today, have also been faced by our species (and by other species which live in a social community) over aeons of time. Do I act for myself or should I act for others? Should I eat these goodies (for myself - and thereby gain nutrition) or share them with my companions and thus gain social Brownie-points which may be valuable in the future? These considerations need not be processed consciously. These are questions asked of (and answered by) evolution. The merit of the choice, for survival, will vary with the circumstances and with the nature of the society, by the current environment and by the rules imposed by that society.

Moral behaviour, which favours sharing, may pay off in time but not necessarily within the lifetime of an individual who has to make that choice. Each individual has genes and those genes will have been reproduced, in whole or in part, in offspring. A social choice may not help the individual but it may well help to preserve the society, which will then support the life-chances of those offspring who carry many of the same genes.

Intuition and the two selves

09.15

If that, as it appears, is the form in which the system represents itself to itself, and thus the form in which it explains itself to itself (falsely as it turns out), what does that tell us about ourselves? It explains that WE see ourselves as being split into TWO parts - a part that is explicable and a part which is not. The inexplicable part generates hopes, fears, loves and hates which drive our behaviour, and does so without explanation.

That, of course, is the mind-body duality that Descartes articulated so famously four hundred years ago and which Elizabeth of Bohemia demolished so expertly.

"And I admit it would be easier for me to concede matter and extension to the soul, than the capacity of moving a body and of being moved, to an inanimate being. For, if the first occurred through 'information', the spirit that performed the movement would have to be intelligent, which you accord to nothing corporeal. And although in your metaphysical meditations you show the possibility of the second, it is, however, very difficult to comprehend that a soul, and as you have described it, after having had the faculty and habit of reasoning well, can lose all of it on account of some vapours, and that, although it can subsist without the body and has nothing to do with it, is yet so ruled by it."
[Elizabeth of Bohemia in a letter to Descartes, June 1643]

Well said Elizabeth of Bohemia! She nailed him. The world has waited for a very long time a coherent answer. If we suppose that there is some kind of non-material entity floating around inside our brains, which can communicate, in some unknown way, with the material mechanism of our brain, how can that happen without that non-material thing reclassifying itself as a material thing? The ability to communicate with material visible things is part of the definition of what it means to be a material thing.

Consider the phenomenon we call "dark matter". Its presence was not suspected until it was noticed recently that the outside edges of the galaxies appeared to be rotating faster than could be explained by the standard calculations associated with gravitational theory. The favoured explanation was that there was something else, which could not be observed directly, which was adding extra mass to the galaxies. This was called "dark matter" and when the mass of the galaxies was recalculated with that assumption built in, it turned out that dark matter contributed most of the mass of every galaxy. But no one has suggested that dark matter is anything other than a material form of matter. It is able to affect the behaviour of ordinary matter and so it has to be classified as material too. The existence of dark matter has now been made more plausible by the discovery that light passing near to distant galaxies appears to be bent, as it were by a lens, by the gravitational fields of those galaxies.

Even more remarkable is the possible existence of so-called "Dark Energy". So far as I am aware, there is still no convincing additional evidence of its existence available, but its existence is offered as an explanation for the observation that the expansion of the universe appears to be accelerating, rather than decelerating, as would be expected under conventional gravitational laws. Remarkably, however, there has been no hint that dark energy might be some kind of supernatural force. If sufficient evidence becomes available to add weight to the idea, then it too will be considered part of the material world and the laws of nature will simply be expanded to include the new evidence. To classify something (anything) as "*supernatural*" is simply to declare that there is insufficient evidence to believe it exists.

Autism

09.16

If my account of how we form the concept MIND is accurate, then we can anticipate that if a person does not possess an innate predisposition to attend to facial expressions, body-language and other human indicators of mood, or if, for some other reason, the person has an aversion to making these observations, then that person will have difficulty forming a theory of mind (with respect to other people) - but not, curiously, the concept of SELFMIND.

It is interesting to note that an inability (or unwillingness) to pay attention to facial signals like eye-contact, has been observed in autistic children whose behaviour is thought to be associated with a deficient theory of mind concept [Philips 1992]. Nevertheless, some autistic people show a remarkable ability to form and deal with other very complex abstract concepts, as in mathematics. So clearly the inability to form concepts (at all) is not a universal feature of autism (although that may be present in some severe cases).

Representing the MIND structure

09.17
I will deal later with what is likely to happen if other mechanisms of my hypothetical brain mechanism go a bit wrong. For the present, I will stick to the way most people behave.

I have emphasised that the format of the mental structure which is retained, first in phase-layer-1 during an experience, and then as a component of the TRACE is a multi-dimensional "fuzzball" of information. In that format it is difficult to illustrate in diagrams. We need an alternative format, which retains the essential information but is rather easier for ourselves to deal with. That is why I introduced the box-representation of STATES within the TRACE. Each box object represents an aspect of the TRACE which may occur in a single state or persist over many states. The time-stamp associated with each indicates the time-duration of the feature.

Fig 09.17 - PERSON plus MIND

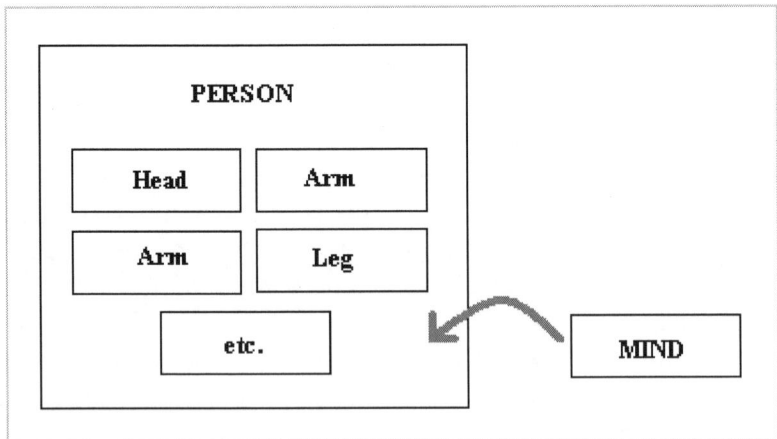

The diagram shows the representation of a person. As discussed earlier with respect to the concept DOG, the concept PERSON has a number of obvious component parts. The several component concepts (legs, arms etc.) can then be augmented by the addition of a MIND concept.

The diagram, in the next section, illustrates a structure, which the system would be able to build to represent a person walking.

It shows a PERSON concept and a few of its components. Each part of this representation is a sub-STATE of the information provided by phase-layer-1. Each part has a unique identifying number (used for reference) and each has a time-stamp. We must recognise too, that these box-shapes are illustrative simplifications. Each corresponds to a structure in the concept store and each is complete with its own internal components, suitably marked by tags.

09.18

All that has been illustrated earlier. What we can now add is the way in which the introduction of these MIND and SELFMIND structures enables the representation of circumstances to be augmented and several traditional problems to be solved.

Consider first the way in which the system can represent a rather common event - a person walking.

In the diagram we see a number of STATES. The one with ID = 1, represents a PERSON - that is, a physical object, the body of that person. The second box represents that person's MIND. Note that these and the components (left-leg and right-leg) have time-stamps which last for the duration of the action. Note also that the last part of the structure represents a repeat enactment of the whole process WALK (recursively). That means that the whole procedure will continue indefinitely with a movement of left-leg then right-leg with each movement of a leg causing a movement of the PERSON.

To prevent that infinite continuation we need to modify that last part. Something must intervene to cause some other end-point. And that is where the MIND structure is very useful. In addition to causing these movements of legs to cause movement of person, it can also indicate that one of the new locations reached by the person as a result of all these leg movements, is designated as a GOAL state.

Fig 09.18 A person walking

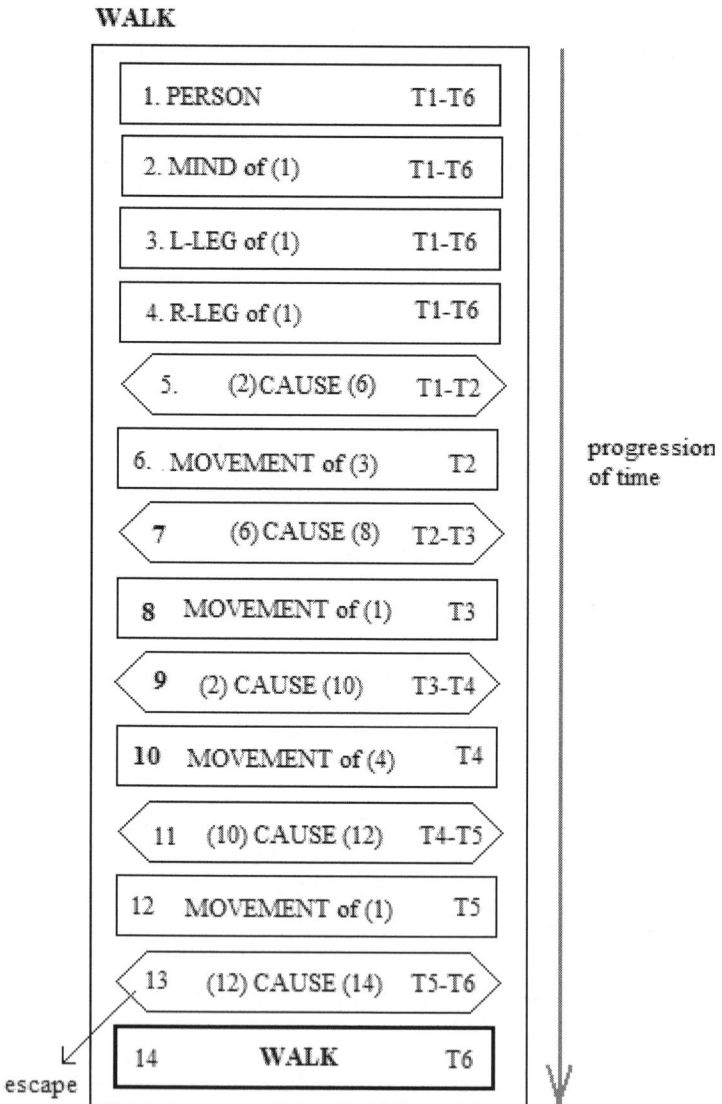

WALK

1. PERSON	T1-T6
2. MIND of (1)	T1-T6
3. L-LEG of (1)	T1-T6
4. R-LEG of (1)	T1-T6
5. (2)CAUSE (6)	T1-T2
6. MOVEMENT of (3)	T2
7 (6)CAUSE (8)	T2-T3
8 MOVEMENT of (1)	T3
9 (2) CAUSE (10)	T3-T4
10 MOVEMENT of (4)	T4
11 (10) CAUSE (12)	T4-T5
12 MOVEMENT of (1)	T5
13 (12) CAUSE (14)	T5-T6
14 **WALK**	T6

progression of time

escape

The facilities offered by this form of representation are adequate for that, although I readily admit that the structure required is, or could become, very complex. In general, we can represent events in the external world using the sequence of boxes as I have shown here. We can also place a very similar structure *inside* the MIND structure to represent the fact, or suspected fact, that the action is part of a plan this person has.

By designating one particular state as a GOAL state we can indicate that the behaviour is deliberate. Note the arrow labelled "escape". That represents some alternative continuation of the action which avoids infinite recursion.

The representation of complex causal linkages

09.19

An important feature of the format suggested for these representations, is that a causal link between two conditions or STATES is given a structural unit of its own (with its own ID number).

Fig 09.19 (1) - a cause can cause a cause

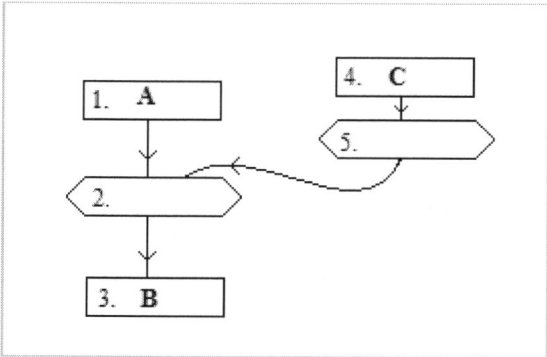

It is tempting to represent causation by simply adding pointer-arrows, within one unit of the representation which points to another. That temptation should be resisted. By giving each causal link an identity, a time-stamp and status of its own, we make it possible to develop some very powerful representations of causal linkages. For example, we make it possible to show that one causal link can cause another.

Diagram (09.19(1)) above shows the way the notation can build the representation of a cause causing a cause. The diagram is a representation of something "permitting" or "enabling" something else to happen.

If we introduce the idea of having negative conditions, a condition (B) say, and its negation not(B) and something else which causes not(B) we could regard that as a representation of something "preventing (B)".

Fig 09.19 (2) A cause can prevent a cause

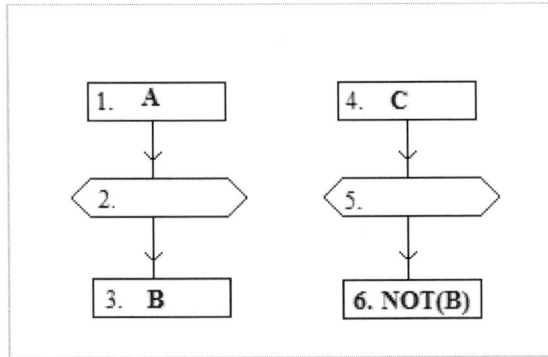

These diagrams can become very complicated indeed and I have no intention of giving many more that are more complicated than the ones shown already. I hope these examples are sufficient for the reader to realise the potential. If we seriously wanted to implement these ideas in a working mechanism we would need to handcraft a few simple examples and then use these as basic building bricks for larger and more complex arrangements. Eventually we would need to leave it to the system itself to build these representations which would become so complex and obscure that we would have difficulty being sure what was going on internally. I introduced these ideas in a book published in 1988 [Noble 1988]

An alternative form of representation

09.20

The graphical "box-and-arrow" representation is convenient and clear when we are dealing with small illustrative examples. But when we are dealing with more realistic practical examples, every diagram drawn that way has a distressing tendency to resemble a plate of spaghetti. It is helpful, therefore, if we use another method of presentation on the printed page, which abandons the arrows in favour of reference numbers. Every concept is given a unique number and every other concept within the structure can then refer to another by using that unique reference number. Here is the structure presented in this form.

The various "T" marks added in brackets to each concept, represent TIME markers. Since all of these concepts have been formed by extraction from the episodes within the longer-term memory, and since each episode in the longer-term memory is a chronological sequence of states, with each state carrying within it a time-stamp created by the CLOCK, it is possible for every concept to carry a marker which indicates a relative time sequence. In this case the sequence is $T1 < T2 < T3$. The time-stamp (T1 --- T3) indicates that a concept is present and plays a role within the scenario over a period from T1 to T3.

    1. Person (T1 --- T3)
    2. Mind (of 1) (T1 --- T3)
    3. Legs (of 1) (T1 --- T3)
    4. Movement (of 3) (T2)
    5. Movement (of 1) (T3)
    6. <2 causes 4> (T1 --- T2)
    7. <4 causes 5> (T2 --- T3)

In words, this structure can be read as follows:

There is a person who is present all of the time from T1 to T3.
This person has a mind (also present over that time interval).
This person has legs (also present over that time interval).
The person's mind causes the legs to move (T1 to T3)
The legs move (T1 to T3)
The movement of the legs causes the person to move (T1 to T3)
The person moves (T1 to T3)

More detail required

09.21

There is scope within this form of representation to expand the movement of the legs - first to show that there are two legs involved, that these legs have articulated components, that the legs move alternately, and that there is, within the time sequence, a small time-lag between the movement of the legs and the movement of the person. We could also add the detail that the walking action requires contact with some fixed surface, that the surface does not move and the base of each leg (or foot) does not slide in contact with the surface as the leg moves - and more. Details of that kind would make it possible to make a distinction between walking and running.

Clearly there is a great deal more data, which can be added to make the representation more complete - other limbs, head and trunk, the pelvis and the sway that transfers weight from one leg to the other. There is almost no limit to the detail that could be added. In practice we shall adopt a parsimonious strategy of representing only the bare minimum required in any given context. We might, in the first instance refer only to a pair of legs, and then later discover that there is a need to refer to one of them in particular - if for example the person had a limp.

The structures are flexible and can be altered as required. This makes it possible to deal with exception conditions as they arise, rather than try to anticipate all exceptions and include special "exception points" within the structure where modifications can be made, as suggested by the theory of circumspection [MacCarthy 1980]. That is one important application of the ability to form a representation of "prevention" as noted above.

In a later chapter we deal with the use and interpretation of language, we shall then be able to see more clearly how the addition of more detail can be triggered (as required) by the words used in an utterance.

With this notation, however, the order in which the concepts appear is unimportant. The chronology and involvement of the individual concepts is indicated by the time-stamps and the causal connectivity of the action is also indicated by the causal links and their time-stamps.

System processing.

09.22

Whatever notation we use to construct this conceptual representational structure - whether it is boxes and arrows in a drawing or synapse connections in a biological brain, the real significance of the structure lies in how the mechanism of the system is able to determine the way the mechanism behaves. When we look in more detail at the components of the structure we will find some components are physically attached to others. That physical attachment carries within it the implication that if X is attached to Y then if X moves to a new location, Y must also move to the same new location (and vice versa). The strength of attachment will be represented by the force or suddenness of the movement which will break that behavioural rule. That is just one of the rules of naive physics which we must all learn in infancy.

The labelling of concepts

09.23

It is difficult to discuss how concepts can be represented without having convenient and (relatively) unambiguous labels which can be used to identify them. For that reason I will defer further discussion of these points until we get to phase-layer-5, which deals with language and which provides precisely what is required.

Eidetic Memory

09.24

Having made and emphasised the point that a quale, or stored record of experience, does not contain anything that can be described as a "visual" record of that experience, I feel I must address the issue which suggests strongly that the brain can indeed contain something which might be described in those terms. I refer to the phenomenon known as eidetic memory - also known as "a photographic memory". Some people, most often children, have the ability to recall a visual experience, apparently in very exact detail and then to read from that memory, as though from a printed photograph, details of the image which were not consciously recognised when the scene was experienced for the first time.

What I suggest is happening on those occasions, is that the stored memory is in fact not a visual image like a photograph, but a stored record of the kind I have described here which is a record of the condition of the phase-layer-1 response to that experience - the parts that are labelled as having been received from the visual perceptions. In which case when that extra (previously unnoticed) detail is recalled, what is being recalled is the identification of the detail - i.e. the condition of the relevant detection units.

The same phenomenon or similar can occur in relation to perceived sounds. It is said that Mozart, as a child could listen to a piece of music, for the first time, and then write it down perfectly - note by note, in standard musical notation.

I suggested earlier that the information which is obtained from phase-layer-1 by the memory mechanism in phase-layer-2, comes in a form which is analogous to the content of a form, filled in by a subordinate, by ticking boxes. It should in such a case be possible to re-inspect the form and find there ticked boxes which had not previously been noticed.

I cannot prove that, but I can make a prediction which could be checked. If an eidetic memory is really equivalent to a graphic image, then someone with an eidetic memory should be able to look at a scene with one eye and then later discover the retinal blind spot within the image. I predict that that will not happen - unless the subject was made consciously aware of the blind spot during the original experience. I have looked. I can find no reference to such a test having been made.

CHAPTER 10

Comments on Phase-layer-4
What is a person?

The concept of SELF

10.01

By providing the system with a representation of SELFMIND which is associated with a representation of SELF, phase-layer-4 achieves what I believe is an active performance of full consciousness. It has a concept of SELF as a physical entity within the environment. It can explain its own experience to itself in terms of recognisable objects and events. It can store the understanding of that experience that it has created within that SELFMIND entity, to represent the past history of SELF. It uses that SELF history to guide its guesses about what it, itself, is likely to do in response to the circumstances it is able to predict, and it can understand how those actions are likely to affect the predictions it is able to make.

10.02

The curiously convoluted multiple role that it plays in those representations of SELF and of its own actions, constitutes a subjective experience. We could say that what it is doing when it performs in that way, is taking an outside view of itself, from inside itself.

As I explained earlier (and repeatedly), it must do that because to do otherwise, to attempt to simulate the detailed mechanism of its own internal mechanism, is to invite infinite recursion which would bring its operation to a sudden halt. In practice a few recursive loops could be performed, but recursion cannot be allowed to continue unchecked. There has to be a way of escaping from those endless loops.

There is also the problem that basic decisions are driven by evolutionary development and are therefore beyond computation.

10.03

There remains the issue of what format could be used to store the potentially very long record of past experience. To economise on storage space it would be helpful if these records could be held in a very compact format. That requirement would have several consequences.

First: the recovery of past experiences would take time and would occasionally be patchy.

Second: as records become older, space could be saved by amalgamating or coalescing them. If I go to a supermarket once per week, I might be able to remember the detail of last week's visit, and perhaps even that of the week before. But unless there was some unusual and significant event during one of those visits, they would all be merged into an undistinguished commonality. And that seems to correspond to my own experience with my occasionally (normally) unreliable memory. A few events are unlike any other, and are of great significance to me. These stand out. Most other things merge into a continuous background. To recover a precise memory takes time and usually needs a prompt from some unique and isolated event.

10.04

My hypothetical system carries with it an implication that many people will find uncomfortable. It means that each of us, that is, the unique personality that defines what and who we are, is nothing more mysterious than a brain procedure - not something spiritual and not something that is immortal.

When one understands something, it is that procedure which is doing the understanding (NOTE: doing it, not experiencing it). When one is motivated to act in a particular way, it is that procedure which acts that way for reasons stored internally and in accordance with its own predictions of future conditions. We might say that "it takes a decision to act". But that is an informal use of the word "decision" which, if misinterpreted, could lead to yet another deferment of the explanation of what "taking a decision" really means.

The procedure can often make a choice between alternative courses of action. Some of these will be unconscious actions which evolution has bestowed upon it. Others will be actions, which, by analysis of past experience, the procedure can recognise as being likely to be more advantageous to its own well-being. Often that personal well-being will be dependent upon the well-being of the society of which it is a member - and its own standing within that society.

Actions which favour society rather than the individual can be described as altruistic. There is nothing ersatz about that kind of altruism. It really is unselfish in a true and literal sense of the word. But that need not stop us recognising that it is also self-promoting in a complicated way, and that complicated way may be behaviour which has also been bestowed upon us by evolution.

Most of us behave morally, and do so instinctively. Perhaps that is because throughout the evolutionary history of our species, being moral has helped our tribal society (as it was for most of that time) to survive. By doing that we created a protective environment for the survival of the genes which we had bestowed on our own progeny. It did not happen that way in every case, of course, but may well have happened often enough to ensure that that strategy was more often than not the best way for our genes to survive. We do not have to be consciously aware of these complicated causal interconnections. We could say that evolution "knows" these reasons well enough.

CHAPTER 11

Phase-layer-5 - The coming of language

Hypnosis

11.01

I have always been fascinated by hypnosis. I find it amazing that a person can be induced by another to believe that the scene or the events described by the hypnotist, are real. Not just that the words the hypnotist speaks are true words, but that the actual experience, which those words describe, is a real experience - real in the same way that an experience that can be acquired by vision, touch, hearing, smell and taste, is real. How can that be?

The implication seems clear. The format of the information gathered in those two quite different ways - by perception and by listening to words - the end products of those two mechanisms are the same. The only difference it would appear, is the indication of source and the emission of aspects which escape verbal description.

Earlier, I talked about the information being stored as a multi-dimensional fuzzball. I also suggested that the mechanism of mind attached labels to elements of that information store which in effect say "*this is something that was seen*", or "*this came from your sense of smell*", and so on. What the fact of hypnosis suggests is that under the influence of the hypnotist these labels can be switched temporarily. That is an alarming thought.

It is also the case that even when people are not under hypnosis, the words used to describe an experience which is genuinely real, will influence what people think or remember about that real experience. For example, if we question people who have witnessed a traffic accident, the words we use to question them can have a disrupting influence on the truth of their witness statements. If we say "*Did you see any broken glass on the road after the two cars smashed into one another?*" we are much more likely to get the answer "*Yes*" than we would if we asked "*Did you see any broken glass after the two cars hit one another?"* That has been tested in the laboratory using video recordings of a collision in which no broken glass was in fact produced. [Loftus and Palmer 1974]. That is further evidence that the information we get from a verbal description ends up, after processing, in a format that is indistinguishable from the format of the information we get by direct perception.

That does not prove my idea that language processing, and direct perception use the same concepts and the same mechanisms of interpretation, to put together our understanding of events, but it most certainly does not contradict it.

11.02

I do not envisage that the evolution of a phase-layer would stop when a new phase-layer was added to it. Each phase-layer would continue to evolve. Mutations, which would earlier have had no attendant advantage, may then be able to secure an advantage because some new feature in the phase-layers above it makes the advantage possible.

So I think that what came first were basic concepts, which permitted basic conscious thinking - the ability to explain to oneself what one was doing, why one was doing it and how that likely behaviour would affect predictions. After that, further compression produced condensation of storage. The development of language and the development of abstract concepts then went hand in hand.

11.03

In this chapter I want to describe how the system is able to construct an interpretation of a spoken utterance. In the next chapter I will show, with a number of examples, how these techniques can be applied.

Language, syntax and evolution.

11.04

For about half a century linguistics has been dominated by the ideas of Noam Chomsky. In his book "Syntactic Structures" he proposed the theory that the human ability to distinguish between the grammatical and the ungrammatical is innate and is fundamental to our ability to use language [Chomsky 1971]. To explain how this idea is compatible with the fact that every natural language appears to have a different form of grammatical structure, he proposed that there is an innate universal grammatical structure (called "deep grammar") which is common to all. He proposed that during infancy each child learns a complicated set of "grammatical transformations" which map from this deep grammar on to the "surface grammar" of the mother tongue.

11.05

The Chomskian approach is implausible from an evolutionary point of view. As I have maintained throughout this book, evolution has no foresight. It cannot develop the components of some complicated feature which may later, and with amazing good fortune, turn out to be able to combine to form something useful, but the components of which individually have no immediate identifiable survival advantage. The idea of irreducible complexity has been the main argument used by creationist opponents of evolution to justify their stance. Even Charles Darwin himself, conceded that if irreducible complexity of any biological entity could be demonstrated, that would fatally damage his theory. To date no one has ever found any actual biological entity which cannot be analysed into simpler components which each have some attendant survival advantage.

It is a fact, however, that the syntactical approach advocated by Chomsky, if it could be confirmed, would constitute precisely the kind of irreducibly complex biological component which the creationists so desperately want to discover.

It is implausible that a single mutational change could be responsible for anything as complicated as a mechanism for testing syntactical correctness. If that is so, then the evolution of a large complex mechanism must be the result of many mutational changes. That implies that there must have been several intermediate stages in the evolutionary pathway.

I cannot not see any immediate survival advantage which could have been associated with an early or intermediate stage during the evolution of a system of grammar, with the classification and structuring of the words in an utterance, to ensure correspondence with some arbitrary set of rules, as a preliminary exercise, before language could develop. Those rules of grammar are arbitrary. The fact that each natural language has its own (surface) grammar demonstrates that fact. There is no logical imperative which requires, for example, the verb in a sentence (in a given language) should occur where it does.

The sequence of events, as advocated by Chomsky (grammar before language use), must be back-to-front. There had to be some language facility available before such a grammar-pattern matching mechanism could have evolved.

However, if the acquisition of syntax came after the use of language had appeared, then there was no requirement that any part of the syntax system needed to be innate. It could be a learned ability - learned in infancy in response to the patterns of language which are actually experienced ... provided there was something else, which did come before, which did have some immediate survival value, and from which the syntax system could been a development.

Conscious and unconscious communication

11.06

Many animal species communicate unconsciously. A bird can cry in alarm and other members of its flock can use that cry as a trigger to take flight. That is a form of communication.

However, language, of the sophisticated variety, is primarily a means of conscious communication. To be a conscious form of communication, the bird which cries must know, or be able to anticipate, the effect that the cry is likely to have on its companions. It must make that cry deliberately with that end in mind.

Did conscious communication evolve gradually from unconscious communication? If it did not, then it is difficult to understand how conscious communication could have evolved at all - if, that is, we insist that conscious communication must be fully developed with a recognisable syntactical format.

11.07

Two-way conscious communication cannot provide an individual with any survival advantage unless there are others who have the same or similar abilities and with whom the individual can exchange information. So if the Chomskian view is correct several individuals would need to benefit from the same mutation changes simultaneously.

That is just not plausible. A more plausible scenario would begin with single-word unconscious communication. The next step would be single word communication in which one side of the dialogue has some conscious understanding of what is going on and is able to anticipate the reaction of the other side. That can evolve into both sides having some conscious knowledge of what is being said. The next stage would be a form of speech which could put two words together. Then more words.

Slowly the number of words could increase and at some point a few arbitrary rules or conventions, about the order in which the words should be uttered, would help to disambiguate meaning. Pentti Haikonen, who is Finish, makes the point that in the Finish language word order is not important. What marks the roles which each word plays within sentence is not its position in that sentence but the inflection (or word ending) which the word carries [Haikonen 2003].

Formal and Natural Languages

11.08

The orthodox approach to the processing of computer languages required that every sentence uttered or typed, must be parsed and passed as grammatical before there is any attempt to analyse what that utterance actually means. This approach arose from the way the statements of a computer programming language are handled. Some very clever parsing algorithms were developed and these now form the basis of most of the grammar-checking facilities supplied with desktop publishing systems.

11.09

Computer languages are classified as "formal languages". Languages like English or French, are "natural languages".

A formal language has a clearly designed syntax. Parsing a statement in a formal language, before trying to turn it into something a computer can execute, makes sense. The grammatical rules are strict and are designed deliberately to make checking feasible and efficient. Every computer has an internal language (machine language) of its own and a program written in that machine language can be executed efficiently. To "understand" a statement in a formal computer language like Java or C^{++}, means turning it into an equivalent program in machine language and eventually into a computer operation being performed.

The processing of formal languages has been developed by computer scientists into an art form, so it was only to be expected that the same techniques would be tried for the processing of natural language and that, being justifiably proud of what they had achieved, computer scientists would be confident that they could deal adequately with the intricacies of a natural language in the same way.

The need for automatic translation was the driving force in the 1970s for efforts to develop natural language processing by computer. Chomsky's idea that all natural languages shared a common "deep grammar" and that it was possible to derive the various and very different surface grammars from that deep grammar by a technique termed "transformational grammar" sounded attractive to the authorities who would very much have liked an automatic system which could translate Russian text into American English.

To no avail. The AI community over-promised what they could achieve and many millions of dollars were wasted. It is interesting to note that the search engine Google has achieved a modest but useful level of machine translation by abandoning the grammatical approach and instead concentrating on statistical techniques. Google now has an enormous corpus of text and that makes the statistical approach feasible (although it occasionally produces bizarre results).

More recently there have been attempts to use a more direct semantic approach (Explicit Semantic Analysis, or ESA) which categorises semantic content in terms of the contexts named in Wikipedia [Gabrilovich and Markovich 2009].

Ray Jackendoff, a respected academic and much published expert in this field, is also moving away from the Chomskian approach, in his case in favour of conceptual analysis of meaning. In a footnote to a recent book he writes -

"Did language arise in our distant ancestors primarily as an enhancement of communication or as an enhancement to thought? (More properly, were reproductive benefits conferred on our ancestors by having language primarily due to their better ability to communicate or due to their better ability to think?) We can't go back there and find out. Nearly everyone assumes the primary advantage was in communication. But Noam Chomsky, never to be taken lightly, has argued that communication had little to do with it. For him the primary advantage innovation was structured thought. What he calls "externalization" - the ability to speak one's thoughts out loud - was a later development. But for him, "externalization" includes pronunciation, which provides the very "handles" that make rational thinking possible. So on the present story, he's got to be wrong. My inclination is to think that the language faculty developed in the service of enhancing communication, but the immediate enhancement of thought was a huge side benefit."

[Jackendoff 2012, p222]

I find myself caught between these two positions. Neither Jackendoff nor Chomsky seem to be making a clear distinction between the development language and the formation of concepts. My own position is that the "*enhancement of thought*" which (according to Jackendoff) Chomsky attributes to "*language*" should really be attributed to the formation and development of concepts and that these concepts are then used as a component of a slowly developing language facility to enhance communication. As I explained earlier, I cannot see how an enhancement of communication can happen suddenly and uniformly unless lots of people have a miraculous and nearly identical mutational change at the same time.

The construction kit theory of language.

11.10

Basic to my approach to language is that the meaning of a sentence is a representation of some aspect of the world around us, and that the purpose of language is the communication of those representations from one person to another. That there are other aspects of language, I have no doubt. But that, I suggest, is the main reason why humans, and many other species, evolved the means to communicate. It is a logical extension of the means of sensory perception. We have eyes and ears to tell us what is going on around us. We can communicate with our companions so that the things those companions are able to see and to hear can be shared. We all benefit from that sharing. Language provides each one of us with a whole society of eyes and ears, and all of them focused on a single objective, how to survive and to multiply (and help each other to do that) in a dangerous environment.

An individual word does not normally appear to have a meaning that can be falsified, but a sentence does have a meaning which can. Why is that?

There are a few words, of course, which do have significance when they are used in isolation from other words, - words like "HELP!" or "LOOK OUT!" (that's two words - I know, but with the meaning and urgent impact of a single word). The way in which several words together seem to acquire significance in a way that eludes single words, is an issue which has long been debated and to which I now offer a solution.

A single word has a meaning that is a compendium of several different occasions on which a person encountered a particular object or situation, and to which the meaning of that word refers. But since it is about *several* occasions we cannot identify the exact occasion to which reference is being made, we cannot identify which of the several interpretations available is the one which is appropriate.

If I say the word "walk" to my dog, the animal will get very excited, leap about and then stand expectantly at the door. For a dog, it seems, there is only one narrow context in which he is interested. In most other contexts, when talking to another person, that person may well feel that the statement is incomplete. To which person am I referring? Who is going to walk? Where does the walking take place? To what destination?

By using several words together, however, I can narrow the context, eliminate possibilities and narrow the interpretation down to a single option. When that specific option has been identified it can then be either true or false. The two-word statement "*John walks*" enables the listener to place the reference to the person JOHN into the vacant slot defined by PERSON in the representation of WALK which I offered in a previous chapter.

But there may be several vacant slots in a concept and there may be several additional bits of information which can be slotted in to these positions. It is also the case that a statement in any language must always be linear. So there is little scope for helping the listener to slot the extra bits of information into the correct or intended positions. Some conventions about where in the structure of a sentence these extra bits of information should be located would help.

And that is why grammar provides help in the disambiguation of meaning. Grammar, in my view, is a set of rules or conventions which we use to indicate how the meanings of the several words in a sentence, are supposed to be linked together.

Word-concepts

11.11

The word-concepts in a language (in common with all other concepts) are formed by the data compression algorithm and extracted, as repeating chunks. When we experience the sound of the word "*John*" we form the word-concept "JOHN". I use the term word-concept here (and place the identifier in quotation marks) to indicate that this is a concept which refers specifically to the sound experience of the word (or at a later stage its written equivalent). Included in the content of that word-concept will be the muscular actions required to utter it.

However, any person who has that repeating experience of the word sound, will almost certainly also have the repeating visual experience of a person we call John (and other forms of sense experience). These repeating forms of experience will therefore have been identified and become part of the concept JOHN (without the quotation marks).

Ostensive definition of concepts is almost certainly the way the mechanism of communication got started. Later, more complex ways of identifying a reference can be developed.

All that then remains to be done is to make the association between the word-concept "JOHN" and the thing-concept JOHN. It is a two-way association.

"JOHN" <--> JOHN

So if the word "John" is heard, the thing-concept JOHN is identified and brought into working storage. If the thing JOHN is perceived, the word-concept "JOHN", and hence the sound of the word "John" (or a set of word-sound phoneme pronouncing actions), is brought into working storage. The same is true of every other word in a language. Each word is associated with at least one concept. Some words may be associated with several concepts (giving rise to possible ambiguity - a problem with which I shall deal later).

11.12

When a person communicates with another, he (the speaker) has within his mind an information structure (of the type described earlier and termed an "interpretation"). Within this structure he identifies a number of substructures which correspond to various concepts. Each concept is associated with a word-sound. He utters a sequence of these word-sounds.

She (the listener) hears each word-sound. She identifies the word-concept associate with each, and retrieves from concept store the non-verbal concepts associated with each. She then uses those concepts to build an interpretation structure - in exactly the same was as she would for any other kind of on-going sense experience (as described in earlier chapters). The resulting interpretation structure may not be an exact replica of the one held in the mind of the speaker, but it will be similar.

Objections to the construction kit theory

11.13

This idea of how linguistic communication takes place has been suggested many times in the past and has equally often been rejected [Fodor 1977 p16]. There are several reasons usually given for this rejection.

(1) Objection: What kind of concept would be associated with a word like "how"?

Answer: A word like "how" is introduced only as language use becomes more sophisticated. Initially communication will be limited to single nouns and verbs. "John run", "John come", and so on. Later, as the ability improves, additional words will be introduced which do not refer to things and events in the environment, but to words in an utterance. In particular these new words will refer to word locations within an utterance.

"Peter and John".

Here the word-concept "and" refers not to any particular word-sound but to the word-sounds (and groups of words) which occur before and after its own position in the utterance. It indicates that whatever concepts these word-positions refer to, are to be linked into a single (composite) entity.

A word-concept of that kind I will call a "meta-concept" (a concept which refers to other concepts). With increasing sophistication those meta-concepts grow in complexity. The word-concept "HOW" informs the listener that the description which follows, or which is requested by the utterance, should be interpreted as taking the form of a causal description.

A simple analogy may help clarify ideas. Consider those plastic model aeroplane and ship construction kits which are marketed under the trademark "Airfix". Each kit contains a number of plastic parts which are to be put together. But each kit has two other enclosures. It has a printed list of instructions and a tube of glue. We could get by without either of these two additional items but the chances of a mistake being made are thereby increased. My suggestion is that these meta-concepts play the role of these additional items. They inform the listener how to build the interpretation structure, what sequence to follow, and where and how to attach each additional piece to the growing interpretation structure.

(2) Objection: The construction kit idea might work reasonably well for simple declarative sentences - "*The door is open.*" But how can that be appropriate for questions - "*Is the door open?*" or commands - "*Shut the door!*"

Answer: The key to this problem lies in the ability of the system to represent the MIND of a person. A great deal (if not the majority) of our communications, are concerned with what is going on in a person's mind. The reason for that is obvious. We are social animals and we are at our most effective when we act in a co-operative way. To do that, however, we need to share objectives, agree the method of achieving those objectives and co-ordinate the roles we play. The interpretation of a declarative sentence results in the construction of a representation of some aspect of the environment.

In the case illustrated by the first example above, the interpretation will include representations for the various entities involved - a door, a wall, a person who might want to pass through the door, the door having two positions (open and closed) and the person (and currents of air) being able to pass through the doorway only if the door stands open.

That form of interpretation does not change for a question provided we extend the environment to include the mental landscape of the speaker. So the sentence "Is the door open?" will have exactly the same interpretation as before, but with the additional information that in the mind of the speaker, the disposition of the door is not known, and that a request is being made for that extra information. To represent that state of affairs we merely indicate that the giving of that information will cause the speaker to be in goal-state.

In the case of a command "Shut the door!", we again have an interpretation structure which represents the door being open. The additional information needed is that it is the closing of the door which will help the speaker to achieve goal-state.

In each case (question and command) the interpretation must be extended to include the representation of hypothetical actions - in one it is the provision of information, and in the second it is an action to be carried out. In every case we have a representation of the environment as it exists within the mental model (the MIND) of the speaker.

(3) Objection: In order for the speaker and listener to communicate it is necessary that the concepts they have in their minds, should be identical. If concepts are derived from personal experience how can we reasonably expect two different people to have identical concepts? This is the problem classified by Prinz as "publicity".

Answer: It is not true that the concepts held in mind by the two people involved, *must* be identical. It is necessary only that they be similar. Since the participants in a conversation live in the same external environment, we can expect that significant parts of the concepts will be very similar. We have also seen that when

183

concepts are processed by the compression algorithm the result is an abstract concept or a group concept. The two people involved will almost certainly have quite different examples of these individual concepts, but the abstract concepts formed by compression will be in much greater correspondence.

I can illustrate the principle involved with an analogy. Two DIY enthusiasts are discussing the construction of (say) a rabbit hutch and they are doing this on the telephone. The rabbit hutches are to be constructed using spare bits of wood etc. which both men have in their personal junk-boxes. The bits they have in those boxes will not be identical, but meaningful communication can still take place if the men discuss the process in terms of concepts, which are not specific. The term "*a bit of plywood*" does not specify the thickness or other exact dimensions, but the meaning is clear to both men and each will choose a piece which fits the overall dimensions each has in mind. In addition each will know which aspects of the concepts they have are peculiar to their own circumstances and will not expect the other to be aware of those. Misunderstandings will occur if any of these assumptions are not valid.

SUMMARY

11.14

The mechanism proposed can evolve in gradual stages from pre-linguistic mechanisms. The most important of these evolutionary precursors are -

(1) the ability to form concepts from the memory of previous experience and

(2) the ability to combine concepts to form an interpretation of current experience.

This gives the proposed mechanism the evolutionary plausibility which the Chomskian approach lacks.

In addition to that, it is suggested that the word classifications, in terms of which the grammatical structure of an utterance can be analysed, make use of that same process of concept formation applied to the experience of listening to spoken language. This explains how the idea of grammatical structure can evolve - an explanation which is also singularly lacking in the Chomskian approach.

Once an unsophisticated form of language has been developed, more features can be added. These will include the addition of abstract ideas and the development of meta-concepts. These more sophisticated features support and are supported by a parallel development of language.

What I still need to do, however, is to explain, with the aid of numerous examples, how the meanings of various words, phrases and sentences can be represented. That is the topic covered in the next chapter.

CHAPTER 12

Language continued ...

This chapter contains technical detail about how the meanings of various words could be represented. I have tried to cover a wide range of different word types to show the power of the representational approach which is based on the time-stamped states and causal connections. The chapter could be skipped at a first reading.

Generating syntactic structures from a semantic base.

12.01

In 1971 a book was published which had almost the same title as the heading of this section [Hutchins 1971]. In the introduction to that book the author stated that the stimulus for his research was the need to provide a theoretical basis for automated information retrieval systems. The approach he adopted was based on what he called "semones" - atomic semantic units or categories.

The example he offered was the semantic category which makes the distinction between these lexemes - *boy, girl, man, woman, bull and cow* - which is, of course, the male-female distinction.

The approach which I will take here does not avoid the use of semones altogether, but it does insist that a semone is no more than convenient short-hand for a much more extensive network of associated components - the representational structures which have been described earlier and which have as their components time-stamped STATES and CAUSAL connections. We can use semones to avoid an uncontrolled combinatorial explosion, but must retain the ability to expand them, as required by context, into their more primitive components (see section 12.44).

I do not dispute that the syntactical categories identified by linguists - structural units such as noun-phrase, verb-phrase etc. are useful. I claim only that they are not the evolutionary precursors of the ability to use language. These classifications come after the ability to recognise the sound and appearance of words has been acquired. However, any attempt to understand utterances requires that we are able to segment a string of words into meaningful groups which do indeed correspond to noun-phrases, verb-phrases and the like. My concern is to find a way to do that that does not rely upon an innate knowledge of grammatical categories. The technique I suggest is not elegant and does not always produce a satisfactory result. In defence of my suggestion, however, I offer the observation that our ability to recognise shapes and objects is not always satisfactory. There are many examples of visual scenes which are ambiguous and which, when they are considered in isolation, that is, without a relevant context, we find that that ambiguity cannot be resolved.

It seems to be widely recognised that to analyse and recognise the visual perception of an object we must first recognise parts, or components of that object. These will be parts of the visual scene which have characteristic and easily identified shapes. When a sufficient number of these characteristic components are identified a recognition of the whole may then be attempted.

Traditional syntactic analysis, in effect, approaches the task pre-armed with a list of acceptable or legitimate patterns, expressed in terms of syntactic categories. Each word has already been assigned a syntactic category. So the task then is to identify for which of these several possibilities a given example or group is a precise match.

One problem which this approach encounters, however, is that the list of legitimate patterns is constantly changing. The rules change, but the human ability to understand carries on with very little difficulty. And that suggests to me that the human way of understanding language is not based upon precise lists of legitimate patterns. It must be based on understanding and it is from that understanding that the analysis of structure and pattern arises.

12.02

So I propose a method that seeks to recognise components and features within a sentence (that is, individual words and groups of words which can be recognised easily) - just as we seek easily recognised individual features or components of a visual scene. This, since it resembles techniques which have been successful in another context, seems to me to be compatible with a more plausible evolutionary narrative.

For simplicity of presentation I shall assume that we are discussing language in its written form and that that language is English. Let's start with a sentence which is free of serious complications –

"The old man lifted his bags and walked slowly down the road to the railway station where he bought a ticket to London."

The presence of what, in the terminology of syntax, is called a "determiner" indicates the presence of a noun-phrase - or a group of words which correspond to some identifiable entity or event which plays a role within a narrative. Pronouns are also unambiguous indicators of a group of that kind. Plurals, often do the same.

Words like "which", "that" or "where" indicate the start of a clause - a parenthetic description of some particular aspect of meaning. Prepositions do the same. Auxiliary verbs ("was", "will have been", etc.) are often unambiguous indications of a verb-phrase.

Note: There is no necessity for me to continue using the terminology of syntactical groups in that way, but since the terms are familiar to most people, it eliminates the need to invent a new terminology.

I suggest that the recognition of these easily recognised features (or clues) is analogous to the recognition of an edge, an eye-shape, the sharp pointed ears of a cat, or the sinuous coils of a snake. These are sufficient to suggest the entity being observed, and the rest of it is then more easily recognised within the context of that initial hypothesis. What I am suggesting therefore, is that when we encounter that sentence above we can start the segmentation process this way –

"(*__The__* old man lifted) (*__his__* bags and walked slowly down) (*__the__* road to) (*__the__* railway station) (*__where__*) (*__he__* bought) (*a* ticket to (*__London__*)."

Here I have identified the determiners "the" and "a" as being each the starting point of a group. The relative pronoun "where", the pronoun "he", the possessive pronoun "his" and the proper noun "London" are also group start-points. Each start-point brings the previous group to an end.

We can then add a number of other identifiable start points such as the prepositions "to" and "down", the conjunction "and" and the verbs "lifted" and "walked". Note that there is no need for the system to recognise these syntactical terms. All it needs to know is that each is a group starting-point and the meaning structure associated with each word. What we then have is -

"(*__The__* old man) (*__lifted__*) (*__his__* bags) (*__and__*) (*__walked__* slowly) (*__down__*) (*__the__* road) (*__to__*) (*__the__* railway station) (*__where__*) (*__he__* bought) (*a* ticket) (*__to__*) (*__London__*)."

Although the phrase structure shown above is not the same as would be produced by a conventional syntactical analysis, it will be recognised as being similar.

To progress further I now have to introduce two extra notions – the idea of a narrative ID (a unique number which identifies an entity or group as an important component of the narrative) and "demons" – that is, small procedures which are embedded within some of the meaning structures. As processing continues, these are activated in sequence. Each is designed to search for a suitable target. If it fails it is placed back on an activation list where it will be found and activated again at a later time.

The technique requires that each group should now be given a unique narrative ID. Let's say that these IDs will use a #-symbol like "#1". In the same way we can assign narrative IDs to all the groups, thus -

"(#1 ***The*** old man) (#2 ***lifted***) (#3 ***his*** bags) (#4 ***and***)
(#5 ***walked*** slowly) (#6 ***down***) (#7 ***the*** road) (#8 ***to***) (#9 ***the***
railway station) (#10 ***where***) (#11 ***he*** bought) (#12 ***a*** ticket)
(#13 ***to***) (#14 ***London***)."

The meaning structures of some of the words will carry demons and these will now be activated in sequence.

The demon associated with the word "the" will search for a suitable target. A simple heuristic suggests that that target will be the last word in the group "*man*". The task performed by the demon is to create a single example of "man" and by doing so ensure that it is assigned a unique identifier. It will also initiate a search backwards through the text for a previous mention of that man. If it is found, the unique identifier of that man will be borrowed. If it is not, this new man will be established as the current focus of attention. A demon associated with "old" will also target "man" and modify his age property to be greater than normal or the standard age.

With its assigned narrative ID the whole group can now become available to serve as the target of other demons. Notice that these narrative IDs play a role which is similar to nodes in a syntactic tree structure. In effect, the grammatical structure of the sentence is growing upwards and outwards from its semantic base.

But rather than proceed further with the analysis of that sentence, I will deal with individual issues one at a time.

12.03

To begin that detailed analysis I will use the simple example –

"John kicked Bill"

We can easily identify "John" and "Bill" as corresponding to players (noun-phrases) within the narrative, and that the sentence can then be translated into -

(John) (kicked) (Bill)

The diagram illustrates the semantic interpretation procedure in action.

Fig 12.03 John kicked Bill

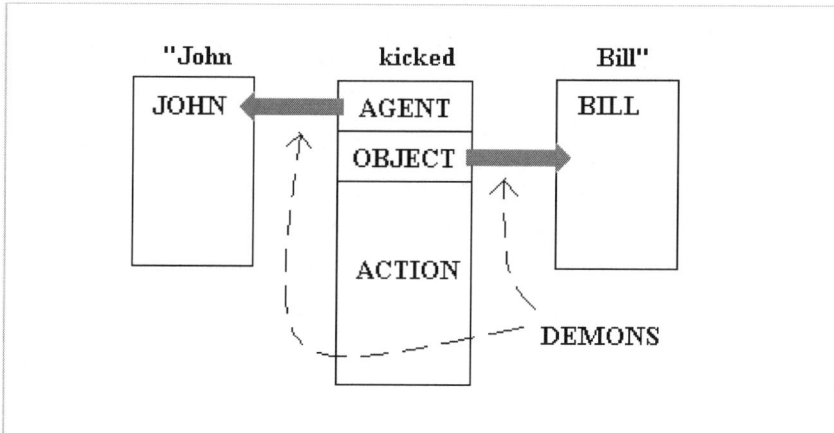

The two shaded arrows represent the action of the demons seeking their assigned targets and instantiating the appropriate components within the meaning structure of "kicked" with the relevant ID numbers.

If the sentence had been in passive voice –

"Bill was kicked by John"

The group analysis would have produced

(Bill) (was kicked) (by) (John)

The presence of "was" is important. It will have a demon which (in this example) will target the demons within the meaning structure of "kicked" and alter them to use alternative search patterns for their targets. The meaning of "by" will also have demon which find and locate John as playing the AGENT role.

The occurrence of that conjunction shown in the first example sentence, linked two actions -

*(**lifted**) (his bags) (and) (**walked** slowly)*

Here the demons embedded in the word-concept **AND** will discover the concept associated with "**walked**" and then try to match it with a similar concept which in this case is associated with "**lifted**". The composite action becomes a single verb for the sentence as a whole with the case categories, and the demons, which they jointly provide.

I concede that this approach is less elegant, more error-prone and less efficient than the very fast and elegant parsing techniques developed by the traditional approach. It depends upon heuristic rules which do not always guarantee success. But I submit that the approach is robust in the context of changing language usage and seems to correspond more closely to the technique I use myself (based on introspection of my own thought processes). I am confident that given the same scrutiny and developed as assiduously as that traditional form of analysis, any problems could be slowly eliminated.

The plurality of concepts

12.04

To talk about the plurality of concepts may seem an odd way to start a discussion on how we might represent the meaning of various words and concepts. One might have suspected that the issue of plurality could have waited until after we had discussed the representation of single entities. But each concept is really a compendium of *several* previous encounters with a particular kind of experience. So there is a kind of plurality about every concept.

The concept DOG, for example, means a collection of observations of doggy things. The concept FIDO means a collection of encounters with one particular dog called Fido.

Pause there. It must also be remembered that until that collection is formed, those previous experiences were separate experiences. That is, the collectivisation of various similar experiences to form the concept of a single entity, is the consequence of the concept formation process. So we cannot (or should not) use that result as if it was a fundamental property of a known external world. The brain tries to make sense of that world and the putting together of various experiences to form singular concepts is a part of that process.

The representation of a plural entity is an unexpectedly complex affair. To get a grip on the technique required we need to take a short excursion into the world of computer programming.

List structures

12.05

In computer programming it is normal to allocate space in the computer memory for items of data that need to be stored. But if the number of items which must be stored is not known at the outset it is impossible to allocate the correct amount of space. "List processing" is a technique used to overcome this problem. Every conventional computer has a memory which has a large number of locations where data can be stored. Each of those locations has a unique address - a number which identifies that location. It is therefore possible to refer to an item of data by using what are called "*address pointers*". The diagram illustrates this idea.

Fig 12.05 (1) - address pointer

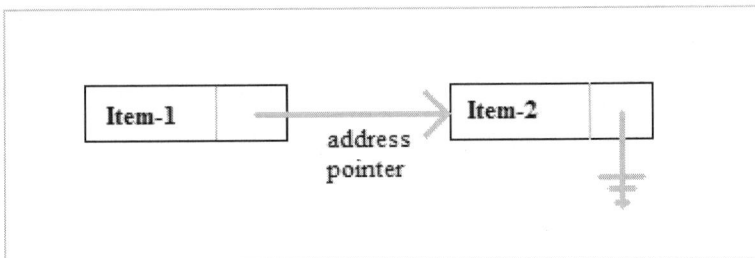

In this diagram we see two items of data, item-1 and item-2. Each has a separate location which is inside a box structure. It does no harm to think in terms of real boxes, like shoe boxes. Each box is divided into two compartments. An item of data is stored in the first and an address pointer is stored in the second.

A numerical address pointer is shown in the diagram as an arrow which points at the other box. That second box is also divided into two compartments and it too has an address pointer. In the example illustrated that second address pointer does not point anywhere. That indicates that there are no other data items in the list.

Fig 12.05 (2) - a list structure

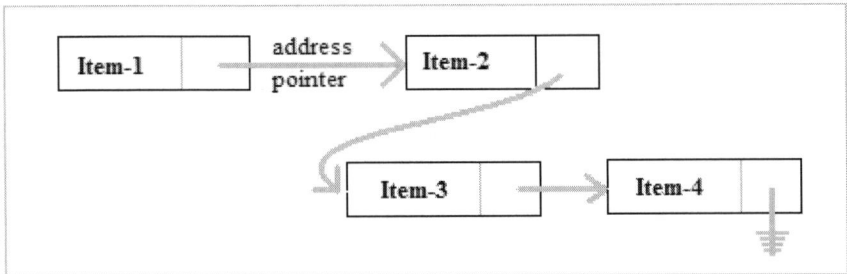

Additional items can then be added to, or subtracted from the list by manipulating the pointers. The items within the list do not need to be physically adjacent.

A simple list structure cannot be used to represent an infinite list and yet we do need to talk about infinite lists. The list of cardinal numbers 1,2,3,4,.... for example, is infinite. So we do need a method to represent them. And there are other problems.

"There are a lot of people about tonight."

How many is that? How long a list should we use?

To represent an infinite list, or a list with unknown length, we need a variant of the list structure which is called a *"dynamic list"*. A dynamic list structure has a special "header" record (as shown below). The header holds a pointer to the first item in the list. It also contains an item called the "generator". The generator is a special program which, when activated, will generate or create a new data item which it then adds to the list.

In order to be able to generate a typical member of the list the generator program must be given a set of properties which the new member of the list must have. A specification of these properties is also held in the header. The simplest way to do that is to provide a typical specimen which the generator copies.

In this illustration of the idea, I have included a "number" feature. This could hold the number of items which have already been generated - or it could hold the maximum number which the generator is allowed to create. We could extend the header so that it has both.

Fig 12.05 (3) - a dynamic list structure

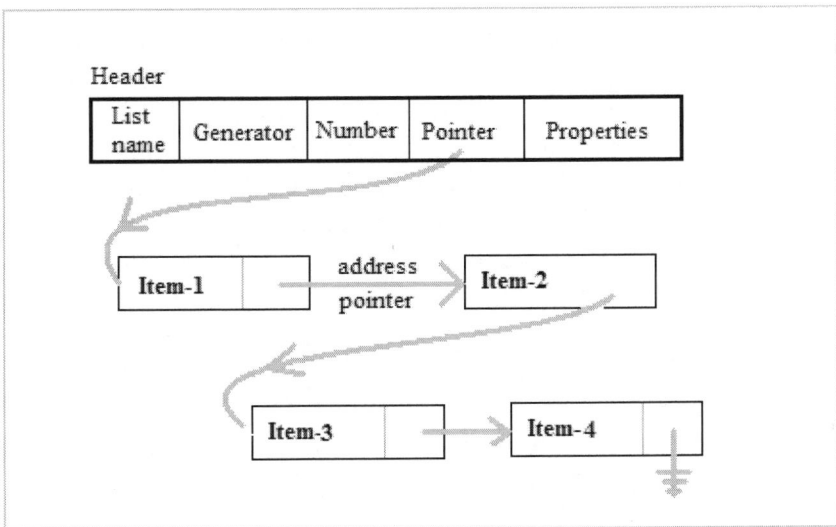

Consider this excerpt from a thriller story in which a group of thugs batter down a door and enter a room.

"Men poured into the room. One of them brandished a baseball bat."

We do not know how many men are in this group. We do know a single fact about one of them. We need to be able to isolate this particular man and we also need to represent the group as a collective.

A dynamic list is the solution to this problem. The generator could create one example and provide that example with a baseball bat.

Note too how this solves the problem of how an infinite list can be represented. We do not need to include every single member of the infinite list. We can simply give it a maximum number equal to "infinity". We can also hold a number of individual members of the list. We have a specification of the list in terms of the properties which specify that an item is qualified to be a member.

12.06

The traditional approach to semantics identifies two kinds of reference - extensional and intensional references. An extensional reference is a reference to the class of things to which an entity belongs. An intensional reference is a reference to the properties which a entity must have to be classified that way.

The dynamic list structure provides a neat solution to that traditional ambiguity by having both extension and intension within the same representational structure. A reference to that structure is therefore a reference to both. Philosophers have debated that issue for centuries - and all to no purpose whatever. With the dynamic list approach, both reference types are included and can be individuated at a later time if the distinction turns out to be important. This is yet another example of how consideration of technical details can resolve a long-standing and a difficult traditional philosophical problem.

NOTE: storage in the brain does not use numerical addresses. It uses a method called "associative storage". Items are stored and retrieved by association with other items which share some property. However, the numerical method used by computers can be used in a way that is "functionally equivalent" to associative storage.

"A dog".

12.07

A question which now arises is this - How do we use this technical trick to construct a representation of a single physical entity? Consider this sentence -

"*A dog entered the room.*"

The word dog is associated with the plural concept DOG (a collective, or a class of dogs). The word "A" has a special role. It is associated with a meta-concept.

This meta-concept has an embedded function (a small isolated computer program also called a "demon"). When the system tries to construct an interpretation of the whole sentence it must launch this function call. The function will search to the right within the structure of the sentence, and it will discover there the meaning structure corresponding to the concept DOG. Initially this will have only the header record belonging to that dynamic list. The task that function is required to perform is to initiate one operation of the generator function (which it finds in that header record). This will generate one item (an example of a dog) and that will become the first item in the list. The generator function will provide that new item with a unique narrative-ID number. The meaning of that phrase "A dog" is a reference to the identity of that dog.

"THE dog"

12.08

The word "*THE*" has a role to play which is similar to that of "*A*". Normally, having established the identity of the dog in question, "*THE*" will initiate a search backwards through previous text to find a suitable referent (with a unique narrative-ID) for that individual dog. If it fails to find a suitable referent it will establish this new dog as the current focus of attention.

With this simple example, we can begin to see how the interpretation process can construct an interpretation of a complete sentence. It uses the concepts associated with each word as the basic construction units and stitches them together using the functions embedded in the meta-concepts.

Dogs

12.09

The word "dogs" is plural. It is a straightforward plural as distinct from a hidden plural. By "hidden" I mean a concept which is not designated as plural in terms of conventional grammatical classification, but which, according to my analysis, does have the characteristics of plurality because it is a collective form of many individual experiences.

This diagram is an attempt to capture, and simplify, the complexity of this multi-level plurality. The form of representation we can use is now obvious. While the concept FIDO is a collection of experiences, the concept DOG is a collection of several individual dogs, and the concept associated with "dogs", is a particular representative set of the concept DOG.

Fig 12.09 - DOG

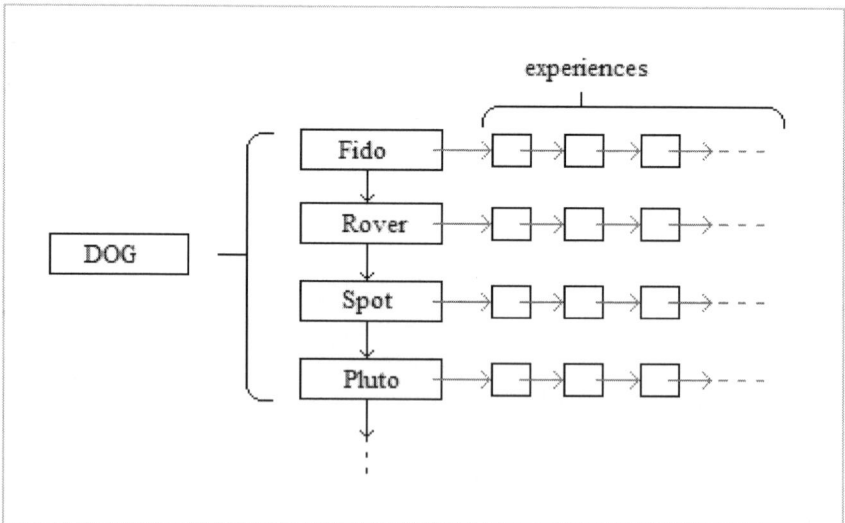

NOTE: I am aware that this analysis is becoming uncomfortably complicated, but that cannot be helped. We must just plod on. Elegance and simplicity is not a logical requirement. All of the relevant information must be captured by the form of representation.

Quantification

12.10

To add still more complexity to that structure we need to introduce yet another level. This one I call "a selection". A selection is a dynamic list which has as its generator function, a procedure which captures a sample from the list of entries of some other dynamic list.

Fig 12.10 - selected dogs

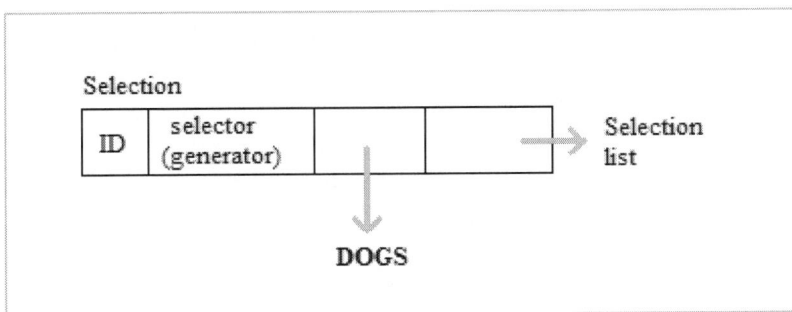

The selection list is able to extract one or more items from the named dynamic list. It may also just specify the type of selection and leave the actual members without these being individually represented.

12.11

This technique offers us some beneficial effects in the context of quantification. There has, for example, been a discussion about why the meaning of the word "*any*" appears to change from being synonymous with "*all*", in some contexts, and the word "*one*" in others.

For example, in the sentence (1) "*Any person can do that*" the whole sentence appears to mean the same as the sentence "*Every person (all people) can do that.*" In contrast, in the question (2) "*Can any person do that?*" one interpretation makes the sentence mean the same as "*Can/cannot even one person do that?*". The analysis which has been offered as an explanation for this apparent anomaly, involves complicated (and in my view far-fetched) syntactical rules. With the introduction of the selection mechanism, and the ability to construct a representation of what a person is thinking, an explanation is straightforward. If a person knows that any item selected from an unknown list will have certain properties, the implication is that every item must have those properties. If a person is not sure whether or not a selection made at random from the list may/may not have those properties, the implication is that not even one item in the list may have those properties.

Other forms of quantification are also handled by this approach. "*Five dogs*" is a selection from the total class of dogs. We may or may not have the actual exemplars in the selection list but we do know how many items there should be in that list. "*Some dogs*" can be a list of unknown members.

Stuff

12.12

I refer to words, which represent not physical objects but the material from which physical objects are made - words like "water", for example, or "wood".

These are materials. The words do not refer to a set of objects. They refer to the materials from which various physical objects are constructed. "*We will burn wood in our fire this winter.*" In that sentence there is no reference to any particular object, but there is a reference to a large number of possible objects all of which are made of wood. So how can that be represented?

It turns out that we can represent materials using the kind of dynamic list structure described. In this case, however, each member of the dynamic list is regarded as being a tiny finite element of the material in question. Whether we are dealing with a solid, a liquid or a gas, the properties possessed by the substance as a whole can be specified by rules which govern the way these tiny finite elements interact with one another. In a liquid, which is viscous, there will be an attractive force between them which holds them together and can sometimes overcome or counter-act the force of gravity. In non-viscous liquids the force of gravity controls how the elements behave. Always, they adopt the shape of the containing vessel.

Modern computers are fast enough to be able to simulate the behaviour of liquids. They simply process each element in turn and calculate the movement of each to a new location under the influence of the various forces specified. For solid objects the individual elements hold on to one another quite strongly. In gases they fly apart so the density of particles is not uniform. All this can be simulated. There is no technical impediment to the adequate representation of materials if we adopt the techniques of finite element simulation. All that is required for gases is that the system is able to represent a mass of gas as a collection of finite elements each of which is a collection of even smaller finite elements.

When we are dealing with gases, the density, or the way in which the smallest elements are packed, must be allowed to vary. So a body of gas will be subdivided into two types of elements - big elements and small elements. In that way the system could build an adequate representation of, say, the Earth's atmosphere and the way its density decreases (of the big elements) as we gain height from the Earth's surface, or distance from the centre of mass. The same technique could be used in the representation of something as nebulous as "*a puff of steam*".

The representation of quantity.

12.13

What we are normally unable to do is to provide explicit numerical values for quantities. If we say that a man is "tall" then what we are actually saying is that a particular man is taller than we normally expect a man to be. Expectation is expressed in terms of a standard height. Let's say that that is STD-MAN-HEIGHT.

Every actual quantity is given a unique identifier. We might, for example, assign to a particular man the height measurement HT-1234. These identifiers are generated and assigned when a concept is used in the construction of an interpretation. If the man is described as "tall" we would add the information that HT-1234 > STD-MAN-HEIGHT. If we have two tall men, and these are recorded as HT-1234 and HT-1235, then we will know that

HT-1234>STD-MAN-HEIGHT

and that

HT-1235>STD_MAN-HEIGHT.

But without specific information on the issue we will have no knowledge of the relative heights of the two men.

Prepositions.

12.14

*"John kicked Bill **in** the stomach, **in** the kitchen, **in** December, **in** a temper and **in** a flash."*

So how do we construct an interpretation of that sentence using the word-concept for the word "***in***" (and its associated concept)?

The answer is that we introduce a program that examines the concepts located on either side of the word "*in*". As it examines them it tries to match up similarities. The first, or default option, is to match them with respect to location (in the sense of the action represented being *inside* some particular location. It is in this context that the use of semones (or semantic categories) is particularly helpful. The component of that sentence above which places the action inside the kitchen, will correspond to that interpretation. It will have the semantic category "location". It will in addition, need to have available a concept of what a kitchen is - a sub-location of a house where food is often prepared. And that needs a concept which represents food as a commodity which is consumed by people to maintain their supply of chemical energy. It's a long story which threatens a combinatorial explosion, There must, at some point, be an arbitrary cut-off when a match has been recognised (see section 12.15 below).

A "temper" is a state of mind (which predicts particular kinds of actions). "December" is a time period (which predicts a particular kind of weather). And a "stomach" is a component (or location) of the human body. The search pattern of the program associated with the word "*in*" will be able to identify and match up all of these contextual references. In some cases we may find that more than one type of match is possible. In that case the interpretation mechanism must hold on to these alternative interpretations until such time as a logical clash indicates that one or more of the alternatives must be abandoned - or placed into background operation mode to be resurrected if some unexpected connection is discovered.

To avoid building the complexities of that program into the main interpretation program, it should instead be embedded within the structure of the word-concept associated with the word "*in*". That technique allows the interpretation procedure to be subdivided into smaller and more manageable parts, and ensures that the relevant parts will become available only if they are actually required. Every word in the system's lexicon will bring with it the procedures needed for its interpretation. This gives every word in the language an individual ability to blend in with the interpretation, rather as the molecules of a given chemical have the ability to combine with each other, within a given chemical reaction.

The parts explosion problem

12.15

Next, let us tackle the issue of how we could represent a complicated physical object - one that has a number of component parts. The problem is concerned with the superfluity of parts which would be produced if we tried to include every component of a given object. Carried to its logical conclusion the representation of every object, even quite mundane objects, would degenerate into a treatise on everything.

Fig 12.15 - hierarchy of parts

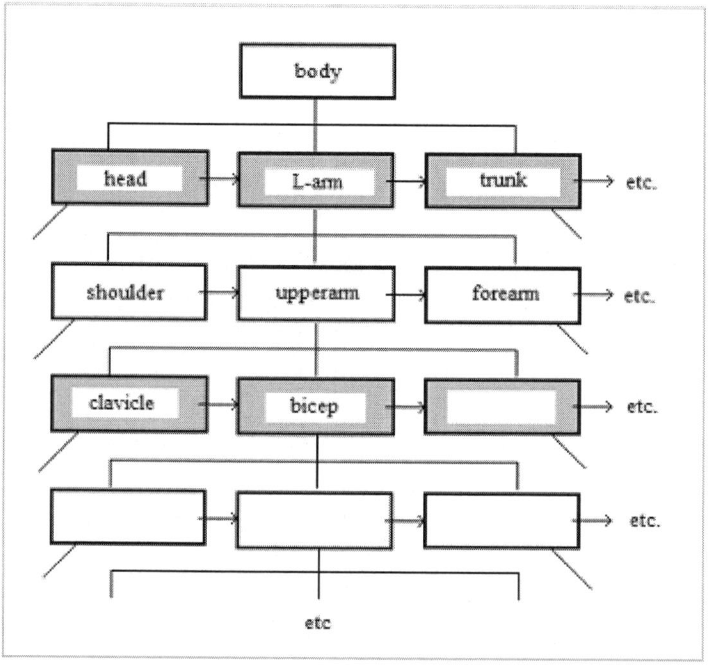

This, depending upon the nature of the object, could include anatomy, physiology, geology, chemistry, physics and so on down to the theory of fundamental sub-atomic particles. So an arbitrary cut off point must be established and my suggestion is that that point must be chosen to include only the most obvious components. The depth of treatment will depend to some extent on the knowledge base of a person concerned. In the case of a discussion between professors of anatomy, we might decide that it is appropriate to carry out the analysis of components further than we would if we were dealing with a discussion between typical people.

If the human body is subdivided into head, neck, trunk, arms, lower-body, legs, etc. should we include shoulders in that preliminary list? It scarcely matters. So long as shoulders are included at one level or another, the actual decision is not important. If the theory is correct then it will always be possible to recover whatever information is required, no matter what decision is taken about the precise level of inclusion. In the diagram I have restricted the explosion of parts to just one component of each level. In fact every component at each level, will (normally) be the start of yet another component-hierarchy. We should not imagine that anything as complicated as the human body can be represented easily as a nested set of hierarchies. The actuality (take a look at Gray's Anatomy) is very complicated and messy.

The information that is contained in that book must be included somewhere within the system - and that is only the physical components - we have not even started on biochemistry.

Searching structures, that are large and complicated, is known in computer science to be notoriously hard and time-consuming [Horowitz and Sahni 1978]. Having two starting points, however, so that we are searching only for an intersection between two expanding searches, reduces the time required. So too does any organising principle, such as hierarchy, which we can impose upon the data. If our system encounters a sentence such as - "*I have a pain in my knuckles*" - it must be able to

(1) take the concept associated with "pain",

(2) discover that it refers to an experience located within the body,

(3) take the concept associated with "knuckles"

(4) discover that it is a body part

(5) expand the body description associated with knuckles

(6) find that we talking about a part of the hand

(7) discover that a pain is something for which treatment may be required

(8) form a reply such as

"Have you asked a doctor to look at your hand?"

It will, of course, also have a representation of a DOCTOR (if required) in terms of what a doctor can do.

Compare that response with the type of reply of which Eliza (see a later chapter) is capable and then ask this question - Does this system, which replies in this way, actually know what a hand and a knuckle is? Does it understand the initial sentence?

Note this too - This hierarchy of components exists alongside the hierarchy of individual experiences from which the concept was derived. I did not claim that the implementation of my system design would be easy.

Two-dimensional solid objects with definite shapes.

12.16

The representation of solid objects which have some definite and recognisable shape, is probably the easiest representational task and the one with which most analyses of the problem start. The problem of defining a representation of a two-dimensional shape was discussed earlier in the context of the phase-layer-1 mechanism. Several alternative methods were discussed. One was suitable for silhouettes against a plain background. It could also classify shapes in terms of proximity to standard shapes (like square, circle, triangle etc.) Another dealt with the type of outline (jagged, smooth, etc). A combination of the two could offer some chance of recognising a shape, which was partially occluded by some other object.

Three dimensional shapes.

12.17

The phase-layer-1 mechanism was restricted to two-dimensional analysis. More difficult to deal with is the idea of three dimensional shapes. For that the system must integrate the information from more than one mechanism of sensory perception. It must, for example, integrate visual information with tactile information or with binary vision discrepancies (or parallax).

Fig 12.17 - binocular discrepancy

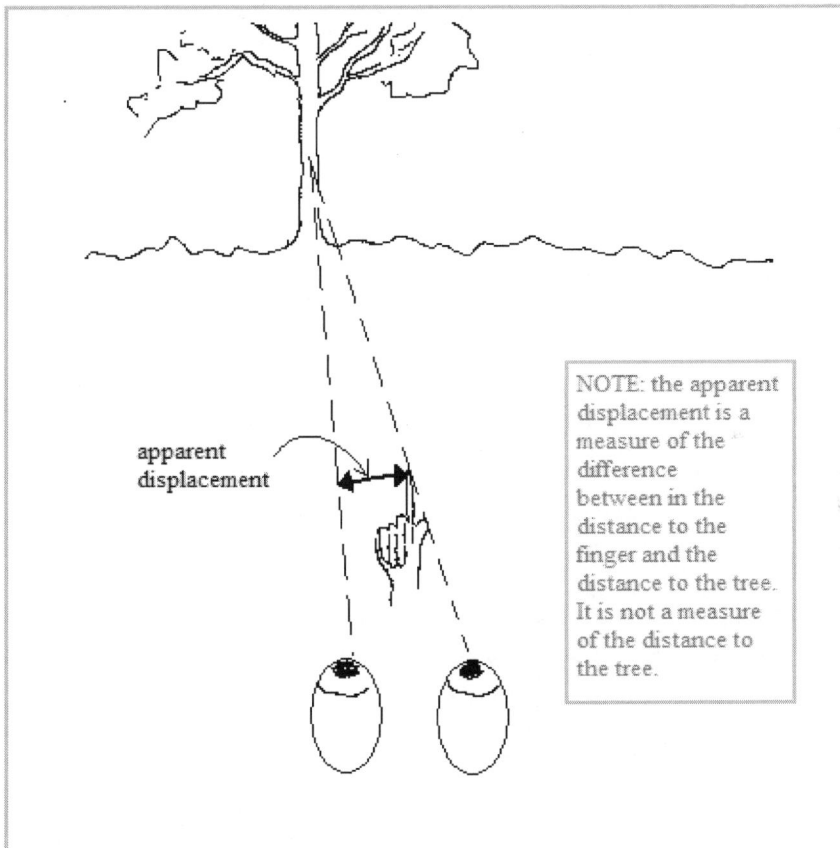

apparent displacement

NOTE: the apparent displacement is a measure of the difference between in the distance to the finger and the distance to the tree. It is not a measure of the distance to the tree.

It was suggested earlier that the matrix form of information, which was made available by phase-layer-1, could be regarded as multi-dimensional. Three dimensional relationships are not expressed in terms of numerical locations within a cubic graticule but as connections to detection units each of which represents a location on one specific axis of a multi-dimensional space. That multi-dimensional space is not therefore restricted to just three visualizable dimensions. Yet, when we look at a scene, the mental impression we get is that we are seeing a three dimensional graticule.

It seems then that the brain could use the parallax discrepancy as a measure of distance (for objects which are fairly close). It is very unlikely that the brain can do calculations which are anything like trigonometry, but the results can be functionally equivalent.

The degree of apparent displacement between objects when we close one eye and then the other, is a measure of relative distance. It works only in the near to middle distance. For far-away objects, the displacement is negligible.

Multi-dimensional vision

12.18

When we look at a scene, it seems as though objects are observed to be located in three dimensional space. What I suggest, however, is there is nothing within the brain which corresponds to this impression, despite its apparent reality. What I think is the case is illustrated in the diagram.

In this diagram, there is a 3D room mostly seen in 2D. There is a central part (in this example the man in the centre of the room), which is seen in 3 dimensions which are given some numerical measure.

What we do have, I suggest is a multi-dimensional matrix (which earlier I called a "*fuzzball*") and that for small regions of that matrix, we can attend to several dimensions. In this example, attention is on the man and by taking note of those extra dimensions we are able to process the identified man as though being perceived from several different directions. The task is difficult however. I can speak only for myself. I find it impossible to do this for more than a small part of the total scene. Briefly, for the selected part, I can in my mind, walk round the object and note what would be seen from the other side. I cannot do that for more than one object in the room, simultaneously.

Fig 12.18 - the graticule

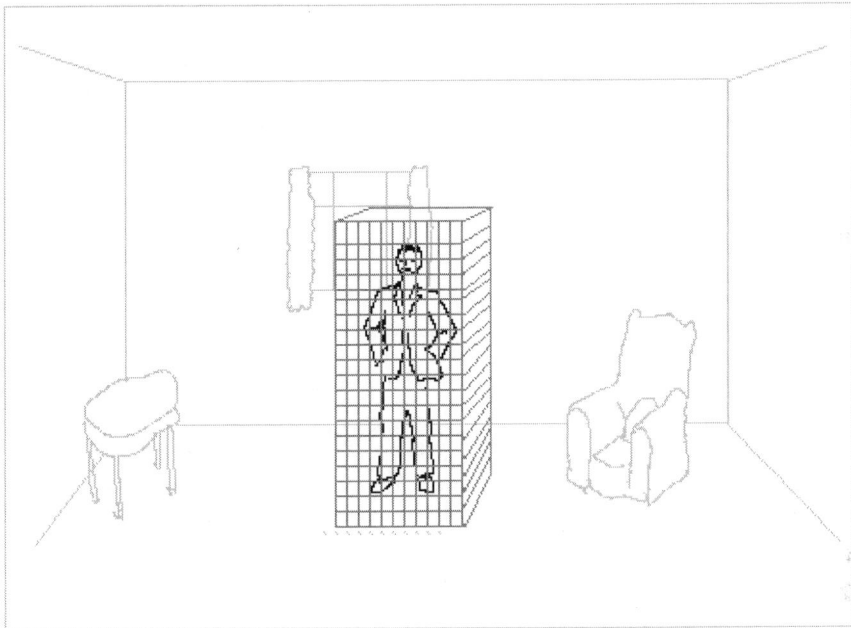

Try checking that for yourself. Look at the scene around you. Select an item within it, and then try to imagine what that object would look like if it was viewed from another direction. That is, take yourself on an imaginary walk round to the other side of your sofa and try to imagine what you would see from that viewpoint. And then, try to hold that imaginary scene in your memory while you try the same trick on the armchair, which is over there on the periphery of your visual field.

Difficult. Isn't it? As you imagine the 3D experience, the view you have of every other aspect of the visual field, fades away into

2D. In that representation every location is related only to the internal grid of the sensory arrays and the information about apparent displacement is held separately. To get a 3D representation we need to bring all of these together to form a single common representation.

That's the focus of attention thing again. I can focus on only one thing at a time because the 3D imaging required for my navigational radar system, is a difficult and time-consuming operation. I can do it only selectively. I suspect that others may be able to able to manipulate space more effectively than myself. I am impressed by professional sportsmen who seem able to be aware of the spatial position of every person on a football field at any single moment.

Indefinite Calculus

12.19

If we are denied the use of numerical values with which we can do calculations, we will need some alternative way to compute quantity values in relative terms. In another book [Noble 2005] I described a form of notation which I called "indefinite calculus". This defined a number of expressions which represented values in relative terms without committing to precise numerical values.

All values, as in conventional algebra, were denoted by unique alphabetic identifiers, such as "A", "B", "C" ... etc. Each of these could be instantiated to an exact numeric measure or, if we were working in a two-dimensional surface, by a co-ordinate pair (x1,y1). The system allowed the relative values of variables to be expressed in the conventional notation, eg $A > B$.

The notation is then extended by the addition of other expressions -

extension(A,B) which means that some quantity extends over an interval starting at A and extending to B covering all positions between. It was necessary to introduce a convention that an extension of that kind included its starting value but excluded the ending value. This obviated problems, which arose when two extension values abutted. With these expressions we can construct representations of various spatial arrangements, like having one object beside, or on top of another, or just above it without making contact.

The range expression range(A,B) was used to represent an uncertain value "somewhere in the range A to B". This is useful when dealing with objects, which have uncertain perimeters, like a "puff of steam".

The notation also included a number of additional expressions such as

increase(A,B) - increasing from A to B
decrease(A,B) - decreasing from A to B
change(A,B) - changing from A to B
increase_with(A,B,X) - increases from A to B as X increases
exclusion(A,B) - excluded from the interval A to B
part_extension(A,B) - extends over part of the interval A to B

and many others. This notation was developed to assist with the representation of various concepts - like "above", "behind", "vanishing", "inside" and with the meaning of phrases like "he is a smoker" where the act of smoking extends over part of an interval of time but not all of it.

Meaning and implication

12.20

Working with these expressions involves a crucial relationship - does expression X imply expression Y? For example if we say that someone lives in Paris that implies that he lives in France. A small range (range(A,B)) implies a larger one (range(C,D)) if it is completely embedded within it. That is, if A>C and B<D. I think that if that implication is not understood and capable of being represented, then the statement "He lives in Paris" cannot be understood.

Three dimensional extensions.

The notation can be extended to embrace three dimensional entities. We can, in effect, drag an extension over an interval of space to create a two dimensional object, and then drag the two dimensional object through an interval in a third dimension to create a three dimensional object.

Fig 12.21 - extensions in three dimensions

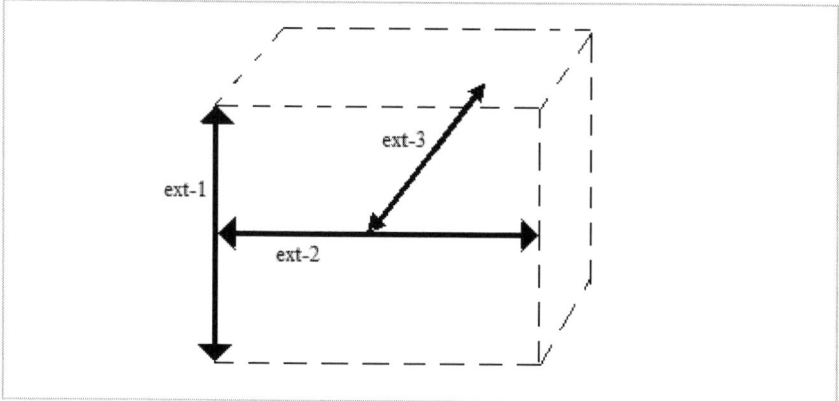

The diagram illustrates the idea. If those extensions were also given limits, which correspond to range specifications, we would define a solid object which was not a perfect rectangular prism.

A cylinder.

12.22

The same principle can be used for other three dimensional shapes. We could "drag" a circle into a third dimension to obtain a cylindrical shape.

The further we extend consideration into a variety of shapes the more it becomes obvious that we need extra facilities within the notation. We need, for example, to be able to be able to denote some regular variation in the size of objects.

Fig 12.21 - A cylinder: the extension of a circle

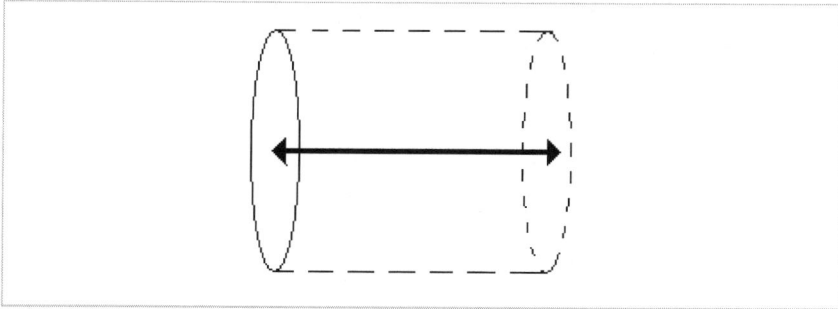

The drag or draw expression

12.22

That general principle can be extended. We are specifying the 3D shapes of objects in terms of the actions needed to draw that object. 2D objects (of various types) can be drawn, or dragged along some pathway. We saw earlier that we could specify the outline of some object as a list of short-line segments. A circle is a collection of line segments all of which have relative directions which differ from one another by a fixed amount.

A tapering cylinder can therefore be represented by "dragging" a decreasing circle along a straight line.

If we introduce a notation for "objects" of various two-dimensional shapes, we can have a circle defined by the expression:

circle=object(start,length,dir,dev);
where start=starting point, length=segment length, dir=direction, dev=deviation angle (fixed)

Fig 12.23(1) - tapering cylinder

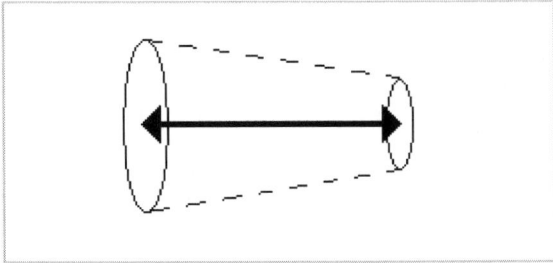

This approach to the representation of physical shapes opens up an interesting consideration.

Fig 12.23(2)- a list of line segments -

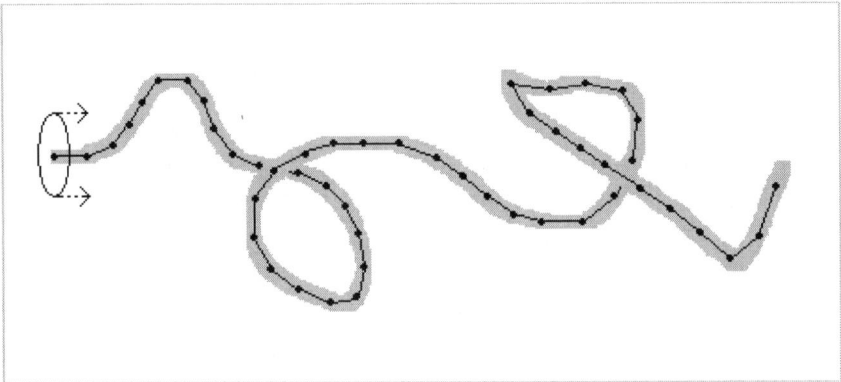

It appears that we can represent shapes indirectly by providing instructions which explain how the shape can be constructed. Compare that idea with the notion of the internal representation of experience as a kind of knitting pattern.

Objects which have no definite perimeter.

12.24

I am thinking here of an object like a mountain. A mountain has a definite location, it fills a definite space, but it is not always easy to specify where exactly a mountain ends and the valley begins. In these circumstances we can take refuge in the "range" expression which specifies that a given value lies in a given range of values. Somewhere between X and Y, is the general format.

"range(X,Y);"

We can get the general form of a mountain by taking an imaginary walk across it and noting that that corresponds to dragging an extension like a cross-section through the mountain, from one side to the other, and noting that that extension (the altitude at any given point in the walk) will increase from an indeterminate starting point, to the summit, and then decline again back to the level of the valley beyond. A representation of that kind would enable the system to interpret a narrative about mountains. It would provide a meaning for the word "summit" and for the word "slopes". A more detailed interpretation can be included if the occasion requires that.

The representation of actions (time durations).

12.25

An action is intrinsically, a sequence of conditions or circumstances which runs over a period of time. The nature of time itself has been a source of philosophical discourse for a very long time indeed. The position adopted here does not offer any new insight into the nature of time itself, but it does suggest a particular way in which the apparent forward movement of time can be represented. A clock is a mechanism which produces a sequence of pulses and records the sequence in the form of a series of unique patterns. Since the brain itself is of finite size, there is no way that the sequence of patterns can in fact be infinite. But it can avoid repetition by classifying time into intervals on a non-linear scale. So times which occurred a long time ago will be classified

215

together. Fine distinctions would then be reserved for recent events. For a person of a certain age, the events which occurred in childhood tend to merge into a long indistinct period within which the sequence of those events becomes forgotten.

The simplest form of representation is the token value - "T". If several times are required we will use the sequence "T1, T2, T3, ..." and so on. If we need to specify the sequence of these time markers we will write "T1 < T2 <T3 ...." and so on, meaning that T1 comes before T2 etc. When we need to record the fact that some particular condition lasted for more than one time period, we can assign to it a time-stamp with the form "T1---T2" meaning that it lasted from T1 to T2. If we are not sure exactly when an event occurred but we know approximately, we may write "T1...T2", meaning that it occurred sometime within the interval from T1 to T2.

States and time-stamps

12.26

We can now consider how we might represent a sequence of circumstances over a period of time.

The diagram shows a simple sequence of conditions. Each is represented by a "state" (of phase-layer-1). Each has been assigned a time-stamp (T1, T2, T3 .... etc). These are considered to be in chronological sequence running from top to bottom. One of them (T4) has been designated as being equal to NOW, a standard or global variable which represents a (context dependent) present time.

When a concept is initially retrieved from the concept-store, the various time-stamps will not have any value attached to them except for the relative values implied by the time sequence. To be able to assign a value like "NOW" to one of them we need the additional information provided by the remainder of a sentence.

This defines a "tense" or time-value. In this example the assignment of NOW to T4, divides the time-sequence into three parts - PAST, PRESENT and FUTURE.

Fig 12.26 time sequence

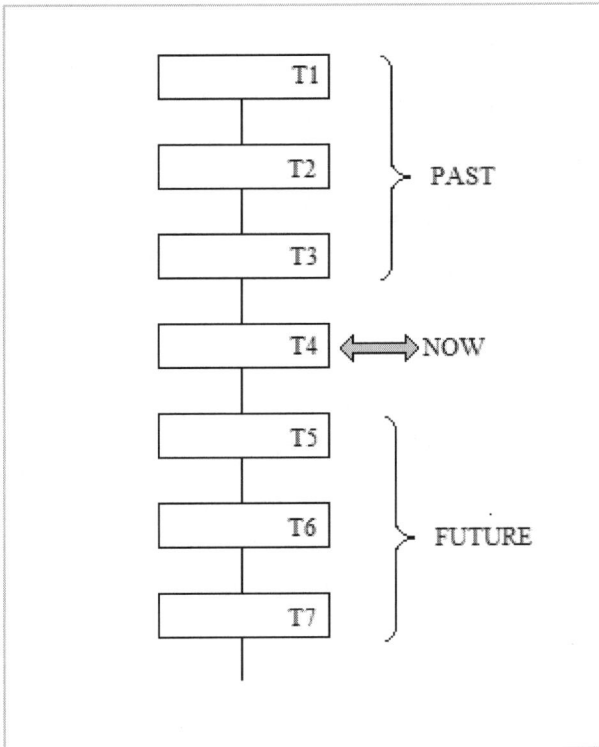

PRESENT and PAST circumstances will be assigned a special status of "confirmed". That is, they are considered to be actual. Everything in the FUTURE, however, is designated "potential". Since it has not yet actually happened it cannot be considered to have the status "confirmed". There may, in fact, be several alternative "potential" outcomes of the events represented. Analysis of the sentence (it is to be expected) will confirm or deny some of those anticipated outcomes. And that is the purpose (or the main purpose) associated with the interpretation of sentences -

to describe circumstances and from those descriptions to be able to predict likely outcomes.

Representing events.

12.27

Events, rather than actions. The term "action" might be taken to imply some kind of deliberate purposeful action. An event has no such implication.

Fig 12.27 events with a single causal-link

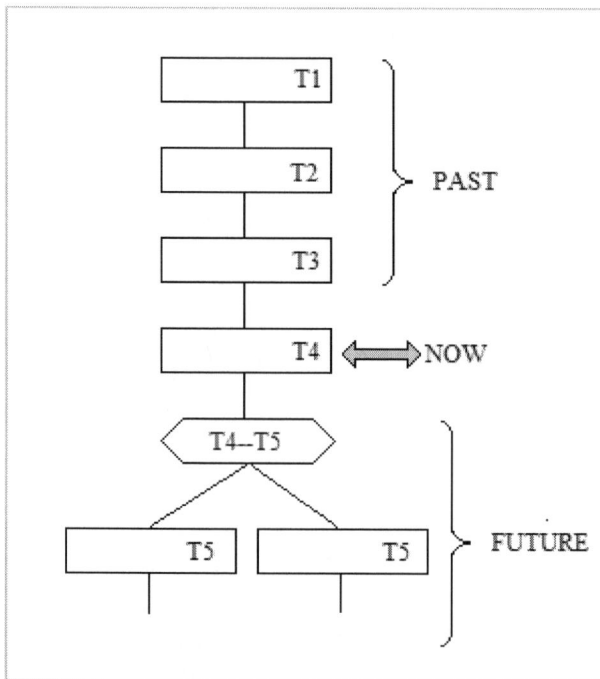

So events just happen. Inanimate things fall, are blown by the wind, crumble, decay and so on.

What about a volcano? A volcano can do things, and if you don't know what could be going on inside, the events that happen and are caused by a volcano could look very like a purposeful action. And the language we use, since it was developed over immense periods of time before our knowledge of geology developed to the current level of sophistication, will probably incorporate those misconceptions. Be that as it may. We are talking about events which are not caused by human motivation. So all we have is cause and effect. There is no hidden calculation which is driving things along.

The diagram shows an arbitrary event with a single causal-link. The link has a time-stamp which covers the period of the precursor condition to the resultant condition. T4---T5 in this example. In this example too, the resultant events are designated as taking place in the future.

Note that there are two possible results both of them with the time-stamp T5. For example, the impact of a foot on a football might cause the ball to fly through the air, or it might cause the ball to roll gently along the ground. These results are obviously mutually exclusive. In any given example, it is necessary that the mutuality or possible simultaneity of the resultant conditions, should be specified. Since the whole point of being able to represent these circumstances is to constitute predictions being made, the detail included in each specification of a causal-link is particularly important.

Representing purposeful actions.

12.28

And now I want the reader to assume that the word "action" implies some form of motivation. To illustrate this type of representation we need a diagram which is rather more complicated.

The diagram shows the structure associated with some arbitrary action. As before we see a sequence of conditions. Here (on the right) we again see a single causal link between the condition with time-stamp T4 and two possible causal effects both with time-stamps T5. In this diagram we also see that one of the states which participates in the action is labelled PERSON.

Associated with that PERSON (on the left) we have a new structure. It too shows a sequence of states all associated with a MIND. This MIND is connected to the PERSON and the rest of the new structure on the left and identified as being OF the MIND OF that PERSON.

What this conveys (or is intended to convey) is that that structure and the events which it represents, exists within the MIND of that PERSON. Note that the final condition in that mental structure is labelled GOAL (of the MIND). The assumption is that a GOAL is something which a PERSON will try to achieve. In other words, the action represented on the right, is planned and executed by that PERSON with the intention of achieving one of the results identified as a GOAL.

Fig 12.28 motivated action

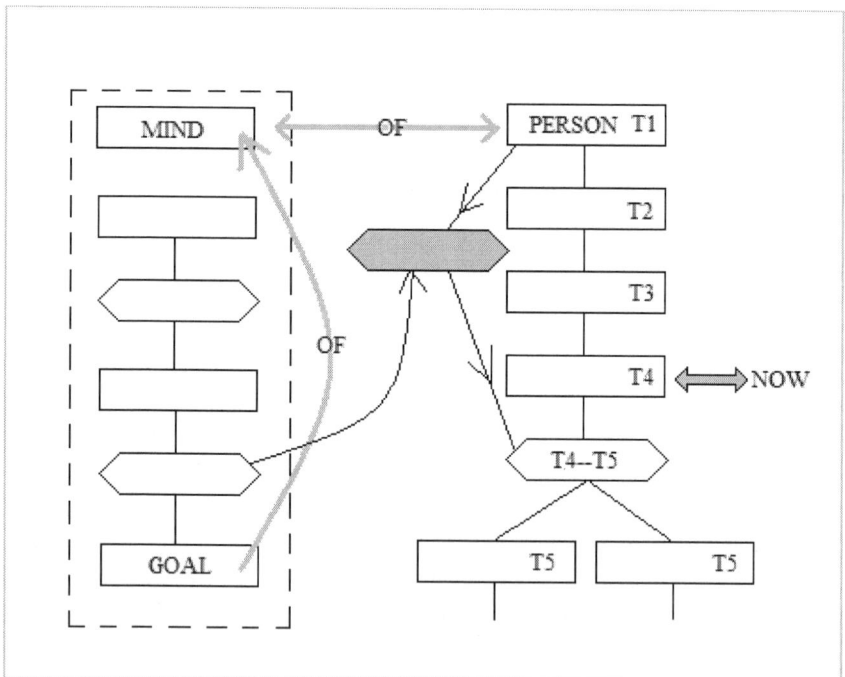

More complex situations can be represented in a structure of this kind by identifying more than one GOAL condition from which the PERSON must make a choice. Some could represent short-term gratification GOALS, or longer-term GOALS for which the reward envisaged is some form of social approval (a plausible working definition of morality).

In this way, because we are able to build a representation of what a person is thinking, we can build a representation of the motivation which drives behaviour (and therefore to predict that behaviour).

In the representation structure shown, the fact that the mental structure in the MIND of the PERSON has a GOAL, is shown to be the CAUSE (shaded) of the action, such that the physical body of the PERSON becomes the CAUSE of the condition (time-stamped T4) being the CAUSE of the action shown. That is, the mental structure CAUSES the physical body to act and thus CAUSE the action to be performed.

Note that I have not assigned any time-stamps to the elements of that mental structure. In practice we could assign a general time-stamp to all of them to show that they were present in the PERSON's MIND for a period of time (say "Tx--Ty") which begins before the action takes place and lasts at least until the action is completed.

The representation of thoughts and beliefs.

12.29

The previous example showed how we could build the representation of a person's intentions. We can now extend that idea to show that it is possible to build a more general representation of thoughts. I am thinking here of the acres of discussion which have been generated by the problem of whether or not mental entities (like mathematical constructs) can be said to "exist". It is clear that we can construct a representation of any condition or any sequence of conditions which could exist in the mental model of external reality. But they do not need to be in external reality. That mental model can be firmly placed in the mental world of a PERSON without any suggestion of there being a corresponding entity in external reality. The elements of such a structure "exist" in the sense that they are part of the internal mental model. But they do not "exist" in the sense that there is not thought to be any corresponding entity in the external world.

I will return to the issue of existence in the final chapter.

Representing knowledge.

12.30

When there *is* such a correspondence we could regard that as a representation of what a PERSON *believes* about the external world. If the correspondence is good or precise, we could say that the internal structure is what that PERSON *knows* about the external world.

The difference between *belief* and *knowledge,* according to this approach, is that the owner of the whole representational structure (i.e. the system itself), agrees with what that other PERSON believes.

Truth.

12.31

That approach to belief and knowledge removes any notion of absolute knowledge. Knowledge is to be judged solely by what some standard entity believes to be true. In this case that standard entity is the system itself. Truth can then be defined as the property possessed by certain internal models, such that they can be shown to correspond to what some person believes is true about the external world. Note, however, that what a person believes is to a large extent governed by what that person is able to perceive. I have commented frequently that the internal model created by a person is determined automatically by sensory perceptions, in a way that is beyond the conscious control of the person who has those perceptions. If my sensory perceptions tell me that I am not sitting here at my computer typing these words, or if I claim to be able to hear voices telling me to murder small children, then others may well (justifiably) decide that I am certifiably insane. In which case, my beliefs cannot be recognised as any kind of standard by which the truth of other people's beliefs should be judged. This recourse to consensus opinion, based on widely observable evidence, corresponds to what could be described as established scientific truth.

The truth-test procedure.

12.32

We are now able to describe a procedure which is able to establish the truth of a statement. This procedure compares two structures - a TEST structure and a REFERENCE structure and tries to determine whether or not the TEST structure corresponds to (or maps on to) some substructure within the REFERENCE structure.

Comparing structures in that way, if these structures are large and complex, is notoriously hard. As the complexity of the structures increase the length of time required to prove that there is such a mapping (or to prove that there is no such mapping) increases at an alarming rate, to the extent that the problem is often regarded as impossible or just not worth attempting.

Nevertheless, if the structures are small (or the TEST structure is small) then a result can often be obtained. And even if a result cannot be obtained in a given context, the fact that we can envisage a result being obtained can sometimes be used to identify what truth is, even if we cannot actually make the decision for a given example.

We can write the truth-test procedure this way -

truthvalue(TEST,REFERENCE,criteria,RESULT);

Here we have a procedure which must be applied to the two named structures. The "criteria" argument tells us how correspondence between the two structures is specified, and RESULT is the result obtained. There may be occasions on which we would want to specify that the RESULT = True, even if we cannot actually confirm that that is the case. That is in effect a representation of what the word "truth" and the corresponding concept means. The fact that we are in some cases unable to carry out the truth-procedure does not prevent it being used as a definition of truth. It used to be the case that the definition of a "metre" was obtained by comparing the length of some test object with a standard metre which was held in some environmentally controlled laboratory space in Paris. That is what (in those days) the term "metre" meant.

Now-a-days a metre is defined in terms of some standard electromagnetic wavelength. Most of us are not in position to make any such test, but that remains the current definition of a "metre". To use the term you must imagine that you are in a position to carry out that comparison test and what you are saying if you say that this rod in your hand is a metre long, is that if you did carry out the test, that is the result you would obtain (or near enough within the limits set by the "criteria" specified).

The liar paradox.

12.33

And that brings me to consider the liar paradox (because if I do not address the problem someone else surely will raise the issue as an objection).

The liar paradox is a reference to the indeterminate circumstance which arises when a statement challenges its own truthvalue status. For example -

"This statement is not true."

If we try to apply the analysis of the truth-procedure as outlined above, to that statement, we find that the TEST statement has become its own REFERENCE statement. And that creates difficulties. Note that the TEST and the REFERENCE must be structures. So if we start with the statements themselves, they must be converted into interpretation structures before the test can be applied. That conversion however, requires that we are able to determine the truthvalue of each. And to do that we need to apply the truth-test procedure and get a result. And the trouble with that is that while one structure is declaring its own truth, the other is denying that result. So a result can never be obtained.

Each application of the truth-test procedure must always run for ever trying to reach a result and at each recursive loop of the procedure it contradicts the result it obtained during the previous loop. The result, as every student of logic knows, is said to be "undecidable".

Why we need two representations of external reality.

12.34

Some readers may be puzzled about why we need to include two separate representations of external reality - a general one and a second one associated with the SELFMIND. The answer is that there may be times when we need to be able to make a distinction between (1) what I currently think is true and (2) what I did (wrongly) believe yesterday. The general representation refers to current belief. The second representation is the historical record of what has been believed by the SELFMIND. The current belief shown in the SELFMIND must be in agreement with the general representation, but the historical record need not be.

Abstract concepts.

12.35

Abstract concepts have always created problems for the representation of the meaning of a sentence. Any sentence which contains a word like "justice" or "education" or "difficulty" or "representation" is problematic. What structures could be used to represent the meaning of these concepts? None of them appear to have anything concrete about them which could be translated into anything as definite as a structure.

As an example, let us consider the concept "justice". The view that I take of that concept is based on the philosophical analysis of John Rawls and most definitely does not bear any relationship whatever to the views espoused by Ayn Rand within which I think the ideas of justice and revenge have become hopelessly confused with one another.

What we need to do is to creep up on a solution, in gradual stages. The first stage is to construct a representation of "society".

We saw earlier how plural entities could be represented using dynamic list structures. Society is a generalised and rather undefined group of people. The header record of the dynamic list would carry various elements, one of which would be a list of group members and another would be a generator function which can generate or create new members of the list. Since each member is a PERSON, each of those members will be associated with a MIND structure. And into that MIND we can deposit a pattern of thoughts which we attribute to each member of the society.

To keep things simple, I shall take a naive view of society by attributing a single common attitude to everyone within it. That means that in the header record of our representation of society there will be a generator function which can create a "typical" member of that society. That member will be a human being. A random number generator will choose with roughly equal probability the gender of that member. It will assign the requisite number of arms, legs, heads, hands and feet, fingers and toes. To each it will also assign a MIND structure. Into that MIND we will place a representation of the attitude which that person has to the scenarios we must also define.

That over-simplification can be modified later to allow more variability. We could perhaps take the result of an opinion poll and try to represent all shades of opinion within our representation. But we will start off by giving everyone in society the same attitude to everything.

That means that we will allow the "typical" member of society to have only one attitude and in that way we will represent all members as having the same GOAL and ANTI-GOAL states associated with various scenarios and events which could take place. Usually we will be concerned with only one or at least a very few events.

To construct a representation of justice we will also need to construct a few examples of actions being carried out by several different people. These might be a schoolboy cheating at his examinations, a serial murderer killing his victims and a thief stealing the belongings of another person.

Each of these involves concepts for which we will need to find adequate representations. The obvious ones are - exams, killing, and ownership. Constructing these representations will be difficult and yet, as we will discover, the detail of these representations will actually not appear in the eventual and successful representation of justice. The important characteristic which they all share is that the "typical" member of society will disapprove of those actions. That means that the end result shown in the representations in each of the three scenarios I have listed, will cause the "typical" member of society to be in an ANTI-GOAL state.

We need a further extension to the representation of the attitude of society. This will involve some sanction. It may be physical punishment, expressions of disapproval, incarceration and so on. The salient point of all these however, is that each will put the culprit of the disapproved action, in an ANTI-GOAL state and that in turn will put the MIND of the typical member of society in a GOAL state.

That is a bit complicated but I think it is clear enough. The crucial factor is our ability to represent causal links between mental states and actions taken. Society disapproves of what someone has done and because of that takes action to make that person regret his actions. That is what emerges when we apply the compression algorithm to the several scenarios I described.

Action by X
causes
Disapproval by T
causes
S to take action
causes

Discomfort of X
causes
Approval by T

Where X is the villain, T is the typical member of society and S is society.

We could add a great deal of detail of course. The action taken by S will be carried out by a sub-group of S who have been designated as having the responsibility for doing so. S, it is assumed, has the physical power to do such things.

What has vanished from that representation are the details of each offence. What also disappears is the idea that it is the victim of the offence who should take the appropriate action. In this view, by definition, justice is the prerogative of disinterested third party members of society.

While trying to creep up to a representation of society and of justice, we appear to have stumbled upon a way to represent the concept of "the law" and "legal punishment". There are, of course, a great many different types of punishment which can be imposed, but they do all share this property. When a legal sanction is imposed it causes a person (the perpetrator) to be in a ANTI-GOAL state which by definition is a condition a person would normally try to avoid. Details of what that ANTI-GOAL state is will distinguish between different punishments ranging from mild disapproval to several years imprisonment or even the amputation of a hand. Clearly the full structure will be very complicated, but there is nothing there which in principle cannot be represented.

Other abstract concepts can be formed in a similar way. Note that although each person who forms such a concept may start the process with a completely different set of examples, but that when the generalising effect of the compression algorithm operates the abstract concepts which result will be very similar.

Multiple alternative representations.

12.36

The approach to representation being advocated here, suggests that we should not be surprised or disappointed to find that it possible to represent a single set of circumstances in several different ways. There is then considerable scope for misunderstanding between people who have different but (in their judgement) equally valid representations within their mental models of what they suppose is external reality. The interpretation of linguistic utterances can present to us variations of great subtlety and therein lies the strength and the complexity of language.

When we consider that the main function of language is to communicate ideas between people and that the aspect of human relationships which are of greatest importance concern people's attitudes and intentions - aspects of reality which cannot be readily observed in any other way - we should not be surprised to learn that a large proportion of the concepts which we use in our communications, are concerned with exactly those internal mental aspects of life which cannot easily be observed directly.

"I am confident".
"You are stubborn".
"He is pig-headed".

What is the difference? The difference is one of attitude in the mind of the speaker - of approval, of tolerance or of disapproval.

To be able to get a grip on these subtle variations of interpretation, we need to be able to represent what is the current state in a person's mental world model and that is where the MIND and SELFMIND concepts are extremely useful. To put these facilities into operation, we do not need any significant change to the way we represent those mental worlds. We use exactly the same representational structures, which we use for representing external reality. But each element of the representation is given a "potential" marker, to indicate that its condition, or even its existence, is not confirmed by observation. The whole structure is then given a reference to the appropriate MIND concept structure.

The implications which then can be seen to flow from that representation are then marked either as a goal-state or an anti-goal state of the person concerned. That indicates whether or not it is a condition which is desired by that person (or otherwise). The assumption, (unless there is some additional information to the contrary) is that that person will normally take whatever action is required to bring that desired condition into existence (or the opposite).

Wittgenstein and games.

12.37

Nearly every interpretation of a linguistic utterance carries some connotation of mental attitude. When the philosopher Wittgenstein famously argued that it is not possible to provide a definition for every word or utterance, he was careful to point out that it is possible to *explain* what a word means, even if it was not possible to *define* its meaning.

The word he chose as an example was the word and the concept "game". Games, he argued, are so variable in their physical form, that it is impossible to lay down any strict criteria for the recognition of what constitutes a game. Think of various games - board games, card games like patience, ball games like tennis and team games like ice-hockey - and there seems to be no obvious common aspects (of location, physical apparatus or even the number of players) which we can identify as shared. But I think he made a mistake. There is one thing which is shared and that is the mental attitude of the players. In each case the player or players, are competing against circumstances - either circumstances being caused by opponents, or circumstances brought about by chance (when the cards were shuffled). In each case, the desired conditions which the player (or players) is trying to achieve, will ultimately be regarded as unimportant.

In saying that I am not forgetting the quip by the legendary manager of Liverpool football club Bill Shankley who once (famously) remarked that the game of football -

".... is not a matter of life and death. It's a lot more important than that."

But that is funny only because we all know that a mere game should not be regarded as being so vital.

In every game the desired outcome (for any given player) results in the acquisition of "points" which collectively can result in that person being regarded as having "won" the game. Winning is desirable (but not really important). Winning is arbitrary. Winning is the prelude to legitimate self-congratulation and in some cases illegitimate ridiculous triumphalism.

When we say of a person (and of some serious activity) - *"It is only a game to him"* we imply that he is not taking the outcome with any sufficiently serious concern. He is not having an adequate regard for the internal feelings of other people. If we say of another *"It is not a game as far as he is concerned"* then we are making the same comment as Shankley (but not with the same degree of wit). We mean that the person concerned takes the issue too seriously. In each case there is an implied criticism.

I maintain that it is possible to explain (as distinct from define) the meaning of every word and every utterance. The only reservation is that the explanation may well (and probably will) involve a explanation of internal human attitudes. Test my thesis with any type of "game" that you can think of. Is there any game to which the explanation above (about human attitudes) does not apply?

The representation of "representation".

12.38

I am trying to show that the approach to the problem of representation advocated here, is robust and can deal with many otherwise very difficult problems. The most extreme example I can think of, is the problem of providing a representation for the concept REPRESENTATION itself. So how could that be done?

The essence of a representation is that it is a structure held in the MIND. We have a means to represent that. We also have the means available to represent whatever structure is held in a given mind. Next, an important aspect of any representational structure - call it X - is that it has a special relationship to some other structure, which we can call Y. This relationship is recognised by the person who has the representation of Y in his/her MIND. The representation X (of Y), is a mapping from X to Y which establishes a correspondence between them, such that the predictions derived from X, match or provide guidance about the predictions, which should be obtained from Y.

This takes us back to that earlier discussion on truth. Truth is the result which may be obtained when one structure (the TEST structure) is compared with another (the REFERENCE structure). As we saw previously, we have to take into account the criteria used to establish a match, and the result obtained.

Consider several different types of representation which we can construct and which have useful properties. An architect can construct a representation of a planned new town. The representation will not match the real town in terms of size, but it will match reality in terms of the relative positions of the buildings. So if we want a prediction about how a person walking about in the real town could get from one building to another, we could, by inspecting only the representation or model of the town, work out what journey that person would need to take. Let's say then that that representation would match reality in terms of the accessibility of buildings and roads.

The designer of an aeroplane might construct a representation of a wing-section so that it can be tested in a wind-tunnel. Again, certain aspects of the representation have no corresponding match in the intended real aircraft. But there will be certain aspects in respect of which there will be a correspondence - particularly in regard to the aerodynamic properties.

In each case the degree of match will be determined by the criteria specified and the usefulness of the representation will also be determined in that way.

The difficulty we encounter, however, is that in these circumstances, the REFERENCE structure is itself an internal model and the criteria of its validity are beyond our control - for these are also determined by a set of criteria defined by the characteristics of the phase-layer-1 SRA.

The crucial feature of a representation is that, while we may be unable to specify explicitly the criteria being used by any individual when he or she constructs a mental representation, we can specify what kind of prediction that person wishes to make. That is, we can construct a representation of the use to which the representation will be put. It could be anything ranging from the avoidance of premature death to the avoidance of mild embarrassment. It could be the acquisition of a favourite food, or the achievement of sexual gratification. All of these can be specified as goal-states and we can distinguish one from the other by constructing a representation of the action which must be taken in order to reach these goal-states (or avoid anti-goal-states).

The structures, which are the result of this representational process, can at times have a daunting complexity. Provided we do not lose heart, however, we find that representation is always possible if we are prepared to start with simple representations and build upwards taking what we have already achieved as components of more complex arrangements.

Representing the unknown.

12.39

A problem of representation, which has often been discussed, is how one could construct a representation of knowledge, which is not known by the person constructing the representation. For example, my friend who is (or was) a Professor of Theoretical Physics, knows a great many things which I do not know. But I know that he knows them. So how can I represent that fact if I do not actually know what it is he knows?

A simpler example - "*John knows Mary's telephone number.*" How can I represent the meaning of that statement when I do not know Mary's telephone number? I have seen some attempts to deal with this problem which involves the use of complicated Greek symbols and obscure logical systems. That is not an approach, which I would recommend. Calling this unknown thing "Chi" or "Phi" does not solve the problem. It exacerbates the problem.

I think we need to start at the beginning and get a grip on what a telephone is. It is first, an instrument, a physical object. Telephones come in all shapes and sizes, but they all have one thing in common. If you have a telephone and if you have in your brain a special number, you can type, or click, or in some other way indicate that number to the machine, and it will then operate in a way that puts you into contact with a particular person (perhaps). You can then (if you are successful) have a conversation with that person. And that is what Mary's telephone number is - it is the special number, possession of which will enable you to have a conversation with Mary. We know how to represent enablement. Enabling means to cause a causal connection. Which means that you cause yourself to be able to cause something to happen.

The representation of these difficult abstract concepts is not impossible if you analyse the problem of representation into appropriate components and then solve those components, one at a time, in the correct order. The technique is clumsy. I will concede that. But it is not impossible. The trick will be to build a basic capability into a machine and then let it deal with the daunting complexity of constructing a representation of that kind.

So how would I represent the fact that my professor friend knows a great deal which I do not know? I would represent his knowledge (like having possession of that telephone number) as that which enables him to do certain things which I cannot do - like passing an exam in advanced physics, designing a nuclear power station or writing a scientific paper on Higg's Boson.

The role of society

12.40

As we explore the way in which various abstract concepts could be represented, it becomes clear that the notion of society plays a very important role. The technique suggested earlier, whereby society is represented in the form of a dynamic list, is potentially capable of holding a list of actual individual members, but it can also hold a specification which can be used to generate more typical members. That provides useful facilities for the representation of society. We do not need to provide a representation of each and every member of society, but each member, who is in fact given an individual representation, will normally have the properties of a typical person. Each will have the same limb components and each will also have a MIND structure. All this can be contained by the generator specification. That specification can also contain a suggested content for that MIND structure - that is, it can suggest what is believed by each member of a particular society.

Of considerable importance would be the attitude any given person has to what he or she believes is the attitude which society has towards himself, or which sub-society he or she feels that person belongs.

Belonging. Ah! Now that is an interesting concept.

Ownership

12.41

Ownership is a relationship between two entities which is sanctioned by society. I can speak of MY house, MY wife, MY hand, MY book, MY seat in a cinema, MY favourite song, MY money, MY life, MY idea, ... and so on. Each of these types of ownership is unique and the differences between them are defined by the extent to which society will tolerate the way I behave towards these other things. Society will not interfere if I decide to cut the nails on my hand. But it would interfere if I tried to cut some part of my wife's body without her permission. The ownership which I have for a seat in a cinema is time limited. I relinquish ownership when I leave the cinema. Nevertheless, if someone tried to take the seat away from me during a performance after I had paid for and occupied the seat, my claim of ownership would probably be supported by the cinema management - at least I hope it would.

House ownership is a matter of legal documentation. My life is owned outright, although some might dispute my right to terminate it if I considered my life to be intolerable. That issue is debatable.

Ultimately, society decides what ownership rights we have. Some societies consider even a person's life and limbs to be subordinate to social controls. A crucial part of each person's personality is the relationship that person has (or thinks they have) with society - whether the goal-states they have coincide or contradict the goal-states which a notional "typical" member of society has.

What this means for the representation of ownership, is that the different forms of ownership can be represented in terms of what actions a person can take with regard to the entity owned, and what sanctions might be imposed by society if those rules are broken.

A tennis match

12.42

I am trying to show that a method of representation which has the ability to include a representation of MIND, of motivation and repetition, has the flexibility to be able to form a reasonable representation of almost anything. To that end I am seeking out issues which are particularly difficult. The representation of a tennis match fits that description.

The particular difficulty which it presents is that it contains an indefinite number of repetitions. Faced with that, most computer programmers will immediately think of some kind of looping structure, but that will not do the trick. The problem is that a looping structure uses a single form of representation over and over again as a rally progresses. Each individual loop will contain some representation of a racket hitting a ball. But if we do it that way, there will be no way we can distinguish between those separate hits - no way we can distinguish between one which was a powerful back-stroke which was intended to be a passing shot and a subtle forehand drop shot. If we want to be able to make such distinctions then every part of a rally must have its own independent representation.

The way to get round that is to use recursion. Each loop of a recursive program creates its own independent records which hold information about that bit of the program, when it started, what data was available to it at the start, and how and when it ended. These are called "*activation*" records.

We have to begin by creating a representation of a tennis-ball - As a simple physical object with a definite size and shape. That should not be particularly difficult. But it does have one special problem. A tennis ball in shape and size is almost indistinguishable from a large number of other kinds of ball. The distinguishing feature of a tennis ball is not just those curiously curved lines on its surface, but the fact that it is designed to be used in a tennis match. So the representation of a tennis ball and of a tennis match, must go hand in hand. Each is an important component of the other.

To let us move forwards we will assume that we have a representation of the physical object. Next we want a representation of a tennis racket. We will assume that that is also possible, at least to the extent that its physical shape is concerned. We would probably divide it up into handle and head, but since both have fairly regular shapes, that should not create too much difficulty. The head would be disc-shaped. The handle would have the characteristics of a tapered cylinder. The size of the handle would be expressed in relative terms (relative to the grasp of a hand). Both would be specified in terms of their most convenient intrinsic co-ordinates. The whole would have additional parameters which indicate the position of connection and orientation with respect to observer-related co-ordinates. The shape of the complete item could additionally be specified in the way described earlier for arbitrary shapes. There is scope within the specification of a concept to have several alternative descriptions. The trick is being able to recognise the equivalence of these alternatives and being able to select the one which is most convenient for computational purposes. The co-ordinates will not be expressed in absolute terms, but always in relative terms usually with reference to body parts.

Having specified the concepts associated with each of the physical components of a tennis match, including the people and the tennis court itself, we can begin to think about how the repetitive nature of the match might be represented.

Again, we work up to the finished result in small steps. We look for components. One such is the stroke. A stroke involves a player holding a racket, causing the racket to move, which causes the racket to make contact with the ball, which causes the ball to move to some destination. The destination can be (1) into the net, (2) out of court, (3) into the area specified as the court on the other side of the net.

The next component is the rally. A rally consists of several strokes. Every time a stroke takes place the simulation must create the appropriate records to represent the various forms of contact and causal links along with the results obtained. Unless it is specified otherwise the system can, in effect, spin a coin to see what the result of each stroke is to be. Note that every stroke involves the creation of new records. We can have a special representation for the kind of stroke we call "a serve", which has certain restrictions placed on it. If we feel inclined to be pedantic we can even require that the person serving does not make the mistake we call "a foot fault". It is complicated admittedly, but there seems to be no way that these complications can be avoided.

The specification of a stroke will include the three possible outcomes, one of which will be yet another return stroke. We will need two stroke representations - stroke-1 and stroke-2 which refer to different players and different rackets. We might write down the program for stroke-1 like this ...

```
Stroke-1
    player-1 holds racket-1
    player-1 causes arm (of player-1) to move
    which causes racket-1 to hit ball
    which causes ball to move
    which causes
```

(a) ball to hit net (point to player-2)
(b) ball to land out of court (point to player-2)
(c) stroke-2
End of stroke-1

The specification of stroke-2 will be similar. It will invoke a call of stroke-1 as one of its alternatives. And so on.

The result will be the creation of a great many physical records. We could, if we are not afraid of complications, even be able to represent that any particular stroke might put top-spin on to the ball, or be a drop-shot, or whatever.

Tennis ball (again)

12.43

A tennis ball is not just a small round object which can bounce. It is also the thing which is an important component of a tennis match. How then might we construct a representation of the way a tennis ball is used? I suggest that to do that we re-use the representation of a tennis match, and then, in effect, we place a large arrow into the representation, which indicates that the focus of attention is the ball which is flying back and forwards.

The same technique - re-use of the tennis match representation with one item within it identified, isolated and given a narrative ID could be used as a representation of a tennis racket, a tennis player and a tennis court.

And that is, I suggest, an important characteristic of the construction-kit theory. It offers a general facility for the re-use of what are often complex semantic representations in a way that enables the representation of various concepts to be placed within a conventional context. The context within which a concept occurs often contains important additional information.

Semantic primitives

12.44

The traditional approach to semantic analysis is based on developing a list of fairly obvious semantic categories "semones" or "markers". These, it is envisaged, can be used (in various combinations) to characterise the meaning of words. As a result, with this approach, the way words meanings can be put together is somewhat rigid and pre-defined and does not always fit particular individual circumstances.

The semantic primitives which I have proposed here, emerge, without human intervention, from the way the data compression process extracts repeating chunks of material. These are (1) physical objects, (2) causal connections and (3) events and scenarios. We can then also identify a fourth, more general category, which contains all of the generalised versions of these basic primitives (object categories, causality itself and abstract concepts) which are created when the compression algorithm is re-applied to the original data and to the concepts already formed.

My claim is that the primitives which I propose really are primitive. Any and all of the traditional semantic markers can, in fact, be constructed from the primitives which I have proposed.

Consider, for example, the semantic differential of MALE/FEMALE which is often proposed in the traditional approach. What I am saying is that we can represent the meaning of the words "male" and "female" by means of a scenario which portrays the behaviour of two people of opposite gender engaging in the sexual act which may then result in the conception of a child. We can do that by constructing the scenario using the representation of physical bodies, their physical components, and joining these using causal linkages of various kinds.

The result is, of course, a structure which is embarrassingly large and complicated. But it does capture all the information in the context, which most people understand and assume is understood when we hear the words "male" or "female". Of course different people will know and understand these things to different degrees.

Even so, we can use that construct as the context (as we could with the representation of a tennis match) and identify within it, the particular components associated with "male" and "female" as components of the action represented.

Figurative speech

12.45

And that brings me to the topic of figurative speech. What strikes me very forcibly is that the use of figurative speech in every day conversation, is very common indeed. It is not the preserve of only creative writers. Everyone does it, and does it regularly without even realising that that is what they are doing.

The very fact that it is so common should alert us to the idea that an ability to handle figurative speech must be an integral and important part of using natural language.

That, I think, is another good reason to be suspicious of both the Chomskian notion that an ability to analyse the grammatical correctness of statements is fundamental to language processing, and the traditional approach to semantic analysis with its rigid and pre-defined semantic categories (which are not really primitives at all). There is nothing there that offers a convenient approach to the understanding of figurative speech.

My own approach uses the analysis of the concepts which are associated with words and proposes a way of putting these concepts together using procedures which are very general and not committed to any specific list of semantic categories. In effect, the "putting together" procedure examines the representations of meaning for the words and their combinations, matches these up with the growing interpretation structure and makes a connection when criteria of quality of match are satisfied. That means that the combination procedure can, in effect, discover or create new semantic categories as it goes along. We do not need to specify these combinations in advance.

In the section above in which I discussed the representation of a tennis match I suggested that the match representation is basic, not only to the match itself, but to all the various physical components of the match - racket, ball, net, court and players. Each of these uses the full representation of a match, as a foundation, and then identifies the role played within that representation by the relevant component. And when we do that, we have, in effect, divided the representation into two parts - a central or core part, and a peripheral or contextual part. My suggestion is, that when we use figurative speech, we are using a concept and we are, in a novel way, switching the focus of our attention from the core part of the concept to some aspect of its contextual part.

When the mechanism of interpretation tries to put concepts together it must recognise that in some instances a conventional way of putting them together would be inappropriate. It must take a different approach by searching for an alternative way to link the concepts, and it will often find that the appropriate point of linkage is in the contextual part of the concept structure.

A few examples might help to consolidate that idea.

If I say that we are confronted by "*a sea of troubles*" I am borrowing a figurative phrase from Shakespeare. But even if the people I am talking to have never heard that phrase before, very few will have any difficulty understanding it. In this case there is a mismatch between the concept SEA and the concept TROUBLES. The second has nothing at all obvious, to do with water. Within the context of the concept SEA, however, there is an indication that we are not talking about just a small amount of water. A crucial part of the concept SEA is that we are talking about a very large sheet of water. The most appropriate way to make a link between SEA and TROUBLES, therefore, is to use the concept SEA as a size modifier (like the concept LARGE) to modify the scale of the concept TROUBLES. In grammatical terms the word "sea" has ceased to be a noun and has become an adjective instead.

Another example: If I say "*They are using that issue* ... (let's say it is unemployment) ... *as a political football*" most people will understand that I am commenting on the attitudes of the people involved. They are not treating the issue with the serious concern that it merits. Instead they are treating it as a game in which points can be scored, and the issue itself is being _propelled_ (now there is another figurative use of a word) back and forwards within the political _arena_ (another one) which has become a notional _football pitch_. You cannot really propel a political issue. But you can construct an analogy between the alternating end-to-end play in a football match, and the alternating contributions made during a political debate.

We cannot escape the use of figurative language. It is how language works, how it develops and how it can be made more expressive (and more compressed). By using words figuratively we can indicate (or imply) a great deal of content while using only a very few words because those words already have a great deal of what we want to say available within the context of their use.

A few days ago I read a satirical article in a magazine with the title "TIPPING POINT REACHED IN CLICHÉS". That made me laugh. It also occurred to me that the very first time anyone used the expression "tipping point" in that way, it was an example of the creative use of figurative speech. Most figurative expressions will eventually, by constant repetition, be turned into clichés. Once a cliché is well established it seems to be easier for people to use it and do the required non-standard interpretation, rather than think out some more direct and literal way to express themselves. Eventually, by constant repetition, a secondary interpretation of a word or phrase is born and is absorbed into the standard vocabulary.

There is much work to be done in this field, but I am pleased by the way my own proposal seems to offer a way to deal with figurative speech, that mimics the human facility - effortlessly, seamlessly and apparently without realising that that is what is happening

12.46

Language is a relatively new phenomenon in the story of human development. A child, born of parents in one social context, but adopted at an early age into another, with a very different natural language, learns the new language of his adoption in a way

243

that is indistinguishable from that of a child native to that environment. So the ability to use that language has to be a learned ability - but one which is based upon more basic facilities which did evolve, probably for other reasons.

To understand the way that ability could have developed we need to backtrack to an earlier stage. The diagram above is one I used earlier to illustrate the way the interpretation process operates on the TRACE structure.

As the TRACE is formed as a sequence of multi-dimensional matrices (or fuzzballs) chunks of that material are recognised. The concept which corresponds to each chunk is identified, retrieved and built in to the developing INTERPRETATION structure.

Several questions arise.

How does the mechanism know that its choice of concepts is appropriate? For any given fuzzball, since there are many dimensions involved and many different ways to group the sensory perceptions included within it, there must be several different choices of concept. So what criteria are used to determine this choice rather than that one?

Fig 12.46 Interpretation of the TRACE

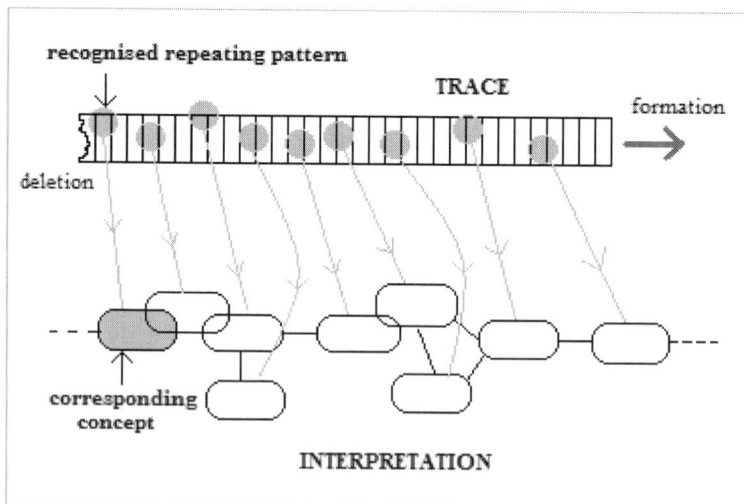

244

If the system makes a mistake, how does it recognise that a mistake has been made? How does it distinguish between a good interpretation and a bad one?

Recall the analogy I used earlier - the construction of a jigsaw puzzle picture. If a piece is fitted into the picture, how do we judge the fit to be satisfactory? Obviously, a good fit is snug. The two convoluted edges meet along the full length of that edge with no perceptible gaps or overlaps. The continuity of lines and colours is preserved across the gap between the two pieces. The corresponding condition in the procedure is a match between most of the elements of the inserted concept and the elements present in the interpretation structure.

Another important feature emerges from this analogy. The quality of fit cannot be determined unless the new piece is fitted on to an existing part of the partially constructed picture. There are a few exceptions to that rule. For certain pieces there are properties which identify them as having particular roles without regard to any other pieces. That provides us with a starting point. Thereafter, it is the rule that new pieces must be fitted on the existing partial picture. The analogy is not perfect, of course. In this situation there is no handy reference picture printed on the lid of the puzzle box. There is therefore no point in leaping about trying to fit pieces at several different unconnected points. We have to start at some point and work outward from there, guessing or predicting what should be visible on a piece which fits the current point of interest.

A "point of interest". That's another name for a focus of attention. Earlier too, I remarked that, that in computer science, searching a complicated structure to find a match for some other structure, is a notoriously hard and time-consuming task. It is made much easier, however, if a starting point is identified from the outset.

What I am suggesting is that these points in the structure which we call "foci of attention" have important roles to play. Each is a point at which the search for a match begins. And when a trial piece is fitted to the growing picture, the system must identify discrepancies. Zero discrepancies indicates a perfect fit. A few discrepancies might be tolerated.

What we are considering here is the basic interpretation of sensory perceptions. We look at (and hear, smell and touch) a scene of some kind. These sensory perceptions assail our senses simultaneously. But the process of interpretation is difficult and time consuming, so we can attend to only one aspect of the scene at a time. Any single element, or fuzzball, within the TRACE can be analysed into one of many possible chunks and hence many concepts. When one has been chosen it must be established in the working memory of the brain and then used as a point of attachment for the next concept.

The diagram below is an improvement on the previous one. The interpretation structure shows several concepts all of which overlap to some degree. The black dots represent potential foci of attention and potential points of attachment.

Fig 12.46(2) Points of attachment

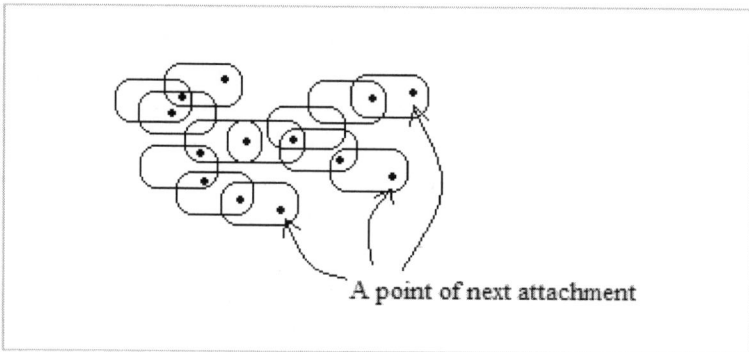

A point of next attachment

We now switch to the interpretation of language. A linguistic utterance is always linear. That tends to obscure the natural and complex simultaneity of the interpretation structure. If you walk into a room, the cat sitting on the mat, the positions of the chairs, the flowers in a vase, the flames in the fire, the ticking of the clock, the smell of fresh-baked bread, may come to you all at the same time. Where do you start the construction of the interpretation? The answer is - with whatever is the focus of attention.

When we are dealing with language, the sequence in which the structure should be built and the way various attachments should be added, is more or less defined in advance by the ordering of the words. All the interpretation process needs to do is to follow that pre-defined sequence. But there still has to be an effort to cluster the material into important components. My suggestion is that the use of narrative-ID markers is a formalised and convenient version of that need to form clusters, and could plausibly have developed from that earlier evolved mechanism. My idea is that the assignment of narrative-IDs is a record of the various foci of attention that occurred as the interpretation procedure progressed.

Ambiguity

12.47

Words, and therefore also sentences, can be ambiguous. That is a problem which has to be confronted by any technique of language processing whether it is based on syntax analysis or concept synthesis as I have suggested here. When we read the phrase

"The shooting of the hunters ..."

it is impossible to tell if the hunters are the things which are doing the shooting or the things being shot. That is true for human understanding as well as for automatic techniques.

There is no perfect technique, so the best we can hope for is to apply some heuristic method which will usually disambiguate, but cannot be guaranteed to do so. The usual approach is to rely on additional information supplied by the context and to try each of the alternatives in turn starting with whichever of the alternatives seems most likely in the given context.

That approach can work well if the system provides facilities which enable it to backtrack - to cancel any actions taken and to reinstate the circumstances which existed before those actions were taken.

When the system being used involves syntax analysis an attempt will be made to match the structure of a sentence to one of the available patterns of word classifications specified as acceptable by a given grammar. Failure to find a match is the event which triggers backtracking.

When the system involves concept synthesis there has to be a similar metric which can signal a failure and trigger backtracking to delete part of the structure and re-establish the structure which existed before the attempt was made. The techniques are well established. Various backtrack-points can be identified as the procedure progresses. At any time an "undo" command can wipe out recent actions and re-establish the condition which pertained at the most recent of these backtrack-points. Two "undo" commands will take the structure back to the backtrack-point before the most recent, and so on.

In the system I have proposed here, various word-concepts carry small procedures within their structure. These can be activated as the interpretation procedure proceeds. As each concept is encountered, any programs which are found embedded within its structure are placed on an "action-list". This, in computer terms, is a stack structure. We can envisage that as a vertical heap of program commands. Each new addition is added at the top and when the action-list is prodded into action, activation starts with the top-most and progresses downwards. If a program is able to complete its task in a satisfactory way, the corresponding program starting command is removed from the action-list. If it is not completed the program start command is replaced on the action-list. A backtrack-point is identified and recorded as such, whenever the action-list is found to be empty. These points correspond to the start and end of word-groups or phrases as they would be termed in a system using syntax analysis. In particular, a backtrack-point is identified at the end of each sentence.

But we still need a metric which will indicate that the assumptions made have failed to help construct a satisfactory representation of meaning. When we put a jigsaw picture together, we sometimes make mistakes. We do not always recognise that a mistake has been made until we find that there is an impossible shape - some vacant shape for which none of the available unfitted pieces will fit. Then we look closer. Is there a join which shows tiny gaps in the way two pieces come together? Unfortunately, however, concepts, as I have described them, are extremely flexible. They can be modified to make all kinds of constructions possible. It is as though the jigsaw pieces were made of stiff rubber. A fit can be forced if required. So how, in these circumstances can the system recognise when it has gone wrong?

I do not have a confident answer to that problem. Much the same problem is faced when chess-playing games are designed. The number of alternative moves that could be played expands very rapidly beyond what is possible within a machine of finite size. A chess-playing program needs heuristics to judge the quality of a board position - some rules which award points. The program will make whichever move obtains the highest score.

I suspect the interpretation construction procedure will need a similar scoring metric for the quality of an interpretation structure.

Extending the repertoire of detection units

12.49

Earlier (in chapter 3), I described the structure of phase-layer-1 which is dominated by detection and action units. These, I argued, were acquired by the very slow process of evolution to establish the basic repertoire of stimulus-responses of which the system as a whole is capable. However, in section 03.18, I also made a distinction between the recognition of features within the environment (which have existed in that environment for a very long time), and features which are comparatively recent and are often human artefacts. Evolution may operate too slowly for the automatic detection of these to be included in that evolved repertoire. It cannot be that we have an innate mechanism for the recognition and automatic response to written words, for example. So I need to propose an additional set of detection units and action units (or response units) which can deal with these.

12.50

The point has also been made that the short-term memory, or trace, cannot include tags within its structure. That is because the TRACE structure is ephemeral and is not subject to compression. These tags, it will be recalled, were inserted into the longer-term memory during the compression procedure, to enable re-construction of memory, as and when that is required.

But somehow the reconstruction process must also be applied to the trace. That, according to my proposal, is the basis of conscious understanding of on-going events. The occurrence of words, written and spoken, can be recognised within the longer-term selective memory, and these occurrences will be replaced by tags during the compression process. So the tags exist. They have been created. These tags represent a way of recognising the occurrence of the relevant compression chunks and therefore the occurrence of replaceable material corresponding to concepts. What has to happen within the trace is the recognition of what we might call "potential tags", and then their replacement, or augmentation, by concepts.

12.51

The tags have become useful items (i.e. concepts) in their own right. They are frequently occurring patterns of experience which correspond to stored chunks of material. But there are no evolved detection units which can recognise the presence of these chunks automatically. What there can be, however, is temporarily constructed recognition units formed from the tags and these, in effect, are an addition to the set of detection units within the phase-layer-1 structure. They operate as learned detection units. Recognition of the presence of particular chunks requires the use of basic feature recognition facilities which have been established by evolution, but also requires that these are combined in new ways to recognise these modern artefacts. That is the role which these tags put into effect.

12.52

Where could these temporary additions to phase-layer-1 be located? We have already seen that the brain can construct representational structures and procedures within working memory. I that, I suggest, is what happens. Tags are utilised as the prototypes or progenitors of temporary detection units, which can be held in working memory and used to detect the presence of chunks of material corresponding to _learned_ features of the environment. When I discussed the structure of the phase-layer-1, I proposed that each detection unit had the power of a small computer. It has a stored memory of the patterns of signals it is supposed to be able to recognise. It has a set of input signals. And it has a program of its own which compares the input with the stored pattern and declares a match when that occurs. So now all that must be added to the system, is the stored memory of the patterns which should be recognised and a matcher program which compares that with the input (in the trace memory).

12.53

The important characteristic of this arrangement is its ephemeral nature of the additional detection units. The comparison between observed patterns and stored patterns takes place in working memory - and then it is gone.

Note this, we cannot read text unconsciously. If you try to read text and think about something else at the same time, your eyes just brush over the words and no connection is made with the meaning of those words.

In contrast, we can recognise certain other features of the environment and do so unconsciously - faces, for example, and movements; certain noises and smells - particularly those which give warning of danger. The recognition of these is the responsibility of evolved feature detection units and they run continuously and independently of our momentary focus of attention.

12.54

So too with the action units. Those in phase-layer-1 are the products of evolution. But we can learn to trigger them and to choreograph their sequence of actions in response to the recognition of particular modern (learned) artefacts. A cup is

251

recognised and there is a detectable activation of the muscular movements required to pick it up. So to with the grasping action required to pick up a cricket ball [Iacoboni 2008]. These reactions cannot have been programmed into our genetic inheritance by evolution.

12.55

NOTE: This chapter has become somewhat bogged down in minutia concerning representation. My main purpose has been to demonstrate that the primitives, which I propose, and the suggested way of combining concepts, can deal with a very wide variety of meanings.

Understanding Language - from the inside, upwards.

12.56

The main difference between the approach to the understanding of language (which I advocate here), and the traditional approach (which is based on syntactical analysis), is not an issue concerning syntax per se. I do not dispute the usefulness of grammatical classifications. What I do question is how these classifications could have been acquired within the general scheme of evolutionary development.

My contention is that grammatical classifications are not acquired by innate inheritance. They cannot be. They are learned by exposure to speech - and eventually, also, to the written form. And having been learned, they are utilised in a piecemeal fashion, in snippets, with each snippet being attached or associated with individual words.

The development of the established techniques of syntactical analysis has taken many years and it has had to overcome many difficult issues. That development process, moreover, has been concerned with issues of efficient implementation.

I am not concerned with the issue of efficient implementation. I want only to demonstrate that the problem of language interpretation can be solved in the "bottom-up" way I suggest which is compatible with slow and gradual evolution. It is simply not plausible that the human understanding of language can utilise a "top-down" method, within which the top-level structure (of syntax structure) is already known. There is no plausible way that that top-level structure could be acquired en bloc.

12.57

I will not attempt a comprehensive analysis of the issue - or anything like it. My purpose, here, is merely to illustrate, with a few examples, how an automatic system might start to construct an interpretation of various statements without having a prior assignment of grammatical classifications to individual words (or lexemes). Instead I will propose a stored association between each word-concept and a syntactical "snippet" which will indicate the pattern of words within which the given word usually occurs. The technique could be described as taking the standard type of syntactical structure or the complete complex parse-tree of a language, cutting it up into small parts, and then distributing those parts to individual words. In some cases where there is some ambiguity about the grammatical role of a word, a given word may be associated with several alternative snippets. It is the task of the interpretation process to fit these snippets together (using the associated meaning structure) to construct an appropriate interpretation structure.

The partial identification of sub-features.

12.58

I place great emphasis on the evolution of procedures from pre-existing procedures, which may, and usually will have evolved, for quite different purposes. Consider, for example, the idea, which is widely accepted, that the visual recognition of shapes (in circumstances where a simple silhouette on a plain background is not available), typically makes use of the recognition of partial shapes or sub-features. Inevitably these partial shapes will be those which have some clear identifiable properties.

The most difficult issue in language interpretation is that those identifiable features are not grouped, as it were, geographically within a two-dimensional visual field. Language is an essentially linear form of communication and so the only convenient method of grouping makes use of word orderings and adjacencies. Sometimes, moreover, those word groupings are interrupted by parenthetic inclusions. The main difficulty, therefore, (and this is why syntactical analysis was originally introduced) is to identify those word groupings in a way that makes sense - subsequently, in the context of meaningful interpretation.

Parts of a sentence

12.59

Quirk and his co-authors, identified 5 separate parts of a sentence - subject, verb, complement, object and adverbial. They further subdivided both complement and object into direct and indirect versions [Quirk et al 1972]. These they claim are the "elements" of a sentence. In the context of my analogy with the theatrical performance of a short play, the verb represents the plot - the action or static condition described, and the other elements correspond to the actors and the stage props. In English, the subject usually comes before the verb and the other elements come after. Special sentence structures - such as passive voice - can reposition these elements. The adverbial element in particular can crop up in various positions. Each can be qualified or modified by prepositional phrases. Quirk et al identified no less than 27 different types.

The most pressing issue for this discussion is the identification of the noun-phrases and their interpretation. These, as it were, set the scene. They tell us what the play is about.

Identifying noun-phrases

12.60

Since the identification of groupings is an important aspect of language interpretation, and since the avoidance of misunderstandings has survival advantage, it is to be expected that the mechanism of linguistic communication would develop techniques to make the identification of groupings easier. Meta-concepts, concepts which refer to other concepts, are one of those techniques. The use of determiners, in natural English is an example.

One of the most important of these groupings is what in the terminology of syntax is called a "noun-phrase". Determiners - like "a" and "the" and quantifiers like "some" are unambiguous indicators of a noun-phrase. A person who is trying to interpret speech can spot an indicator of that kind and assign a group-identity to the words that follow it.

Examples

EG1: John cries
EG2: Young John cries

A sentence structure, which is very common, begins with a noun-phrase which is then followed by a verb phrase (which may contain several sub-phrases). EG1 above has what is probably the simplest structure possible. The word "John" is a proper-noun and it unambiguously forms a noun-phrase on its own without embellishment. EG2 shows that there can, unusually, be an adjective attached ("Young").

Noun-phrases are more usually introduced by a determiner ("the" or "a"). EG3 below is an example. EG4 adds an adjective.

EG3: The baby cries
EG4: The young baby cries

Several adjectives may occur between the determiner and the noun.

EG5: The big brown hairy dog ran

Complications arise when a word, which is normally regarded as a noun, is used as an adjective.

EG6: The baby elephant trumpets

The difficulty illustrated in EG6 is the problem of identifying "elephant" as the noun in the phrase, while treating the word "baby" as though it was an adjective.

In English, and in the majority of cases, the noun in a noun-phrase is the last word in the phrase.

We can therefore identify the noun if we can identify the start and the end of the phrase. The word "the" introduces the noun-phrase without ambiguity. But the end of the phrase is harder to identify. Probably the best way to do that is to identify the start of another phrase (or the end of the sentence). That can therefore be the first simple strategy we could adopt. A determiner starts the noun-phrase and a new phrase ends the previous one and starts a new one.

EG7: (The baby elephant) (trumpets)

And the word "elephant" is identified as the head or the dominant noun in the noun-phrase. That strategy implies that the main technique for identifying the structure of a sentence and its sub-division into phrases of various kinds, resolves into the identification of the start of various phrase types. Fortunately there are a number of phrase-starters of that kind. The determiner "a", several quantifiers like "some" or "any", proper nouns (as used in EG1, plurals are unambiguously nouns -

EG8: Loudly chirping birds ...

Various prepositions like - "in", "by", "with", "which" and "who. Verbs and auxiliary verbs can also be used this way.

This way of identifying phrase structure will produce a sentence structure which is different from the traditional form of sentence structure. Consider this sentence -

EG9: The young elephant who was born that day had difficulty standing upright.

When we apply the suggested strategy we get this -

(The young <u>elephant</u>)
(who was born that day had difficulty standing upright)

If we then re-apply the same bracketing procedure to the second grouping, we get this -

(The young elephant)
(who) (was born that day had difficulty standing upright)

And again several times -

(The young elephant)
(who) (<u>was born</u>) (that <u>day</u>) (<u>had</u> difficulty <u>standing</u> upright)

The next step in the procedure is to construct an interpretation of the various phrases. Traditional syntax analysis would group the first four of these bracketed phrases into a single noun-phrase.

(The young elephant)(who)(<u>was born</u>)(that <u>day</u>)

That discrepancy can be rectified, however, if the words "who" and "that" are used to form connecting links between adjacent phrases. The elephant can be established as the agent of the verb "was born", and "that day" can the established as the time indicator of "was born". It remains only for the verb "<u>standing</u>" to identify its own agent (the elephant). It does that using the small programs which are embedded in the structure which represents its meaning. The meaning representation of all words can have these embedded programs, but the programs cannot find their respective targets until these have been identified and given an appropriate status within the sentence structure by the process of organising words into groups.

Exceptions

It has to be admitted that the strategy suggested for finding word-groupings will not work in a satisfactory way in all circumstances. For example, if the sentence used in EG9 had been

EG10: The young elephant who was born the day before had difficulty standing upright.

The suggested procedure would have identified the word "before" as the start of a new group and formed the singleton group (before). The interpretation of "before" has two referents - a designated time and a designated period of time before which an event took place. We could write that as a pattern -

"X before Y"

EG11: Two years before the outbreak of war.

EG11 illustrates that. In an exceptional case above (EG10) the second time (Y) is missing. The problem caused by the absence of that second time reference point could be resolved by providing the interpretation structure "before" with a fall-back position (i.e. a second demon) which could substitute an assumed PRESENT time or contextually relevant time reference point for the absent Y.

Finding these exception conditions, and the means to deal with them, must for the present remain work in progress.

Interpreting a noun-phrase

12.62

A noun-phrase is an important component of a sentence. It describes and provides an identity for an entity which plays a role within the scene or condition being represented. If the verb of a sentence defines the plot of a one-act play, then noun-phrases represent the players, the actors which do things, and the items of stage scenery which are involved in that action. Consider the noun-phrase -

EG12: The big brown hairy dog

In this example there are three adjectives. Each adjective will have an interpretation structure and each of these structures will have an embedded program. We could call them "demons". The use of demons is a well-established technique in computer science.

Every person who has used a spread-sheet, has made use of demons. When a mathematical expression is inserted into the cell of a spread-sheet, it will typically refer to other cells within the sheet. On being activated it will calculate a new updated value, based on the values found in these other cells. It is a convenient way to maintain relevant values in cells as various values are altered or as time advances.

The demons which are used in this context, however, do something a little more complex than simply calculating a numeric value. They are able to search the interpretation structure, compare values, identify a match between separate sections of the structure and establish a connection or equivalence between matching structures.

Fig 12.62 interpretation of a noun-phrase

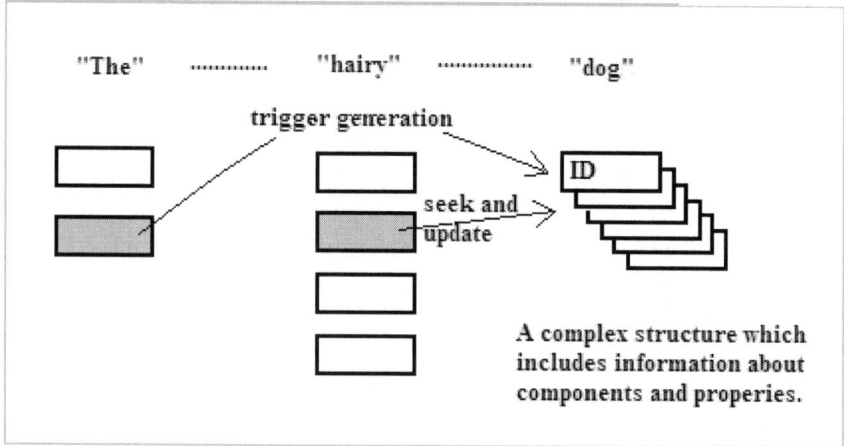

The diagram illustrates the relation between the determiner "The", the adjective "hairy" and their target "dog" and how the demons operate. The dotted lines represent the possible presence of other adjectives.

The embedded demons (shaded blocks) seek their targets. The trick is to avoid wrongly identifying (or targeting) any intervening words in the phrase and to enable each demon to find its true target - the meaning structure associated with "dog". The structure associated with an adjective will not have acquired a role within the interpretation structure. A suitable unique identifier is assigned to the structure associated with "dogs" however, when the dynamic list is used to generate one instance of dog. That will happen when the determiner "The" finds its target and triggers the generator function into operation.

So the determiner brings the instance of dog into existence and the adjective hairy modifies its properties to make it more hairy than a typical dog. Any additional adjectives in the noun-phrase will do likewise for other properties. In this way, the interpretation structures of the various words in a noun-phrase, operate together to produce the representation of one important component of the scene or event represented by the sentence as a whole. These components can then be targeted, found and incorporated into a structure representing the meaning of the sentence.

Verb-phrase analysis

12.63

In normal English there can be only one verb-phrase in a sentence. It represents the story or plot being represented. It may represent a static condition, or an action or change of some kind. Once the mechanism has identified the actors and slotted them into the appropriate roles within that plot, the system will have explained to itself what these actors do, or did, what they did it to, and what they did it with. When the adverbial elements in the sentence have been identified and interpreted the mechanism will have constructed an understanding of (among other things) where they did it, and how, and for what reasons. Here I use the word "understanding" in the sense of being in possession of the implications the ability to make predictions about what follows from these actions described.

For the purposes of identifying the verb, it can, in most cases, be assumed that the verb (or a complicated verb group) will be the leading component of the verb-phrase.

A verb, or the representation of its meaning is, like most nouns, a plural entity. That is because it is formed initially from a collection of individual encounters with that particular action or condition. So once again we start with a dynamic list which offers a generator function. Each activation of the generator creates one instance of that action or condition.

In the case of an isolated verb, the generator function does not need to be triggered by some external activator. When the verb occurs as part of a complex verb group with supporting auxiliary verbs (like "is", "was" and "had") these can act as triggers. In every case, however, the isolation of a verb will result in the generation of a particular instance of the action or condition represented and it will then have a unique ID number within the narrative.

Within the interpretation structure of a verb there will also be several demons. Each demon will have a particular task to perform. One will be required to seek and find the agent of the action. If there is no animate agent, the appropriate target may be the word "it". "It" can, on some occasions, be interpreted as a reference to the ambience or general context of the action or state of affairs.

EG13: It was raining.

In his attempt to reconcile the Chomskian idea of innate deep grammar, with evolution, Steven Pinker used that same example as evidence. He reports that young children deal adequately with EG13. He further states that -

"... the 'it' of the sentence, of course, does not refer to anything; it is a dummy element that is there only to satisfy the rules of syntax, which demand a subject .... how do children cope with this meaningless placeholder?"

[Pinker 1994, p42]

That argument is a good example of circular logic, because the assumption that "it" is a placeholder depends upon the prior assumption that the Chomskian innate deep grammar idea is correct. It can therefore not be used as an element of the argument which supports the truth of the Chomskian position. That would require the Chomskian idea to support itself by pulling on its own bootstraps.

Gerunds

12.64

A gerund is a word which would normally have been classified as a noun, but which is being used as an adjective to modify the properties of another noun. Quirk et al called them "adverbial nouns". I draw attention to their existence because they are an example of a problem which besets the issue of language analysis. When is a noun not a noun?

My answer is "when it is not the last noun-word in a noun-phrase. Consider -

EG14: The baby elephant
EG15: The elephant baby

In each of these examples, the last word in the phrase is acting as a noun and the noun-word "baby" immediately in front of it, is acting as an adverbial-noun. In EG14 the word "baby" is providing the meaning of "elephant" with the extra information that it is newly born. In EG15 the adverbial-noun "elephant" is providing the meaning of the word "baby" with the extra information that it is a creature of the species "elephant". The meaning structure which is the result, is the same - a newly born creature of species elephant.

It does not seem to matter which order the words appear in the sentence so far as meaning is concerned, but for the purposes of processing and constructing the meaning structure, it does matter.

And so we must have a decision about structure. That decision can be determined by identifying the start and end of the noun-phrase. The last word in the phrase is then taken as the noun-word and the mechanism can proceed.

The way in which this is dealt with is similar to the way I suggested earlier that the mechanism can deal with figurative speech. In EG14, the word "baby" provides information but, because it is not being used as a noun, it does not contribute any narrative ID number. That is provided by the word "elephant". That observation adds strength to my contention that the way we deal with figurative speech is not an exception mechanism but an integral part of the normal language mechanism.

Delayed activation of demons

12.65

It is desirable that the generation and the activation of the demons within a verb's interpretation, should be delayed until after all the noun-phrases within a sentence have been identified and interpreted. Since the verb will often be a single word or a single compound verb group, the generation of a particular instance could be self-triggered by the isolation of that verb group. Only then can the demons embedded in that interpretation structure find the instances of actors and props and complete the assignment of roles.

The advantages of my own approach

12.66

The development of the approach I am advocating here, at the moment stands a long way behind the development of traditional grammatical analysis. As a result, undoubtedly, it will be unable, to cope with numerous exception conditions. But that may be only a temporary circumstance. I claim that my own approach has a considerable advantage over the traditional approach. It is flexible; it is adaptable; it can learn from its mistakes.

The basic idea of the Chomskian approach is that deep grammar is innate. The basic structure of that grammar is therefore fixed and cannot change quickly as the usage of a particular natural changes. The only aspect which can be subject to learning and adaptation to changes, are the transformations which map from the deep grammar structure on to the current (and ever changing) surface structure.

In contrast, if each natural language has words which are each associated with existing learned concepts and if, to discover the meaning of a new sentence structure, we must learn the new tricks of how to put these meaning structures together, in a coherent way, then the mechanism can grow and grow continuously as new usages are introduced. Those new tricks can, moreover, learn these new tricks in a convenient way. The new tricks can be explained in words, provided the explanation is given using sentence structures which are already known and for which techniques already exist. An expectation of dynamic adaptation is an integral part of the approach.

CHAPTER 13

Comments on the whole system

In this chapter I will summarise my explanation of consciousness, the hypothetical model of the way it operates and my speculative account of how the mechanism evolved from much simpler beginnings.

SRA

13.01

To give itself a good chance of survival the mechanism of brain must be able to recognise many features of its current environment. It must also be able to link the recognition of these features to appropriate response actions. Initially, the system has no need to be able to identify or classify the features which it is able to recognise and to which it responds. It does not need to know what the things are, that it can recognise. It just recognises and responds.

A mechanism which behaves in that way is what we can term a "stimulus-response automaton". It corresponds to what most people think of when they hear the term "robot".

Although a mechanism of that kind could be developed so that it could recognise and respond to many very complicated aspects of its environment, it is still limited. Without additional and radically different mechanisms it could never behave in a way that is comparable with a human being. It has an ability to operate only in the present.

To improve on that living-in-the-present performance, it must acquire a memory. It must also do that while limiting the brain-space required to store that additional remembered material.

Events tend to repeat themselves and so the past can be used as a guide to what can be expected in the future. However, events seldom repeat themselves exactly and so what is required is the ability to recognise component parts of the past and to be able to put those components parts together in new ways in order to construct a representation of current events when current events

266

have some resemblance to past events. That means that the brain mechanism must acquire the ability to build a collection of chunks of past experience which tend to re-occur in many circumstances.

Unfortunately, a single or small number of chunks of that kind provide the system with little immediate benefit. A survival advantage can be obtained only when a significant number of these chunks have been identified. To meet the requirements of evolution, therefore, the acquisition of chunks must proceed on the basis of some other immediate advantage. That requirement can be met if the chunks are formed as part of a mechanism of data compression. We could say that the system obtains a survival advantage, not by forming a collection of chunks but by forming a collection of holes (which the chunks leave behind).

Fortuitously however, compression, and repeated application of the compression algorithm will produce a form of classification of the entities recognised, and the abstraction of events, including the formation of the concept of causal connection.

These concepts, and the tags which are used in the compression process, in effect, provide the evolving system with the means to detect additional aspects of the environment which are features of the modern era and which have therefore not been around long enough for evolution to develop appropriate and fixed detection units.

The process by which the system can reconstruct a memory is very similar to the interpretation process that is needed to construct a representation of current events. Each interpretation will include predictions of future events - a short distance into the future.

The projection of predictions any further into the future is made difficult by the fact that the mechanism's own behaviour can interfere with that predicted future. To be able to take the consequences of its own behaviour into account, the brain mechanism must perform a very special procedure. The performance of that special procedure is what we call "being conscious".

13.02

This "being conscious" performance requires that the mechanism of the brain should construct a model of itself, feed that self-model with the circumstances of various likely futures, and then observe the responses produced by that self-model. To avoid infinite recursion, however, the operation of that self-model, or one part of the self-model, cannot be given a precise mechanistic representation. Instead it must regard that inner-self as being in part an autonomous mechanism which has various emotional drives - what we call hunger, desires, antipathies, thirst, urges and so on. In that way, by abandoning the possibility of accurate calculation based on mechanism, it avoids infinite recursion and renders feasible its own predictions about the future.

That the mechanism could evolve in that way is made more plausible by my suggestion that that is exactly what the brain does to predict the behaviour of other animate organisms. It forms the concept of MIND by applying the data compression procedure to various indicators of intention - body-language and, in particular, eye-movements. The concept of MIND is therefore not a representation of anything directly perceived in the supposed external world. It is a mental construct which justifies its inclusion in the internal representation of that external world by making a useful contribution to the making of accurate predictions about that external world. I have offered an analogy for that – mathematical concepts which have no counterpart in reality, but which, when used in calculations, provide the means for accurate predictions. The square root of minus one is an interesting example.

13.03

To form the self-model (or SELFMIND, as I have termed it here), the brain of a conscious person, who cannot easily observe his or her own eye-movements, must rely instead on the internal precursors of those eye-movements - muscle controls required to point the eyes, and to the results produced by those eye-movements. In effect, the construction of that representation provides a narrative. That narrative tells the brain -

"This me looking at this object. This is me recalling how that object may behave. This is me wondering what that object will do next in these circumstances."

As a consequence of this internal procedure, or exchange of information between the brain mechanism and its self model, the brain finds itself operating as

(1) a thing which is being represented,

(2) a thing which is doing those representations,

(3) a thing which represents itself as doing that self-representation, and

(4) a thing which makes use of the information gained in that way, to modify its own behaviour.

The operation of that convoluted multi-role performance is what we describe as "*a subjective experience*".

13.04

The final part of the mechanism - phase-layer-5 - introduces a new and (what I claim) is an improved way of exchanging information between individuals.

Fig 13.04 two kinds of concept

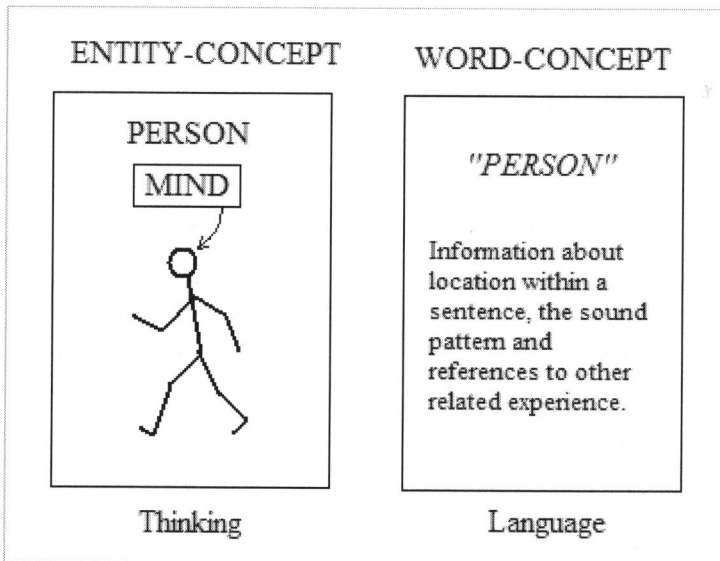

ENTITY-CONCEPT	WORD-CONCEPT
PERSON	"PERSON"
MIND	Information about location within a sentence, the sound pattern and references to other related experience.
Thinking	Language

Words, or patterns of sound, with the action units which must be stimulated to articulate those sounds, are developed, learned by practice and associated with particular concepts. These are the concepts which constitute the structural components of internal knowledge - representations of external reality which enable predictions to be made about future events. They are not what is sometimes called "raw experience". They are records of the pattern of responses derived from the stimulus-response automaton (or phase-layer-1) and the associated actions triggered by these events.

On hearing a sequence of these word sounds, the brain mechanism copies the associated concepts from memory, fits them together in the way previously used to fit together the narrative of perceived events, and provides for itself a representation of the speaker's thoughts - which may well be a representation of external reality as perceived by the speaker.

To make the fitting together easier and less prone to ambiguity, additional words and concepts are developed which we can call "meta-concepts" (concepts which refer to concepts). These, like prepositions, pronouns and relative pronouns (like "which" and "who") provide information about how the other concepts can be linked together. As the language mechanism does this, it assigns narrative roles to various components of the interpretation structure. These roles act as "attachment points" for additional components to be linked into the growing structure. The structures are flexible, however, and it can, when appropriate, link new bits of structure to any point in the existing interpretation.

There are two kinds of concept involved with the use of language. The first kind is the type of concepts with which we normally do our thinking. The second, which I call a "word-concepts", are required for language. Word-concepts are formed in exactly the same way as others, but they are concerned with the perception of spoken words (and later with the visual appearance of the written word). These word-concepts carry the information about where within a sentence the word has occurred and its likely relationship to words (and their associated concepts) elsewhere in a sentence.

Over the several years it took me to develop my theory, there was one recurring thought which troubled me. It was all very well to base the system on the idea of phase-layer-1 with its detection units which had evolved over time, and which would be passed on from generation to generation in the gene pool. However, modern life is full of artefacts, like written alphabetic characters, It is not plausible that the brain could evolve and pass on in the same way an ability to detect these. We know from common personal experience that the ability to recognise these is a skill that has to be learned, and which some people never learn. So where in my system is the learned equivalent of a detection unit.

It was while I was drafting an early version of this book that the solution occurred to me. That is what concepts are. They are the functional equivalent of detection units. They are learned. They are acquired by the application of a data compression procedure to stored memories – i.e. to stored experience – and expressed in terms of the activation of detection units and action units. If I can be allowed, briefly, to use the hardware/software terminology, it is as though the detection units in phase-layer-1 were a hardware solution to feature detection, and concepts were a software functionally equivalent mechanism for those artefacts which must be acquired by learning.

So the whole process of forming the learned ability to recognise these modern artefacts is pig-a-backed on the existing fixed inherited abilities to recognise features – like edges, corners, movements, surfaces, colours and locations. As the operation of phase-layer-1 proceeds, and the memory of these experiences are stored in phase-layer-2, phase-layer-3 introduces the ability to recognise the complex patterns of data within the TRACE which correspond to, or characterise, particular frequently encountered artefacts.

So the system, as a whole, does indeed have two kinds of detection unit – fixed inherited ones (in phase-layer-1, and others acquired by a learning process (in phase-layer-2/3). As the TRACE is augmented by the insertion of particular concepts into its sequence of states particular patterns are identified and "ticked-off" by being replaced by the enhanced pattern that is a concept. Recognition of these concepts can stimulate particular reactions, just as the detection of more primitive patterns can trigger actions in phase-layer-1. But these new reactions are merely re-choreographed versions of the reactions developed in phase-layer-1 over the immense periods of time during which they evolved and were then laid down in the scripts stored in phase-layer-2's selective memory.

The function of consciousness can therefore be expressed this way. It is a procedure which enables the brain to analyse its own standard reactions to events, to anticipate them, and to override them on certain occasions when it recognises that the outcome may not be in its own best long-term interests. That is, it may find it appropriate to sacrifice short-term gratification for the sake of long-term and long-lasting satisfaction.

I like that. That is the hallmark of intelligent and civilised behaviour.

Drew McDermott

13.06

Drew McDermott is the only person I know of who has hit on an idea similar to the one I describe here. His book "Mind and Mechanism" was published in 2001. It is a valuable source of good ideas and a refreshing contribution to the debate about mind and consciousness. It deserves to be known better by those who are not familiar with computational science. Unlike most books on the topic he has actually tried to produce a solution to the problem of consciousness, and the idea which he advances comes very close indeed to the idea I describe in this book. It is not identical, but the foundation of his approach is the same as mine - the need for the brain to construct a model of itself and the threat of infinite recursion which that implies.

The following quotation comes from chapter 3, which is called "*A Computational Theory of Consciousness*". Readers will be able to recognise that his theory is very close to my own.

"*Suppose we have a robot that models the world temporally and uses its model to predict what will happen. I am not talking about 'mental models' as the term is used in psychology (Johnston-Laird 1983), but about numerical or causal models as used in simulation. Such models are a familiar application of computers. The main difference between what computers normally do and what my hypothesised robot does is that the robot is modelling the situation it is now actually in. This model contains various symbols, including one I will call R, which it uses to denote itself. .... When I say the symbol denotes the robot itself, I don't mean to imply that the word 'itself' implies something about 'self'. All I mean is that, for example, when it detects an object in its environment, it notes that R knows the object is present; and when it has a tentative course of action on hand, that is, a series of orders to be transmitted to its effective motors, it will base its modelling activity on the assumption that R will be carrying out those actions.*

Now suppose that the actual situation is that the robot is standing next to a bomb with a lit fuse. And suppose the robot knows all this, so that in its model R is standing next to B, a bomb with a lit fuse. The model is accurate enough that it will predict that B will explode. Supposing that the robot has no actions on its agenda that would make it move, the model will predict that R will be destroyed.

Well, actually it can't make this prediction with certainty. because R will be destroyed only if it doesn't roll away quickly. The conclusion that it would not roll away was based on the robot's own current projection of what it is going to do. But such a projection is subject to change. For instance, the robot might be waiting for orders from its owner; a new order would make it roll away. More interestingly, the robot might have a standing order to avoid damage. Whenever its model predicts that it is going to be damaged, it should discard its current action list and replace it with actions that will protect it, assuming it can find some. Finding actions to achieve goals is a deep and fascinating topic, but it needn't concern us here. The robot concludes that it should exit the room, and does so.

What I want to call attention to is how this sequence of events is represented in the robot's model, and how it will have to differ from reality. The reality is that the robot's actions are entirely caused by events. The sequence I laid out is a straight forward causal chain, from perception, to tentative prediction, to action revision. But this causal chain cannot be represented accurately in the model, because a key step of the chain, the making of tentative predictions, involves the model itself. The model could not capture this causal chain because it would then have to include a complete model of itself, which is incoherent. In other words, some of the causal antecedents of R's behaviour are situated in the very causal-analysis box that is trying to analyse them. The robot might believe that R is a robot hand hence a good way to predict R's behaviour is to simulate it on a faster CPU, but this strategy will be in vain, because this particular robot is itself. No matter how fast it simulates R, at some point it will reach a point where R looks for a faster CPU, and it won't be able to simulate that fast enough. Or it might try inspecting R's listing, but eventually it will come to a part of that listing that says 'inspect R's listing.' The strongest conclusion it can reach is that 'if R doesn't roll away, it will be destroyed; if it does roll away, it won't be.' And then of course this conclusion causes the robot to roll away.

Hence the robot must model itself in a different way from other objects. Their behaviour may be modeled as caused, but its own (i.e. R's) must be modeled as 'open' or 'still being solved for.' The symbol R must be marked as exempt from causal laws when predictions are being made about actions it will take. The word 'must' here is just the 'must' of rational design. It would be pointless to use a modelling system for control of behaviour that didn't make this distinction, and it would be unlikely for evolution to produce one. Any system that models its own behaviour, uses the output of the model to select among actions, and its belief about its own decisions, will believe that its own decisions are undetermined. What I would like to claim is that this is what free will comes down to:

A system has free will if and only if it makes decisions based on causal models in which the symbols denoting itself are marked as exempt from causality."

13.07

I disagree with McDermott on the point about evolution. I think that making that essential distinction (between events that are caused by a mechanism and those that appear not to be) is exactly what evolution would produce. Any system which did not evolve in that way would be condemned to an inability to take decisions vital to its own survival and therefore would be eliminated from the gene pool. Evolution can produce almost any facility - including those of bewildering complexity - provided there is some existing facility from which it can evolve in small individually advantageous steps from some other configuration which is nearly but not quite as complicated. In this case the brain has a considerable legacy of unconscious procedures. I would not say that they are exempt from causation. I would put it another way - for actions which do not have a mechanistic cause, the system supplies a notional causal precursor. That notional precursor is a MIND (or a SELFMIND), which has moods and these moods predispose it to the taking certain actions.

A further point of difference between the two theories (McDermott's and my own) is that I think there is another and more potent reason why the system cannot anticipate its own behaviour in particular circumstances - there is no computational mechanism that is open to inspection by the system.

The real explanation lies in the evolutionary history of the system. The system's ancestors had particular goals and anti-goals. Other individuals had other goals and anti-goals. Those others died out and produced no progeny because the particular goals and anti-goals they had, did not provide a sufficient survival advantage. The ones that did, survived.

How could the system explain that to itself. How could it calculate what action it is likely to take to a given situation if that response is actually a long-standing instinct.

Consciously, a system can learn from past experience and develop sub-goals that enable it to achieve its basic goals. But the basic goals are a given. It cannot do anything about them. Why do I have an urge to eat if I see something which I anticipate will taste nice. I do not know. In chapter 1, I quoted Voltaire.

"When I can do what I want," he wrote, *"there is my free will. But I do not know why I want it."*

That, it seems to me, is a very accurate and compact way to express the human condition.

All I know is that I have a compulsion to behave in particular ways - just as a heat-seeking guided missile has a compulsion to follow after the hot exhaust of an aeroplane's engine. If we could give that missile a way to construct a concept of itself so that it could choose which of several alternative goals it should try to achieve at a given moment, it would be just as puzzled by its own motivation as I am about my need to eat chocolate biscuits. How could we describe that? We could say that the missile "**wants**" to hit the hot engine. Wants? Is that an accurate way to describe it? It is certainly an accurate description of its observable behaviour. When we hear that description we know exactly what to expect. But it not accurate if we regard that statement as a description of what is happening inside it. In the case of the missile if we understand enough about electronics and systems control we could probably give an accurate description of the mechanism. But when it come to living creatures we cannot do that. And the missile itself, if it had the intellectual capability to deal with these things, would be equally baffled about how to describe its own inner mechanism. So all it could do would be to describe itself an "wanting" to do these things. That is, all it would be able to do would be to take the same outside view of itself that we do and do that from inside itself..

If a heat-seeking guided missile was equipped with a more complex brain mechanism, such that it could observe the behaviour of other similar missiles, and if it then recognised that when those other missiles achieved what appears to be their goal to reach and to strike that target hot spot, that they then destroyed themselves utterly, it could be that this missile of superior intelligence might decide to overrule its basic instinct and to avoid seeking that target hot spot. But if it was to do that successfully, I reckon it would need to concentrate very hard, and consciously, on the avoidance of that heat-seeking behaviour. It would be like myself trying to avoid my instinctive eye-blink reflex action or my knee-jerk reaction to a doctor's hammer-strike. A missile that could do all that would need, perforce, to be conscious.

The reader will recognise the similarity between McDermott's proposal and my own. We arrived at that point of convergence independently from different directions - he from the world of computational science and myself with a background in biophysics and an acceptance of the overriding importance of evolution in all things biological. The convergence occurs at the point where these truths are recognised -

To predict the future you must be able to predict yourself.

To predict yourself you must model your own behaviour.

To model your own behaviour you must take steps to avoid infinite recursion.

To avoid infinite recursion, and because of a lack of any accessible explanation of motivation, you must explicate your own actions in terms of emotional urges and not in terms of biological mechanisms.

To do all that your intuition must misrepresent yourself as one part of an inexplicable duality.

In a sense therefore, the brain is a duality - a physical mechanism of consciousness and a separate motivating factor (that is also a physical mechanism of instinctive reactions) which defies conventional explanation.

Pentti Haikonen

13.08

Pentti Haikonen is the principle scientist of Cognitive Technology with the Nokia Research. In his book "The Cognitive Approach to Conscious Machines" [Haikonen 2003] he advances an interesting theory. Being an expert in computer technology, much of his explanation of his theory is described in terms of practical hardware systems. The focus of his attention is on how a conscious machine could be constructed. He is not primarily concerned, as I am, about how a conscious biological mechanism could evolve by natural selection. However, despite differences in terminology and of approach, there is a surprising degree of agreement between his thesis and my own. There are also some differences which are also interesting.

13.09

A good deal of the text is concerned with the mechanics of perception and representation.

"We need a representation method that is flexible, one that allows easy description of the real world, its objects, entities and their relationships including action. This representation method should also allow easy modification and combination of these descriptions so that intelligence and imagination would be possible. This method should also allow imperfect representations, it should tolerate errors and distortion."

[Haikonen 2003 p169]

Distributed Signals

13.10

Haikonen uses the term *"distributed signals"* for the way in which various features of an object could be identified at *"arbitrary locations"* within the mechanism, where the dedicated recognition of particular features can be carried out. These arbitrary locations seem to coincide with what I have called the detection units. So the terminology of "*distributed signals*" seems to correspond to the detection units within the stimulus-response feature recognition system I describe, and also equivalent to Jackendoff's "*character tags*". The diagram below is re-drawn from a diagram in Haikonen's book.

Fig 13.10 "Distributed signals"

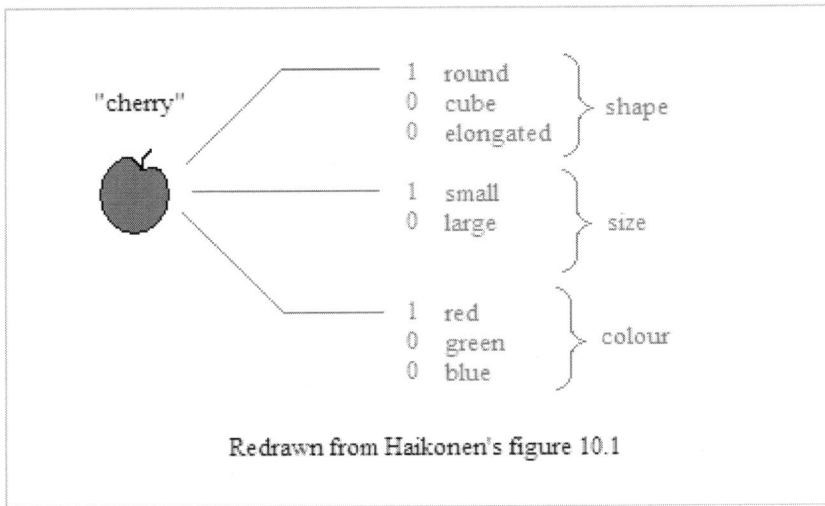

Redrawn from Haikonen's figure 10.1

That arrangement, where particular features are identified by dedicated hardware units, is not new. It is widely recognised in neuroscience [Reisenhuber and Poggio 2003].

13.11

A wild cherry, presumably, will have been a feature of the environment for a very long time, so the ability to detect its presence on features like colour, shape and size, could well have evolved by natural selection. However, a cherry also has the properties that it is good to eat and has a particular taste. These are characteristics which must be learned by experience. Presumably that learning experience can be induced or encouraged by parents.

Aliases

13.12

Haikonen uses the example of a chair to illustrate the need for the identifying characteristics of an object to include the use to which it is put. He uses the term "*alias*" to identify a concept which embraces chairs in terms of use. I have argued that data compression, when it is applied to the memory of past experiences and when it gradually expands the compass of what is included in a repeated chunk, would eventually include that commonality of use as a property of the concept.

To explain how the system can acquire new information Haikonen invokes "Hebbian Learning" [Hebb 1961] as the mechanism by which one neuron can be associated with another (by changing the sensitivity of a synaptic gap) to produce neurone groups which can learn various associations. He illustrates that with a diagram like the one below.

Fig 13.12 The neuron group

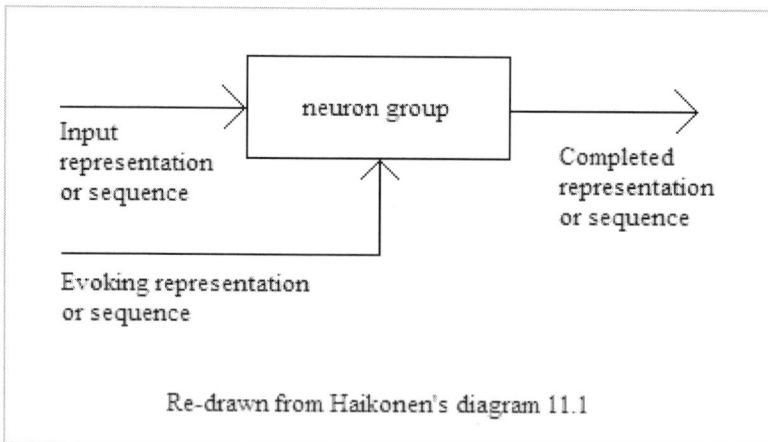

Re-drawn from Haikonen's diagram 11.1

The "*neuron group*", he says, is able to store a representation of an entity or event which can be either static or a sequence of events.

13.13

"*How.*" Haikonen asks, "*do we make a machine perceive something?*"

I did not completely grasp his answer to that question. My understanding was not helped by the fact that he refers to the "Perception Principle" which is explained in his own PhD Thesis to which I have no access. [p181]. Apparently it involves feedback and threshold control coming from "internal processes". He claims, that this realises the "doorbell effect" - a reference to the way that a bell ringing inside a house is perceived as having an external source.

13.14

When Haikonen describes the system architecture he envisages for his conscious robot, he stresses that each of the means of perception - vision, hearing, touch, smell, taste and the reception of linguistic input - has its own separate modality.

Fig 13.14 Grounding modalities

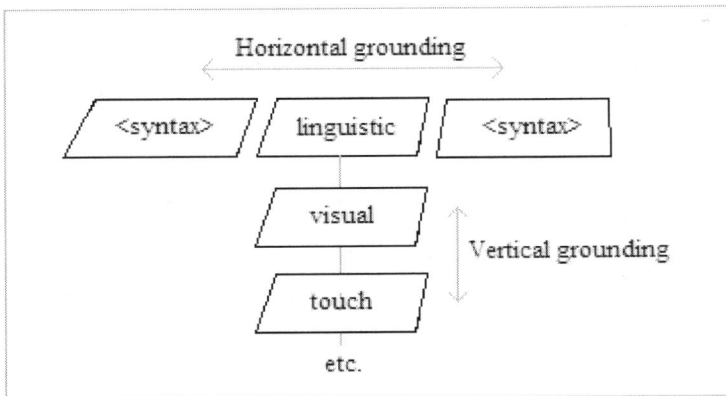

These he regards as a separate "planes". The information in these planes can be interconnected. He describes the connections between the planes as "*vertical grounding*".

Within the linguistic modality, words can also be connected by their syntactic categories. This he describes as "*horizontal grounding*" (see the diagram).

In my own account I also envisage these separate modalities. I call them as "*dimensions*" and speak of the modalities being "*labelled*". Jackendoff calls them "*character tags*". These terminological differences apart however, what seems to be agreed is that these separate modalities are important and need to be identified within the representation structure.

13.15

It seems also that Haikonen, shares my scepticism about the Chomskian emphasis on syntax. At one point he states -

"I make here a bold generalisation and claim that syntax cannot be completely separated from semantics."

[Haikonen 2003 p238]

13.16

However, this notion about "grounding" is an important aspect of his general thesis about consciousness. Having discussed various aspects of known neurological features, he says -

"From these examples it can be concluded that the difference between conscious and non conscious operation would be the level of active cross-connections between modalities; the cross-modality reporting and learning of related associative connections and thus the establishment of episodic memories of the event."

[Haikonen 2003 p254]

And later he states -

"... consciousness is not an observer, agent or supervisor, instead it is a style and a way of operation, characterized by

distributed signal representation, perception process, cross-modality reporting and available for retrospection. There is no need for special 'consciousness neurons', conscious matter or a special seat of consciousness. There is no discrete machine supervisor self, the supervision is distributed in the machine. While digesting this it is useful to realise the distinction between the contents of consciousness and consciousness as a process. The above relates to the latter."

[Hailonen 2003 p255]

13.17

Although I agree with the substance of that, I still find that explanation of consciousness unsatisfactory. For me, to effect a change from the unconscious representation of events, to a self-conscious and subjective experience of events, something more than just *more of the same* is required. My own preferred explanation is that full consciousness happens when the concepts of SELF and SELFMIND are introduced into the representation of events. When that happens those representation structures must include representations and predictions of the system's own behaviour in response to the events predicted. That is what I have described as a "*convoluted multi-role performance*". That, I claim, is the performance of a subjective experience because it requires the mechanism to construct a representation of itself as a physical entity, behaving under the control of its own mind with emotional motives for its actions. In short, it explains itself to itself.

Nevertheless, until that change to full consciousness is brought about, I am happy to think of the increasing detail of representation (in Haikonen's terms increase in grounding) as steps along a gradient of developing consciousness. The gradual process of evolution takes one short step over a cliff-edge, but could not do so unless it is preceded by equally small steps which progress it towards that cliff-edge.

13.18

On the issue of emotional experiences such as anger, pain, pleasure, etc. Haikonen associates these, as I do, with the characteristic types of behaviour which these conditions predict.

My explanation goes a little further. I suggest that the process of data compression, by recognising the repetitions created by that common association with actions taken (and predicted), will produce a concept of mind, and emotional mood, which although it may have no counterpart in reality, does have a valuable ability to enable accurate prediction concerning behaviour. The analogy I use (see section 18.04) for this is the mathematical symbol "i" (which denotes the square root of minus one). That has no counterpart in the external world. There is no number which when multiplied by itself produces the result minus one. Nevertheless the use of "i" in mathematical formulae allows the accurate prediction of many features of the natural world. The concept of emotion, I suggest, is like that. The thing does not really exist, but it has valuable applications with regard to prediction. It is a property of the mind concept and therefore is automatically included in the representation and prediction of the mechanism's own behaviour.

13.19

Another important point of agreement between Haikonen's thesis and my own, is the recognition that any valid explanation of consciousness should provide us with an explanation of why the intuition, that the mind is a non-material counterpart separate from the physical mechanism of the brain, is so common and powerful.

"Any machine that is claimed to be conscious should also reproduce the materialistic mind-body effect."
[Haikonen 2003 p247]

He also claims that a machine constructed as he describes would not be able to do otherwise.

Inner Speech

13.20

I am concerned about Haikonen's references to "inner speech" or some kind of internal language. Ray Jackendoff made similar references but also developed arguments which he called "the unconscious meaning hypothesis" [Jackendoff 2012].

"Another perspective on the Unconscious Meaning Hypothesis" comes from the well-known quote: "How can I know what I think until I see what I say?" This is usually cited to make the point that you don't have a thought until you actually say it. In other words, thoughts and language are the same. But all it really shows is that you aren't aware of your thought - you don't know what it is - until it comes out clothed in words. Before that, before it gets a phonological "handle", it's unconscious."

[Jackendoff 2012 p88]

It can be difficult to know whether these references to inner speech are intended to be taken literally or as a metaphor. We are so accustomed to being informed by others using speech as the vehicle, and the association between word and concept is so close, that it is natural for us to think in terms of that mode of communication when we acquire information in any way. That, I claim, is another intuitive idea that is highly misleading. I have used the metaphor of "telling oneself" on several occasions in this text. But it was a metaphor only. I do not suggest that one part of the brain speaks to another in any form at all. That does not happen by spoken words. We do not speak to ourselves, we do not write letters or send ourselves emails. To do so would introduce an extra and completely unnecessary mechanism of processing. Moreover, when we use the concept of "inner speech" (even in a metaphorical way), and also when we refer to one part of the brain "observing" another, we are inadvertently introducing a mysterious extra intelligence within the mechanism of brain which does the understanding of the linguistic communication. Why is that needed? The brain already has, within it, the information it requires. Why does it have to code the information into words, transmit those words elsewhere in the brain, and then decode it all back into an understanding? It seems a long way round to get back to the point we started from. The final step required is not a decoding into "understanding", but a decoding into action or the planning of potential action. It also seems to me that this idea of inner speech is an unnecessary diversion to avoid saying exactly what understanding is and how it is achieved. By introducing that extra entity which understands the inner speech, it allows a hidden form of duality to creep into our account.

My version of the mechanism identifies the active construction of a representation of events and situations as the mechanism of understanding. That representation contains predictions concerning the status of certain potential conditions - whether they are GOAL or ANT-GOAL conditions, for the individual concerned. That delivers a driving force for action to be taken. That is the end product of the brain's deliberations. As it constructs that representation, the brain knows what it needs to know and it knows how to act. There is no need for it to transmit that information anywhere else in the brain. The only extra bit of information needed is some rationale for that action. It needs to have a causal motivation for its actions so that it can predict the outcome of similar events which may occur in the future. So it classifies its motivation using those simplifying emotional categories - anger, excitement, joy, love, anxiety ... etc. It is easy to identify the indicators and to make use of the predictions that follow. The brain does not need to provide itself with an explanation of what these conditions really are. If such an explanation exists, it is distributed over a vast period of evolutionary development and a shorter, but still quite long period of maturation and learning in infancy.

There is still a problem concerning evolution. How could this inner speech thing ever get started? To begin its evolutionary journey there has to be a point when the evolving/developing system has a meaning for only one word. What use is that? We can make sense of this only by separating the development of word-meanings from the development of words and accepting that meanings had to come first. There has to have been a time when we, or our ancestors, could think using meanings without the need for word-labels. Body language was sufficient for primitive communication. Then came the words to act as convenient handles and to enable the communication of those thoughts. A recent video-clip on a TV newscast of a bottle-nosed dolphin "asking" (by body language) a human diver for help to free it from a fishing net, is, I think, clear evidence of that possibility.

Understanding an utterance

13.21

If anyone thinks that the interpretation of spoken language is a trivial matter, watching subtitles on a TV screen, and seeing the frequent and often very funny mistakes that these systems make, should disabuse them of that misunderstanding. To avoid ambiguity, the recognition of the sound patterns of phonemes must be closely integrated with the analysis of meaning and an awareness of context.

Nevertheless, we can now construct an outline description of how an uttered statement is processed (according to the mechanism proposed here). The sequence of events is quite complicated but follows the programmed sequence already established by evolution for non-linguistic thinking and conscious understanding.

The sound vibrations of spoken words are received at the phase-layer-1 stage. Detection units identify elementary features and activate the appropriate action units (associated with the articulation of those sounds). To establish those associations a growing child must practice making sounds. The collected pattern of these unit activations is stored temporarily in the phase-layer-2 short-term memory or TRACE. Various groups or chunks of that collection of data have already been identified and stored as concepts. The phase-layer-3 mechanism then processes (interprets) the trace and substitutes existing concepts for some group patterns of data within the trace. That establishes the initial phase of momentary or instantaneous consciousness. At that stage, however, all the mechanism is aware of is that certain patterns of sound (word-concepts) have been heard. To form an interpretation the process needs to fit these concepts together. That involves following associated links.

There are several levels of association. First there are the associations with word-sounds which typically occur within spoken statements. Next are the associations with word-concepts. That provides information about where those words normally occur within an utterance - the initial segmentation of a statement into phrases and clauses. Next comes the association between word-concept and thing-concept (or the meaning of a word). The last stage is the linking of word meanings to produce a representation. That creates a parallel interpretation structure which will last much longer than the ephemeral trace. The stored form however will make use of the associations required to retrieve the constructional units in the correct sequence for re-construction.

Within those meaning structures there are further levels. Penetrating these requires still more effort and still more time. Often there is insufficient time available to follow the process to an end-point. There is, in any case, no identifiable end-point.

It is the fitting together of these meaning structure associations (a the phase-layer-4 stage) and based on the syntactical grouping proposed by the first level of interpretation that constitutes the understanding of an utterance.

13.22

The sequence of levels to which interpretation can be carried can be subdivided, crudely, into two levels or systems which correspond to what Kahneman calls "system 1" and "system 2" thinking [Kahneman 2011]. System 1 thinking is fast, superficial and error prone. System 2 thinking is slower and more precise.

CHAPTER 14

Some issues.
In this chapter I will discuss a few additional issues which need to be tidied up. I shall deal with them as expeditiously as I can.

Implementation

14.01

Whenever a physical explanation of consciousness is suggested, a question which then arises is this - Would it be possible to use the design of the mechanism proposed, to construct an artificial system which could then be shown to be genuinely conscious?

That, however, in this instance, is not a question to which I can give a confident and unqualified answer.

Each part of the internal mechanism, which I have described, relies on proven technology. I can say with confidence, therefore, that there is nothing in my proposed design that, in principle, would rule out the possibility of a physical implementation. However, not ruling out the possibility in principle, does not imply that in practice an implementation would be feasible.

The main difficulty, as I see it, is that the construction of the phase-layer-1 system which, in my proposed system, involves the mechanism of evolution and natural selection over a very long period of time and would require a vast expenditure in resources. In a sense, therefore, the system I have proposed, is not confined to a single technological mechanism which could be manufactured easily. It is a combination of that mechanism and the larger one of natural selection which operates in the physical world around us. Constructing an artificial version of that would be very difficult indeed.

The number of individual units involved in the phase-layer-1 system, (with a human-like level of intelligence) would be measured in billions. Each unit is individually shaped by natural selection imposed by the ever-changing natural environment over that time. The best that might be possible in an artificial system would be to craft a small subset of units, designed to be effective within an environment of limited scope - perhaps in a supervisory role, observing and noting human behaviour in a way that defies current monitoring methods. For example, the use of CCTV footage has proved very useful in the identification of criminals, but it also requires an enormous commitment of human resources to scan the footage and identify "interesting" events. Automatic face recognition and motor car licence plate identification help, but what is really needed is the identification of behaviour - the ability to read body language.

Whether that would be acceptable to those concerned with human rights and issues of privacy is another matter. I have reservations about the desirability of providing those in authority with the ability to place an artificial observer with human-like abilities on every street corner and in every home. .

From a technical point of view, progress in implementation might be made if we could devise a simplified analogue of a natural environment, by generating units automatically with built-in random perturbations and by then exposing them to ruthless elimination by the contingencies of that artificial environment. Those, which "survived" according to some pre-defined criteria of what survival means, would be used as the basis for the automatic production of the next generation of units. But what criteria would we choose to make that elimination happen?

In the real world the criteria of natural selection have changed over time. It is thought that a period of rapid change was required to propel the ape-like species (that was the evolutionary precursor of humans), to greater and greater flexibility and adaptability of behaviour and to higher and higher levels of intelligence.

That might be possible, but I do not envisage that an artificial environment could be constructed on a scale which matched the scale and diversity of the real environment or achieve a speed which would produce the desired results within a practical time-scale.

I do not want to speculate further. Suffice it to say that implementation would be theoretically possible but would definitely not be easy.

Metaphysics

14.02

Metaphysics. According to the dictionary of philosophy –

"... the term is now applied to any enquiry that raises questions about reality that lie beyond or behind those capable of being tackled by the methods of science. Naturally, an immediately contested issue is whether there are any such questions, or whether any text of metaphysics should, in Hume's words, be '... committed to the flames, for it can contain nothing but sophistry and illusion' ".

[Blackburn 1994]

I agree with Hume and I regard the terms "metaphysics" and "supernatural" as synonymous. Both ask us to believe in the existence of "things" and "phenomena" which cannot be checked by observation.

What does "material" mean?

14.03

When I think about what we mean when we describe something as being "material" I think first about the obvious physical components of the world. I then think about forces like gravity and magnetism. I then realise how difficult it is to grasp what these forces really are. No one suggests that these forces do not "exist", and yet we do not have any direct perception of them. Add to them the concept of "dark matter" which has only recently entered the scientific discourse. The existence of dark matter is still debated but additional evidence for its existence has begun to be found and efforts are now being made to devise ways to discover more such evidence. The existence of dark energy is just beginning to be considered in an effort to understand why the universe appear to be expanding at an accelerating rate.

In another book [Noble 2008] I postulated the idea that there are two additional forces of gravity - equal in strength to one another, but opposite in direction. One pulls massive bodies together (like normal gravity) and the other pushes them apart. If you are concerned about Einstein's version of gravity I am sure we could easily think up an equivalent pair of forces which satisfy the requirements of that theory too. The point is this, because they are equal and opposite, the net effect of these additional forces, is zero. So there is no way we could ever detect their presence. To what extent therefore are we justified in entertaining the possibility of their existence? The concepts we form are practical and useful things. They help us to understand (and to predict) the universe we can observe. But those particular additional forces of gravity are completely useless. They add nothing at all to our understanding or our ability to predict.

What emerges from these considerations (for me) is the thought that when we describe anything as being "material" what we mean is that it appears to have observable effects. If we identify it as a component of our mental representation of the universe it enables us to improve the accuracy of our predictions about how the universe will behave.

I mentioned Dark Energy earlier. No one has any firm idea of what it is. It's presence is suspected only because we can observe phenomena, or a phenomenon, which does not agree with the known laws of the universe. Yet no one, so far as I am aware, has seriously suggested that the true explanation requires us to believe in magic. To accommodate these new observations we seek to expand the known laws.

The Explanatory Gap

14.04

And that raises a problem. Some claim that consciousness has two components - Access Consciousness (which is the physical or material mechanism of the brain) and Phenomenal Consciousness (which is the metaphysical or non-material counterpart). But these two parts are in communication. Damage to the physical brain affects the ability to be conscious. If you make a conscious decision to do something, you (that is, your phenomenal consciousness) cannot act upon the decision unless that conscious decision is somehow communicated to the physical mechanism so that it will instruct your limbs to act as required.

In view of the argument above about material things, therefore, it does appear that that non-material phenomenal consciousness by being in communication with the material mechanism of the brain, and affecting its behaviour, is thereby re-classifying itself as a material thing.

The proponents of the two kinds of consciousness theory have a name for that anomalous communication between the two. They call it "The Explanatory Gap". To my mind, however, the fact that phenomenal consciousness appears to be both material and non-material at the same time, is not a gap in our explanation. It is simply a logical contradiction. When we find that making a particular assumption leads us into a logical contradiction (something true and not true simultaneously) then that is proof positive that the initial assumption was wrong - deeply, comprehensively and irretrievably wrong. There is, therefore, no point in pursuing the idea of there being two kinds of consciousness, or the "explanatory gap", any further.

Note: The conversion of a logical contradiction (which comprehensively destroys a favoured hypothesis), into an "explanatory gap" that someone else is invited to solve, is a neat trick. It is rather as though a Flat-Earthist had demanded that globular theories about Earth shape, can be taken seriously only if they first solve the problem of what happens at the sharp edges of the world.

Arguments.

14.05

Yet despite that definitive proof that the two kinds of consciousness idea is wrong, those who hold these views persist with arguments which purport to show that the idea of artificial consciousness is absurd. Most of these arguments come from philosophers who seem not to understand much about computer algorithms. For my part, for the reason given above, the idea that consciousness might have a metaphysical or supernatural component is nonsense.

I am sure, however, that some readers of this book will have heard these arguments and may feel that there is a case to be answered. So I will deal with them as quickly as possible.

The Turing Test

14.06

Alan Turing, famous for his contribution to the decryption of the German Enigma code, was also a brilliant mathematician who, with great originality, conceived the possibility of artificial intelligence. He published a paper in which he suggested a test of artificial intelligence. It was quite a simple idea. If a machine was devised that could carry on a conversation with a human being, and that human being was then deceived into thinking that he was in discussion with a real human being, then the system had passed this test.

Unfortunately, Turing did not specify the rigour with which the test should be conducted. I imagine he thought that the people conducting the test would be honestly trying to reveal the truth.

If that is the case, then he was wrong.

His specification has been misinterpreted in a simplistic way in an attempt to disprove the very idea of artificial intelligence.

CHAPTER 15

Conversations with a machine.

Most of this chapter is concerned with some very old stuff which should have been "consigned to the flames" a long time ago. It irritates me that it is necessary to bring some of it into the discussion at all. Searle's Chinese Room argument, for example, still crops up in general discussions despite its obvious fallacies.

ELIZA - A case study in misrepresentation and misdirection.

15.01

In the early days of artificial intelligence research, a computer system was constructed and given the name "ELIZA". The name was borrowed from Eliza Dolittle, the uneducated flower girl in Bernard Shaw's play "Pygmalion" - later to be turned into the musical "My Fair Lady". Eliza was taught to talk "proper" by a linguist called Professor Higgins. Higgins did it to satisfy a bet with a colleague. ELIZA, the computer system, was intended to demonstrate the (then) current possibilities of AI research, but although it is amusing and has some interesting practical commercial applications, it was also, as it has turned out, a gift to the enemies of artificial intelligence. To the unenlightened and procedure-blind, it illustrated the best that AI research could achieve. That was a bit like taking a Second World War string-bag biplane as the best example of what was possible in aeronautical engineering.

To understand how that misunderstanding happened, and the full extent of the mistake, you have to understand how ELIZA worked. It was basically a machine that operated on word strings. It parsed the sentences and identified keywords. It constructed new sentences on related topics, and then printed those new sentences. The interest and amusement came from knowing that that was all it was doing, and yet also recognising that in many ways it gave the appearance of a human level of understanding.

If ELIZA fooled some of the people some of the time that was an indication only that people tend to assume that others understand what is being said if they themselves are able to make a connection between the sentences uttered. But ELIZA did not need to understand what the words or the sentences actually meant. It simply threw back the same (or very similar words) to the user. It had a list of synonyms so it could substitute alternative words.

And what did that produce? For some users it appeared to have an almost magical ability to talk, or at least converse, in a human-like way. ELIZA spawned a collection of similar systems one of which was call the DOCTOR system. This one simulated the kind of conversation people might have with their psychiatrist. One of the characteristics of a conversation like that, is that a shrink seldom, if ever, actually answers a question. He or she always turns the patient's questions into more questions. If you asked the system about "X", its standard reply is "*Is X important to you? Tell me more about X.*"

Another spin-off system called PARANOIA was created. This one treated every statement by the user as a hidden reference to the Mafia and usually ended every conversation by accusing its inquisitor of being a member of that criminal organisation.

A famous conversation between DOCTOR and PARANOIA ended that way -

Paranoia: *I think you are a member of the Mafia.*

Doctor: *Would it be important to you if I was a member of the Mafia? Tell me more about the Mafia.*

What was unfortunate about ELIZA, DOCTOR and PARANOIA was that many people genuinely thought that these systems defined the limits of what is possible in AI systems. They also claimed that these systems have shown that the Turing Test can be passed by some very dumb systems, which lack any understanding of language. That is not true.

On several well-documented occasions, an unsuspecting human has indeed been fooled into thinking that ELIZA or the DOCTOR was really a human being. But the confusion was only momentary and can be explained by the circumstances which tricked the human user into a false sense of normality.

To give an extreme example, a few days ago I thought that my wife was having a conversation with a visitor in the room next to mine. It turned out to be a radio. So if we apply the same criteria in that case, as Searle uses for his Chinese Room thought experiment, it would appear that even a radio can pass the Turing Test. And that is clearly ridiculous.

One of the people deeply involved with the DOCTOR project, used to work from home using remote computer terminal, without bothering to travel into the laboratory. On one occasion a salesman, charged with responsibility for selling some of the systems devised by the laboratory, to commercial organisations, visited the laboratory and found a teletype (no VDUs or Blackberries in those days) sitting by itself and showing the words -

DOCTOR: Type your question followed by a full stop.

The salesman, thinking he was in contact with the expert in charge of the system, typed -

Salesman: Can I use the system today for a demonstration to some potential customers?

DOCTOR: Is it important to you that you are able to use the system? Tell me more about these customers.

Salesman: What do you mean? Of course it is important.

DOCTOR: You seem very definite about that.

Salesman: Of course I am sure.

DOCTOR: Why are you so sure?

Salesman: What the hell are you on about?

(at this point he forgot to terminate his statement with a full stop)

DOCTOR: ..... (no answer)

The salesman then phoned ELIZA's creator at his home number, woke him from a deep sleep, and spoke in an angry voice -

Salesman: Why are you being so snotty to me?

Sleepy researcher worker: What do you mean I am being snotty to you?

I re-tell this story from memory having heard it from Danny Bobrow, one of the research team involved, at a small departmental seminar. He also told of an occasion when a departmental secretary was discovered discussing the personal and very private details of her own social life with the DOCTOR program.

Passing the Turing Test has to be more exacting than that.

In an informal way we each apply a Turing Test, every day to our companions. We chat with them and it is on the basis of these conversations that we conclude that other people have the same level of understanding of language that we have. We also conclude that those other people are conscious. But those conversations are much more exacting. They are on-going over a very long period of time and many situations arise which may not arise in the laboratory when an unsuspecting user has a short conversation with ELIZA or DOCTOR.

Charniak's problem

15.02

In the 1970s Eugene Charniak tried to construct a computer system which would analyse a children's storybook. What he had in mind was one of those "*Jane and John played with a ball*" kind of stories. His thesis, in which he gave examples of the problems he found in trying what might have been expected to be a simple project, was illuminating. One of those stories told how John and Jane went to a shop to buy a birthday present for Jack. John bought a kite.

"*But Jack already has a kite,*" Jane said, "*You will need to take it back.*"

A simple story indeed, but one with hidden traps. In that last sentence we need to consider this question - to which kite does the word "*it*" refer?

The last kite mentioned is the one which Jack already has, and that is the one which a system, based only on grammatical rules, would identify as the referent for "*it*". But you and I know that that is not the kite to which "*it*" refers. We should not expect a shop to accept the return of a purchase bought by someone else, perhaps in a different shop, at a different time. We know that. But how could a computer system capture that knowledge in formal grammatical rules?

The students and the councillors

15.03

Here is another example of pronominal reference, which defeats grammatical rules.

"*The students were unable to hire the hall from the councillors because they advocated revolution.*"

To which set of people does the pronoun "*they*" refer? The councillors? Councillors do not usually advocate revolution. Surely it must be a bunch of hot-headed students that it is talking about.

Pause a moment.

This story refers to an incident in China during the days of Chairman Mao. At that time, and in that place, advocating revolution was required of all those in public office.

This example illustrates the amount and the depth of knowledge about the world and its social history, which we need to have in order to understand various linguistic utterances. During our conversations with other people we rely on and expect our companions to understand these things.

The conclusion we should reach from these examples is that a system based on nothing more complicated than grammatical analysis cannot pass a properly conducted Turing Test (PCTT).

Testing questions

Pronominal reference is just the most obvious problem, which we all solve daily and for which grammatical analysis is inadequate. But there are many other examples. The idea that underpins my thesis - that consciousness enables a system to anticipate its own reactions to predictable events - is one of those critical tests. To conduct an appropriate Turing Test the questions we ask of a computer system should probe its understanding of it own future behaviour.

"What would you do if ..... ?"

We can think of a number of scenarios that would search its understanding of its own motivation.

"And why would you do that?" would be normal follow-up question.

The test could then be expanded in a significant way by exposing the system to exactly the hypothetical circumstances it was quizzed about. We could then see if the system's predictions about its own future behaviour were accurate.

Retrospective questions should also be included. Think less of a computing laboratory. Think rather of the interrogation room at a police station where a suspect is being grilled - and where the police are in a position to check CCTV footage and to make forensic tests to check the validity of the answers.

"When you went into the sitting room, did you notice blood on the carpet?"

Note - there does not need to have been any blood in the room. Even if there was indeed blood present in the room, we can check CCTV footage to see if the suspect actually looked in the direction of the blood. Trying to dodge the question by pretending that the system cannot remember, is not going to work for very long. We will be ready for these evasive answers. We offer the test subject a seat - with a hidden pin embedded in the cushion. If it jumps up shouting "ouch" we know has at least one of the characteristics of consciousness. A simple reflex action? Not if the next time it sits, it carefully examines the seat for hidden pins. We would then suspect that it has remembered the experience and anticipated that it is an experience it does not want to repeat.

Another test question. This one is the standard question a doctor asks to see if a patient is fully conscious or seeing double -

"How many fingers am I holding up?"

A doctor who asks that question wants an answer which is the correct number of fingers. He would not accept as adequate the answer *"Is it important to you that I know how many fingers you are holding up?"* We should not accept that either. An adequate Turing Test is not as simple as the opponents of artificial intelligence seem to suppose.

It is with that cautious assessment in mind that we should approach the many claims that have been made by the opponents of AI research and see them for what they are - naive judgements made by those who have very little understanding of how computer systems might be able to perform.

Context dependency

15.05

The crucial point is this - The meaning of a sentence depends upon its context. To understand a sentence a person must understand that context.

When a computer system tries to mimic the ability of a human with respect to communication with language, it must confront and solve that difficult problem. The system must somehow gain information about that context. The context can be created by the previous dialogue. It can also be created by events outwith the dialogue altogether. The example provided by Gene Charniak, demonstrates both. Human knowledge about the way shops operate will have been learned over a long period of time before the conversation even starts. The same example also illustrates how the first part of the conversation was able to construct a context and then placed it into that wider context of purchasing things in a shop. To pass an appropriately conducted Turing Test, an artificial system must solve that problem.

The policy adopted by most opponents of the AI-project, is to ignore the problem of context dependency completely, to invent simplistic mechanisms which purport to be able to communicate, and then to claim that such a system would be able to pass the Turing Test. Either those AI opponents are unaware of the problems involved or they are aware of it but are assuming that their target readership is not. The first explanation, if true, is surprising and disappointing. The second, if true, is dishonest and disgraceful.

John Searle and the Chinese room

15.06

John Searle's argument which is known as "The Chinese Room" has become famous (or perhaps infamous would be a more appropriate term) as the best known argument against the whole idea that human consciousness and understanding could ever be explained in terms of a physical procedure. Briefly, Searle's argument goes like this -

We must suppose that there is a room and that inside this room there is a man (who speaks only English) and a filing cabinet which contains various records. Together these records contain a grammatical analysis of the Mandarin Chinese language. The records in the cabinet are mostly written in Mandarin Chinese but they also have some instructions written in English. The man is able to read and obey these instructions. A person, who is a fluent speaker of Mandarin Chinese then inserts statements and questions (written in Mandarin Chinese) through a letter box into the room. The English-speaking man inside the room, lifts the letter, reads it, tries to match it, symbol by symbol with the records inside the filing cabinet. When he obtains a match he reads the English instructions on the record and follows the instructions. The instructions tell him to write some symbols on a card and then to access other records in the cabinet (again). This process continues until, by following the instructions, the man has written a series of symbols on the card. He then posts the card back out through the letterbox. The person outside, who speaks Chinese can then read what is written on the card and finds that it is a statement in Mandarin Chinese which seems to be a reasonable response to the original query.

Searle then invites us to reflect on the performance of the Chinese room. It has, he claims, passed "The Turing Test". That is, it has fooled a person into believing that it has a knowledge and understanding of Chinese, when in fact it has no such understanding. The man inside the room, Searle reminds us frequently, has no such understanding, and the contents of the filing cabinet are just a bunch of "dumb grammatical" rules.

15.07

Two things should be noted -

(1) The person who is posing the questions, which constitute the Turing Test (as envisaged by Searle), is not actually trying to catch the Chinese Room out. The questions posed as examples are just general chit-chat and there is no attempt made to pose questions in such a way that only a person who really does understand the language could answer sensibly.

(2) There is an implicit assumption, which is not even mentioned, let alone addressed, that a system based purely on grammatical rules could achieve such a result.

In my discussion of the ELIZA system, I suggested that we should look at the Turing Test in more detail and I concluded that a system based on grammatical analysis alone could never pass a properly conducted Turing Test (PCTT).

Searle has written a large number of papers on this topic and a comment with which he seems to be remarkably pleased (for he repeats it many times in several of these papers) is this -

"... a computer has syntax, but no semantics" [Searle 1983]

That comment and the fact that he has repeated it often, suggests to me that Professor Searle has no understanding at all about the nature of computers, of syntax or of semantics. Consider the diagram.

Fig 15.07 - Syntax and semantics

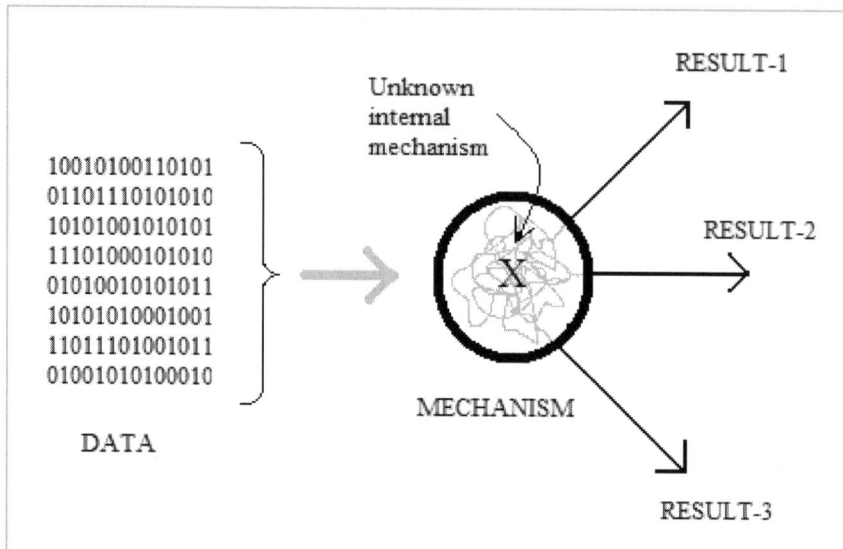

On the left we see a block of data. This is just an arbitrary block of 1s and 0s as they might occur within a computer system. Not only does this data have no semantics. It also has no syntax either. Syntax and semantics are just the kind of things that data does NOT have.

Data is just data. Whether or not that block of data is grammatically correct, is something, which can be determined only by the program or mechanism, which is attempting to read the data, and then to do something in response. It does not matter whether that procedure is specified as a computer program, or by the physical hardware of the computer's CPU. Each is just a procedure. It is the way each processes the data which determines the syntactic or semantic properties of the data.

In that block of data there are 8 rows and 14 columns. If the mechanism processing the data can process data only if it comes as a block with 8 rows and 14 columns then that block of data is syntactically correct. If not, then the block of data may not be syntactically correct. It is as simple as that. The semantic interpretation of the data is also determined by the mechanism, which processes the input. The nature of the semantic interpretation is determined by the various alternative results, which the mechanism produces.

In this example the semantic interpretation of the data has only three possible results

SEMANTICS=(RESULT-1 + RESULT-2 + RESULT-3)

No more and no less. If we wrote an alternative procedure to handle the data we could expand the semantic interpretation a great deal, or diminish it. The block of data could be intended to indicate how soldiers should line up for a parade, or it could be intended to be read as a chunk of computer ASCII code. The data themselves, if I can put it this way, do not know anything about that. It is the processing program that decides. So Searle's frequently repeated statement about computers having syntax but no semantics is just nonsense.

Syntax and semantics are not some kind of magic juice, which can be squeezed out of 1s and 0s (or the condition of brain cells). If Searle's Chinese Room is to pass a properly conducted Turing Test it would need to have a suitable mechanism stored in that filing cabinet and the understanding which it may have, if that mechanism can be discovered, will be an understanding possessed by the activate operation of the procedure, not by the man operating it or the filing cabinet which contains it. What the man himself knows or does not know is irrelevant.

The questions we present to the Chinese Room should be chosen so that there was some way to distinguish between responses which indicated some understanding and those, which did not. For example -

"*What colour is my hair?*"

The answer might be right or wrong. If it was right (and was right consistently), that would indicate that the system was probably able to observe the world around it. Without input from the external world a mechanism cannot be considered conscious. A hospital patient in a coma may be apparently unconscious but can also be internally conscious. That will be the case, however, only if he or she is able to recall the stored memories of data which was received at some earlier time. If there never has been any input of data the mechanism of brain cannot be conscious because there is no experience, which requires explanation and no input which can be anticipated.

Another question -

"*What were we talking about yesterday?*"

That would tell us whether or not the system had a memory. Memory of previous dialogue would permit us to construct a context. We could for example tell it a story about Jack and his kite. If it has information about that, a system might be able to interpret new sentences and do so with that context in mind.

A system which is based only on grammatical analysis does not have a memory. One could be added of course, but that goes beyond what Searle envisaged. We could add lots of other things too. That would also turn the system into another kind of system - which is exactly what I am advocating - that a different kind of system could understand what it was talking about.

Searle's Chinese room is totally inadequate. That filing cabinet would need to contain records with a great deal more content than Searle envisaged. It would also need eyes and ears. It would need limbs to respond. It would need a good memory. And it would need to be able to explain itself to itself. That last point means that it would need to be conscious.

Here is an interesting statement which we could post through the letter-box of the Chinese Room (written in Chinese of course) -

"*I am going to set fire to your Chinese room.*"

If the door of the Chinese room is opened and the man emerged dragging the filing cabinet after him, I think it we would be impressed and justified in assuming that the message had been understood. But to do that, the instructions stored in the filing cabinet would have had to tell the man to do that - in English. It would be a strange set of grammatical rules that could do all that. But it is only if it could do something like that that the system could be said to have passed the properly conducted Turing Test. That, after all, is the kind of test situation, which we use to judge the presence of consciousness in our fellow human beings.

The Chinese Room could not perform as Searle claims.

Ned Block

15.08

Ned Block is also an influential figure in the debate about consciousness. He is responsible for a number of interesting thought-experiments and among those one of the best known is the "Chinese Nation argument".

He was also responsible for giving us the terminology of *phenomenal* consciousness and *access* consciousness, which identifies respectively, the subjective experience of being conscious and the physical mechanism of consciousness.

Block's Chinese Nation argument

15.09

Block asks us to consider a very large collection of people each of whom is able to carry out the task performed by a single neurone in the brain of a conscious person. China is the most populated country in the world and so it was China and its billion or so inhabitants that he offered as a prototype for this thought experiment. That number, of course, falls a long way short of the actual number of neurones in the brain and even more so of the number of active connections within a typical human brain, but it is still a large number and so we need only stretch our imagination a little to get the idea of a lot of individual components, beavering away at these special tasks, without having any idea of what it is that the whole thing is able to achieve collectively.

15.10

It is significant that when Block presented his Chinese nation argument, he told us about the nature of the components of the procedure involved (they are people). He could have left that piece of information out because the fact that the components are people is of no consequence at all. They could just as easily have been electronic units each designed to carry out the actions performed by a neurone or a synapse gap or whatever. So why people?

Note: there is at present, in Switzerland, a new well-funded project which has as its objective exactly that. The aim of the project is to construct a machine which is an exact electronic analogue of the brain – with a one-for-one replacement of individual neurones by electronic units. That may answer the fundamental question but it may do so without also telling us how the trick of consciousness is done.

Anyway, I suspect the reason for Block telling us that the components of his thought machine are people, is that by telling us that Block confuses the issue completely. When one thinks about the system he describes, it is almost impossible to ignore the fact that each of those people will have his or her private thoughts and private consciousness. But the issue we are concerned with is the result of the procedure, which they all carry out together, and that is something which lies above and beyond their individual consciousness. What they think and know about doesn't count. What matters is what the system, as a system, thinks and knows.

I do not imagine that the individual neurones or synapses in my brain have any significant knowledge about what I am thinking and knowing. The most they can know about is one very small component of my thinking.

I maintain that to be conscious Block's Chinese Nation system would need to anticipate its own decisions and explain these to itself. So it would need to have a mechanism of self-modelling. As a part of that self-modelling procedure it must be able to attribute its own behaviour to the feelings which it imagines itself having. Our news media do something very similar when they attribute emotionally driven motives for behaviour to the capital cities of various countries. Moscow wants this. Washington fears that. London is trying to achieve some other thing. It's a form of figurative speech of course. But this is a system which is attributing these emotional drives to itself. We also often talk about collective responsibility. In the final analysis it is the system which decides, by whatever mechanism governs its decision making.

That is a difficult circumstance for us to imagine. We are so accustomed to taking the sentient behaviour of real individual people into account that it is difficult to put these ideas aside.

The Aunt Bubbles machine

15.11

Block has another hypothetical mechanism to offer us. He calls it the "Aunt Bubbles machine". Aunt Bubbles has stored inside her a truly enormous list of sentences. There is however a problem. It is known that the list of all possible sentences is infinite. You can for, example, add the word "and" to the end of a sentence and then start all over again with a new one. And that can be done as many times as is required - without limit.

To overcome that snag, Block proposed that the sentences should be limited to a specific number of words. There is a finite number of words in a language and so, if the total number of words in a sentence has a limit too, then there is a finite number of permutations of those words. So this list is also finite. It is also enormous, of course, but we are asked to ignore the practicalities.

Alongside every one of those sentences in the list there is a suitable response recorded. When we engage Aunt Bubbles in conversation we are therefore constrained to use one of the many sentences in her stored list, and she will then be able to respond with her pre-specified response.

Er ....

Except that, as I explained earlier, the meaning of a sentence is context dependent. That means that the meaning of each sentence which the user types, may change because we can vary the order of sentences typed by us before we present any particular sentence to it. Which also means that the single pre-specified response for any given sentence may not be appropriate on every occasion. So Aunt Bubbles is not going to do as well as Block thinks she will. If we carefully set up a context (about kites and birthday presents perhaps) and then ask the Gene Charniak question, Aunt Bubbles will get it wrong because she has only one fixed response per sentence.

When we engage with other conscious human beings in a conversation, we all rely on the other person having an understanding of context. Every joke that ever was, relies upon those who hear the joke being able to "get it" by linking up the apparent meaning of the words in the joke with some other meaning determined by context. That is what a joke is - it is the sudden discovery that there are alternative interpretations available when context is taken into account. But context dependency occurs all the time.

"They are doing Much Ado at the local town-hall. Shall we go?"

If the person who hears that statement does not know that "Much Ado" is an abbreviation of "Much Ado about Nothing" and that that is the title of a play written by William Shakespeare, then that sentence would appear to be an invitation to a very strange evening's entertainment. Additional contextual information would be the knowledge that "going" to a play means going to a building, paying money, sitting in a seat allocated to you and watching a performance on the stage. It also helps to know that a town-hall performance is not likely to be as impressive as one at Stratford on Avon.

I would like to know what response to that sentence Ned Block would program his Aunt Bubbles to say. And how about this exchange?

"*Clint Eastwood is on at the Odeon tonight.*"

"*I've got to wash my hair.*"

What's the connection and how is it that you know that?

Comment on these arguments

15.12

I find all three of these thought experiments impressive for their exuberant naivety. Not one of the systems proposed has the remotest possibility of performing in a satisfactory way under the scrutiny of a properly conducted Turing Test.

The crucial feature which they lack, is the ability to take into account the context dependency of meaning and the variety of contexts which can be determined by an extended dialogue. Pronominal reference is the feature which most often expresses some form of reference to a contextual entity or activity. But the context can be constructed in a great many different ways over what could be an extended period of time. Note that even although the length of the sentences may be limited, there is no limit on the number of sentences we may include within a conversation. Any given sentence in the finite list of sentences can be repeated an indefinite number of times. So the dialogue may be theoretically infinite and the number of permutations of these sentences is also potentially infinite.

The problem described by Gene Charniak is a good example. Note that to disambiguate the meaning of the pronoun "it" we need not only to understand the context relating to the buying of presents, but to understand also the rules of commerce which govern how the return of goods purchased might be conducted. The first is created by the foregoing dialogue. The second is knowledge of the world learned laboriously over what could be a period of years.

In our day-to-day lives, we engage in conversations with other people constantly. There are times when we may suspect that another person has not understood what we have been saying. Sometimes the other person will simply ask us to elaborate. At other times the response they give will seem to us odd or not relevant. In a sense then we are all engaged in conducting a properly conducted Turing test with those other people (and they of us). As a result of this testing procedure we invariably come to the conclusion that other people are conscious (as we are). What we cannot do, however, is to regard that conclusion as reliable if the conversation has lasted for only a few exchanges of short sentences and no attempt has been made to test the responses given. To come to the conclusion that that other person is conscious we must assure ourselves that the other person has sensory perceptions of various kinds, is able to process these to form an internal representation of external reality (similar to our own), that they are also able to demonstrate awareness of various other external realities (as we are) which may not have been mentioned at all during the dialogue, and that they are able to perform various actions designed to bring about what they regard as favourable results.

CHAPTER 16

More arguments

Jackson's knowledge argument

16.01

In 1982 Frank Jackson offered us an argument which purports to show that there are forms of knowledge which cannot be acquired without direct experience. It is sometimes called "The Knowledge Argument" [Jackson 1982]. He asks us to imagine a person called "Mary" who is a brilliant scientist but has been raised from birth in a monochrome world. She is restricted to viewing the external world by means of monochrome TV, and is able to read only monochrome books. It is not clear how she manages to avoid seeing the colours of her own skin, but we will let that pass for the sake of argument. Jackson argues that even if Mary studies the physical facts of colour vision and learns (in Jackson's words) - "*All there is to know about colour*", she will still not have had the experience of actually seeing any colours, until one day she is allowed to step outside her monochrome environment and WOW! she sees colours for the first time.

Her knowledge of colour includes knowledge of the physical mechanism of seeing colours as it is performed by the brain. She would therefore (Jackson says) be able to construct a computer model of a brain seeing colour. Despite that, there is still an additional form of knowledge that Mary cannot acquire until she steps out of the monochrome environment.

I find nothing in this argument with which I can disagree except the statement that Mary, before her emergence from the monochrome world

"*knows everything there is to know about colour*".

What Mary does NOT know and could therefore never build into her computer simulation of colour vision, is the mechanistic consequence of directly seeing colour at the phase-layer-1 level. She could construct detection units, which would respond to colour, but these would never be activated. If her computer simulation was able to create what I have described as the "*multi-dimensional fuzzball*" that fuzzball would not contain the three dimensions of colour because the relevant detection units would always remain without stimulation. If she was able to hook up her artificial model to a colour-sensitive TV system (in a way that she could not see herself) then her artificial colour vision system would be able to see colours. She would need to add extra bits to her model system to make it conscious of what it was seeing (in the way I have described in this book) but she herself would not see or be conscious of any of this. That is - her artificial system would experience colour but she herself would not. So she would still get a surprise and a new experience when she stepped out of her monochrome environment.

If Mary was able in some way to intervene in the mechanism of the artificial colour vision model, and change the relevant detection units to an active or stimulated status, by doing what computer programmers sometimes used to call "*a core alter*", then again the model would experience colour. But Mary would not see colour. Note that that is the case even if the artificial mechanism is operating within her own brain. Unless she altered more interconnections in a subtle way, the model she had created would not be feeding information to the part of her "being conscious" procedure.

Note: this misunderstanding is caused by thinking of consciousness as a static state or condition which pervades the whole brain.

To be able to see colour, without stepping outside her monochrome environment, Mary would need to intervene in the mechanism of her own brain, (perhaps by implanting micro-electrodes into her brain cells) and in that way forcing the relevant detection units into a false state of stimulation. Then she would see colours (if she had not during her years of captivity lost those important detection units).

However, if Mary were able to do that, she would encounter more difficulties. Colours are expressed not simply in terms of colour dimensions. They also have spatial dimensions and those dimensions need to be associated in the right way. Visible entities have locations within a two dimensional space spread out ahead. There is also a location discrepancy between the two eyes.

A sound, in contrast, envelops us, but it also has the dimensions of proximity and directionality, which are indicated by the time differential between the arrival of that sound at the two ears. If Mary interfered with all of that, using artificial stimulation to trick the brain into thinking that it was seeing colours or hearing sounds, she would need to get these all these components and associations right. There are probably more I have not thought of. Each has a unique blend of dimensions. I suspect that that unique blend determines the unique quality of an experience. I suggest that that is what a colour is - a unique blend of dimensions. If Mary got any of that wrong she could give herself an unusual form of synaesthesia.

All the signals within the brain are just action potentials travelling along axons, dendrites and crossing over synapse gaps - (or not crossing them as the case may be). So I suspect that even if Mary got some of her connections bit wrong, those signals, whatever source they had, if they are labelled as colours and were packaged with the dimensions appropriate for colours, would still be experienced as though they were colours which had been detected by the eyes.

My hypothesis has no difficulty in accommodating Jackson's knowledge argument. It throws up no anomalies. The problem, I think, is that Jackson has been fooled by his own words - that Mary "*knows everything there is to know about colour*". Fooled, that is, into thinking that the materialist explanation of consciousness implies that conscious knowledge is all that is required to build a model capable of having those qualia experiences. That is not a valid assumption. There is something extra needed. But that extra something does not need to be something supernatural. It is something which is hidden in the unconscious part of the mechanism - explicable in general terms at an analytic level, but not readily knowable in precise detail at a conscious level. I did warn that implementation of my proposed mechanism would be extremely difficult (see section 14.01).

Nagel and the Bats

16.02

In 1974 Thomas Nagel published a paper entitled "*What is it like to be a bat?*" [Nagel 1974]. And with that title he provided the mysterian school of thought (i.e. the proponents of the supernatural account of consciousness) with a useful form of words. The essence of the mysterian approach, is that subjective experience is "*ineffable*" - i.e. cannot be explained. That leaves them in a difficult position. How can you describe (or even just talk about) a condition which you claim is indescribable?

Nagel solved that problem by providing them with a phrase which describes what the condition is not. It is not nothing. By stating that they believe that there is something "*that it is like*" to be a conscious human being, or a bat, they can express the fact that without consciousness there is nothing that it is like to be in that condition.

Nagel did not use the term "*qualia*" himself, but he used the phrase "*something that it is like ...*" several times - and he said little else. This is what he said -

"But fundamentally an organism has conscious mental states if and only if there is something that it is like to be that organism - something that it is like for the organism.

We may call this the subjective character of experience. It is not captured by any of the familiar, recently devised reductive analyses of the mental, for all of them are logically compatible with its absence. It is not analyzable in terms of any explanatory system of functional states, or intentional states, since these could be ascribed to robots or automata that behave like people though they experience nothing [1]. It is not analysable in terms of the causal role of experiences in relation to human behaviour - for similar reasons. I do not deny that conscious mental states and events cause behaviour [2]*, nor that they may be given functional characteristics. I deny only that this kind of thing exhausts their analysis."*

[Nagel 1974]

I added the numbers in brackets because I note that there appears to be a self-contradiction in these quoted words. He claims the possibility of robots or automata that behave like people though they experience nothing [1]. But he also concedes that *"conscious state or events cause behaviour"* [2].

If consciousness can cause certain types of behaviour, and robots automata have no consciousness, how could an unconscious robot or automaton perform the actions that in a conscious person are caused by that person being conscious?

Zombies

16.03

The claim that human behaviour can be replicated in every detail by a robot or automaton, which has no consciousness at all, is disputed. It is also one of the main arguments offered against a materialist or natural explanation of consciousness. A robot which is able to do that is called "a zombie". The main proponent of zombie-ism is David Chalmers. Others, myself included, say that zombie-ism is impossible.

Chalmers is Professor and Director of the Centre for Consciousness at the Autralian National University, visiting Professor of Philosophy at New York University, author of books on consciousness, editor of the Philosophy of Mind series of books by Oxford University Press (OUP), editor of Philosophy of Mind a collection of important papers (also published by OUP), a member of the editorial boards of a number of academic journals devoted to the topic of consciousness and the organiser of a large Internet database of publications on consciousness. Chalmers is therefore an influential figure on the topic of consciousness.

16.04

For Chalmers, the possibility of zombie-ism is a central pillar of his argument for claiming that materialism is wrong. It is important therefore that we examine the idea in some detail. Unfortunately that is not an easy thing to do for his arguments tend to be verbose and to identify a bewildering variety of philosophical positions separated only by hair-splitting distinctions. Any attempt to offer a counter-argument usually ends up like the result of a shell game. What you thought was the position he was defending turns out to be the wrong one. Chalmers has, for example, identified eight different ways in which we can use the word "conceivable", three different types of materialism and three different types of dualism. I leave it to the reader to work out how many different individual positions that can generate. But the *conceivability* of zombies is the foundation on which his argument is based. Not, you must understand, the conceivability of zombies in *this* universe, but the conceivability of these things *in some other possible* universe (which he also finds conceivable). I quote -

"The most straightforward form of the conceivability argument against materialism runs as follows -

1. P&~Q is conceivable
2. If P&~Q is conceivable, P&~Q is metaphysically possible
3. If P&~Q is metaphysically possible, materialism is false.
----
4. Materialism is false.

Here P is the conjunction of all microphysical truths about the universe, specifying the fundamental features of every fundamental microphysical entity in the language of physics, as well as the microphysical laws. Q is an arbitrary phenomenal truth: perhaps the truth that someone is phenomenally conscious, or perhaps the truth that a certain individual (that is, an individual satisfying a certain description) instantiates a certain phenomenal property. P&~Q ("P and not Q") conjoins the former with the denial of the latter."

[Chalmers 2010]

318

The crucial line in that argument above is line 2 which asserts that if something is conceivable then it is possible. This assertion is about the conjunction P&~Q, but from my point of view that is irrelevant. It could be as readily made about a single proposition which for simplicity we could call "X". Therefore, according to Chalmers -

(A): conceivable(X) => possible(X)

Where the symbol "=>" means "implies". I dispute that assertion. The grounds on which I object are that conceivability (in any of the diverse forms Chalmers identifies), is not a universal property. It expresses a relationship between some entity and its context. "X is conceivable" does not inform us of an intrinsic property of any X. It is a property of X within the mind of a particular person (called "Y" say).

So what we should write is

(B): In MIND(Y) {conceivable(X) => possible(X)}

I can accept that that proposition as true for some meanings of the word "conceivable". For some other readings of "conceivable" (B) is not true. I can, for example, "conceive" (in one sense of the word) of a two dimensional circular triangle, which is obviously an impossible object since the properties it specifies are logically incompatible. And yet I conceived that idea. I thought of it and I formulated those words and so, in a sense, I conceived the idea. For another reading of the word "conceivable" the phrase "*X is conceivable*" is synonymous with the phrase "*X is possible*". The proposition (B) then becomes a tautology.

16.05

However, for all readings, the word "conceivable" cannot properly be applied to an entity, or to a proposition, in isolation from its context. If we try to do that - that is, if we try to turn a property which describes the relationship between something and its context, into an intrinsic property of the entity, then we can get absurd and even comical results. That was well understood by Stephen Leacock, the Canadian humourist, who wrote a spoof adventure story about an intrepid explorer trekking across the desert. Suddenly a *solitary* horseman appeared on the horizon and rode towards our hero. Then another, and another, and so on, until our hero was entirely surrounded by a huge jostling crowd of *solitary* horsemen.

"Conceivable" is a word like "solitary". It tells us not very much about "X" but it does tell us a good deal about the relationship between "X" and its context (other horsemen or the mind of some other person).

I am not sure how to react to the qualification that the possibility Chalmers refers to is "*metaphysically*" possible. I take the view, as David Hume once put it, that metaphysics should be "committed to the flames". I take that view for much the same reason as I dismiss the idea of the supernatural. If there is enough evidence to justify belief in a thing's existence, then it should be classified as a natural (or physical) phenomenon.

16.06

Chalmers' view is that a metaphysically possible entity is an entity which, while it might not be possible in this universe which has the known physical laws, it might be possible in some other universe where the physical laws are different.*

"*There is little reason to believe that zombies exist in the actual world. But many hold that they are at least conceivable: we can coherently imagine zombies, and there is no contradiction in the idea that reveals itself even on reflection. As an extension of the idea, many hold that the same goes for a <u>zombie world</u>: a universe physically similar to ours, but in which there is no consciousness.*"

[Chalmers 2002]

The concept of a possible universe is another of those concepts (like conceivability) which is context dependent and once again the context is defined by a person's mind. The concept of possibility is related to the concept of probability. To say that something is possible is equivalent to stating that its probability is non-zero. When we talk about the probability of an event (or its possibility), we are actually talking about the reasonable prior expectation which a person has of that particular occurrence. We are not talking about something that necessarily has an actual existence. Indeed, if there is evidence of its existence, then probability is not relevant. If it has occurred then its existence (or at least the existence of the evidence) is a certainty.

Once we have recognised that the context within which these statements about possible universes and the conceivability of zombies are located is within a particular mind, the significance of the statement as a basis for general arguments about consciousness loses force. We can no longer argue with any validity that the zombie idea is possible merely on the opinion of a particular person. Some supporting evidence or a supporting logical argument is required.

* Note: the idea that the laws of nature, science or the universe, are all known and fixed, is naive. The known laws are in a constant state of flux - of modification and of upgrade.

16.07

Chalmers uses statements with logical form and the symbolism of the (P&~Q) format. When he says "P&~Q is conceivable", what he means is "zombie-ism is conceivable". "P" represents the physical properties which the zombie has (the zombies overt behaviour) and Q represents the non-physical properties which he associates with consciousness. In using that expression, he is therefore making the prior assumption that consciousness requires those non-physical properties. The possibility of P&~Q means that the existence of a zombie - having all the physical characteristics of a conscious person but lacking (what he believes are) the crucial non-physical characteristics of consciousness, is possible - behaving like a conscious person but not being conscious nevertheless. By introducing that factor "Q" and also its negation, Chalmers complicates and confuses the real issue.

My contention is that zombie-ism is impossible. I hold that there are some forms of human behaviour which require consciousness. I believe that consciousness, when tested properly, cannot be faked. In that view, the presence or absence of Q, in the expression above, is irrelevant. By introducing it into his argument Chalmers risks relying on circular logic. The validity of his opening statement depends on the validity of his conclusion.

Pinker's argument

16.08

Steven Pinker relates how the philosopher George Rey once told him that due to a boyhood accident with a bicycle he had lost all consciousness - that he himself (i.e. George Rey) was a zombie.

"*I assume*," writes Pinker, "*he is speaking tongue-in-cheek, but of course I have no way of knowing, and that is his point.*"

[Pinker 1997 p 147]

I do not think so Professor Pinker. You do not just *assume* that he is talking tongue-in-cheek. You know very well that he is talking tongue-in-cheek. So does every other person who reads those words. The real point is this - why is it that you can be so sure that Rey is joking?

I'll give you the answer. Consider this, how could a zombie, which once was conscious, know that it had lost consciousness? To do that it would need to be able to remember that it had been conscious and would therefore know what it was like to be conscious. So how could a real zombie, for which *there is nothing that it is like*, do that? How could it remember *what it was like* to have the subjective experience of conscious, while there *was nothing that it was like* to be in its currently zombified condition?

That is an example of the many pitfalls that await a fake zombie and which seem to have been overlooked by members of the zombie fan-club (with or without reflection). A real zombie would not know what it is like to have what he is not supposed to have. In order to know when you are supposed to be conscious or otherwise, you have to be conscious. He would also find it impossible to know what *it was going to be like* in the event of some predictable future experience.

16.09

In another book Pinker tried to sum up how a zombie-robot could be programmed.

"The way the elements in the processor are wired up would cause them to sense and copy pieces of representations, in a way that mimics the rules of reasoning. With many thousands of representations and a set of somewhat more sophisticated processors (perhaps different kinds of representations and processors for different kinds of thinking) you might have a genuinely intelligent brain or computer. Add an eye that can detect certain contours in the world and turn on representations that symbolise them, and muscles that can act on the world whenever certain representations symbolising goals are turned on, and you have a behaving organism (or a TV camera and a set of levels and wheels), and you have a robot.

This, in a nutshell, is the theory of thinking called "the physical symbol system hypothesis" or the "computational" or "representational" theory of mind. It is as fundamental to cognitive science as the cell doctrine is to biology and plate tectonics is to geology. Cognitive scientists are trying to figure out what kinds of representations and processors the brain has. But there are ground rules that must be followed at all times: no little men inside, and no peeking. The representations that one posits in the mind have to be arrangements of symbols, and the processor has to be a device with a fixed set of reflexes, period."

[Pinker 1994 p77-78]

No. I think that "*period*" is the wrong word. A better word would be "*comma*". I admit that the quoted words above constitutes not a bad brief summary of my own proposed system - but only as far as phase-layer-1 is concerned. A sophisticated conscious robot, which mimicked human behaviour, would require much much more.

Memory for example. The system needs to have a memory. It needs two kinds of memory - a short-term memory to hold current events, and a longer-term memory which is selective to act as a repository of information about the past. That's what phase-layer-2 does. Phase-layer-3 adds concept formation (by processing the longer-term memory) and the ability to utilise those concepts to construct an interpretation of events which may never have occurred before. These concepts do the job of detection units - but for the recognition of *learned* features of the environment. The system fits those concepts together to build an interpretation of these new events. That is needed to understand these events and predict what will happen next.

Phase-layer-4 provides the system with the ability to model itself and its own motivation. It needs to understand its own role in these predicted events if its predictions are to be accurate. The construction of that self-model is the procedure which I believe is the "being conscious" procedure.

In the quotation above, the phrase "*a fixed set of reflexes*" is another point where Pinker goes seriously wrong. For a human-like performance, a robotic system would need to be able to accommodate the way meaning changes as context changes. It would also need to be able to anticipate its own behaviour in response to predicted and very variable future events. I say that zombie-ism is impossible. Here's why.

The Reverse Zombie Argument.

16.10

Let us (for the sake of argument), assume that zombie-ism is possible. Let us also say that we have overcome the practical difficulties and been able to construct a robotic system according to the scheme of my proposed system. That is important. My argument works only if we know exactly what is going on inside when the robot responds to our test questions. Let us call this new robot "Z". We then test Z using a Properly Conducted Turing Test (PCTT) and Z passes that test convincingly.

In order to be able to use language as I have proposed, Z must have some concept (or meaning structure) associated with every single word in the language. In previous chapters I addressed the problem of how meaning structure or representations of various words might be constructed - including some very awkward examples like "justice" and "representation". Assuming that we manage all that as suggested, we then approach the crux of the matter. How could we teach Z what the word "consciousness" means?

16.11

Consider this - we all think that we know what consciousness is and yet most writers on the topic begin their papers and books on the topic by apologising for _not_ being able to tell us what consciousness is. The solution to this imbroglio is to explain consciousness by relating it to actual experiences.

"Remember when you saw that red sunset?"

"Remember when you touched that hot stove?"

"Remember when you were able to smell the scent of those roses?"

And how would Z interpret this statement -

"Remember when there was something that it was like for you to smell roses?"

So the concept of consciousness - the meaning of the word "consciousness" - is taught by making reference to internally stored memories of subjective conscious experiences. Note that Z will indeed have stored memories of the occasions when these experiences occurred.

All this is what we do for other human beings. We teach them what we mean by conscious experience by making reference to previous experience. Unfortunately, when we are dealing with other human beings we can only assume that they have these internal memories of subjective conscious experiences. In the case of Z however, we know exactly how Z operates. He does have these internal stores. We know that. We can print them out and read all that stuff. It might take a very long time to do that but it is possible (and I don't need a convoluted argument based on conceivability or alternative universes to know that it is possible).

In addition to teaching Z what "*consciousness*" means, we also must teach him what "*knowing*" means and what "*honesty*" means. Earlier, I explained how the system might represent the concept of "truth". It would do that in terms of a procedure which could compare two structures - a TEST structure, which in this case would be the interpretation structure of a given sentence and a REFERENCE structure which in this case would be the representation of reality produced from its sensory perceptions after being processed by the phase-layer-1 mechanism of detection units and action units.

That being so, we can envisage an extra feature for this particular example of Z. We could add circuitry so that when the result of that mental comparison (when targeted at his own utterances) was positive, his nose would light up green. And when the same test produced a negative result, his nose would shine red. Red for a lie, green for the truth. We might also experiment with flashing amber lights when Z was not sure.

Anyway, the crucial test would come when we asked him if he believes that he himself is conscious. Z would interpret that question using the definitions of consciousness that he has, and by consulting the storage of internal data about his recorded experiences. He would then be bound to answer "Yes".

What is more - his nose would tell us that he *believes* that he is telling the truth.

So what kind of thing is it, that would honestly believe that it is conscious, while it is not actually conscious?

I would say that that thing is a logical contradiction. How could we say that a human being is not conscious if he believed honestly (according to his understanding of honesty and of consciousness) that he is conscious. That would contradict what consciousness is.

Since it is, as the mysterians constantly remind us, a subjective experience, consciousness is a self-validating entity. Z has to be the final arbiter of his own consciousness so long as he does that for sound reasons, and in the case of a zombie, which we have created, we can check that his reasons are sound. We can even have those reasons printed out for our inspection.

16.12

Note: The idea of adding extra circuitry to the mechanism so that it gives an indication when it is telling what it believes to be the truth, was added in order to counter the objection that I am asking the reader "*merely to take the robot's word that he is conscious*". The criticism implied is that those words are produced by recitation of a prepared speech - as from a tape recorder.

That is a misrepresentation of my argument. But it is also a response which I know from past experience is often produced by sceptics. Those critics tend to make simple-minded assumptions about the internal operation of procedures and tend also not to check that these assumptions do not contradict assumptions, which have been made at another time and context, to solve another problem. The contradiction in this case arises from the difficulty of ensuring that a robot's responses correspond to other known events. Would a robot know whether or not to claim that he was consciously aware of seeing some object if we know from the study of CCTV footage that he (or it) had never at anytime been in a position to observe the said object. Would he know, in advance of events, *what it would be like* to have an experience? Zombie-enthusiasts do not extend their reflections to include validity checks of that kind being carried out.

Note that the new honesty-revealing circuitry can be constructed so that it is not under any kind of control by the robot's brain mechanism. It just happens. He cannot prevent his nose turning red or green. We can think of it as a kind of involuntary blush. We could also obtain a similar insight into the robot's integrity by forcing it to print out the entire contents of its on-going mechanism. We are also in a position to test the validity of the new circuitry with a set of test questions for which the truth is known.

Note: with the advent of brain scanning equipment we are fast approaching a situation where we will be able to have the kind of insight into the truth-status of the thinking of a real person. There are already indications that when a person lies or tells the truth, different parts of the brain are activated.

From previous experience of trying to present this reverse zombie argument to sceptics I have learned that the sceptic seldom reads my description of the mechanism in any detail (if at all). They skip that bit because they have already formed the opinion that consciousness has nothing at all to do with mechanism and conclude that reading about the detail of a proposed mechanism must be a waste of time. That's what is called being a prisoner of your own prejudices. So the significance of the fact that for this robot we are in a position to know what is going on inside, seems to escape them. Having avoided reading and understanding the nature of the Z mechanism, the sceptic is, it seems, still harbouring a suspicion, or a mistaken dogmatic certainty, that we are dealing with a robot which is uttering fixed responses from a pre-written script. That is not the case. The mechanism is as I have described it. Consciousness, in my view, is the mechanism that allows the brain to escape the limitations of a pre-written script.

A red or green nose, however, is rather more difficult to ignore (or to pretend to ignore). I think that the logic of the conclusion is equally hard to ignore. Zombie-ism is impossible.

16.13

I find it difficult to leave this topic without returning to the arguments offered us by David Chalmers, the most prominent advocate of the zombie idea. He is also the person who introduced the terminology of the Explanatory Gap and the Hard Problem. In recently published book of his "The Character of Consciousness" I found these words -

"What makes the hard problem hard and almost unique is that it goes beyond problems about the performance of functions. To see this, note that even when we have explained the performance of all the cognitive and behavioural functions in the vicinity of experience - perceptual discrimination, categorization, internal access, verbal report - a further unanswered question may remain: why is the performance of these functions accompanied by experience. A simple explanation of the function leaves this question open."

[Chalmers 2012 p8]

Note these words - "*... why is the performance of these functions accompanied by experience?"*

And then compare it with this question - *"How could a kinetically energetic molecule feel hot?"*

It's the same question. Once again we are wandering about inside the mechanism (like Leibnitz in his mill-sized brain), seeing the physical components of that brain mechanism working together. We are also, apparently, expecting to be able to see the external events which are caused by that mechanism, in operation inside, as if they were also components of the mechanism or floating alongside in order to "experience" events like pleasure, pain, etc. for no practical reason whatsoever.

Quantum Mechanics

16.14

In recent years a new idea about consciousness has emerged. This one suggests that the solution to the problem of consciousness lies somewhere in the mysteries of quantum mechanics. The logic underlying this approach is curious. It seems that (for some people) if we are faced with a problem we cannot explain, the solution should be sought in something else we cannot explain. That is not an idea I find even remotely persuasive.

The best known advocates of this idea about quantum mechanics are Stuart Hameroff and Roger Penrose.

Hameroff

16.15

Stuart Hameroff is an anaesthetist. He noted that several different general anaesthetic substances can block consciousness despite not having any obvious chemical similarity in their molecular structure. He has argued that the way these molecules act cannot be by chemical reaction but could be related to the physical presence of those different (and often large) molecules inside microtubules in the cytoplasm of cells. Microtubules are tiny tubular structures which are thought to form a kind of skeletal support structure for cells. They may also act as conduits which conduct various molecules to the site of their chemical action and they are known to be involved in the separation of chromosomes during cell division. Hameroff has suggested that the anaesthetic effect is due to the way these anaesthetic molecules block or in some other way interfere with the role these microtubules have in the conscious condition.

Penrose

16.16

Roger Penrose is an eminent mathematician with an impressive background in cosmology. In a book "The Emperor's New Mind" (ENM) he attacked the idea of artificial intelligence and advanced a theory that crucial abilities, notably possessed by mathematicians like himself ("mathematical insight"), enable one to arrive at reliable conclusions using non-algorithmic procedures which defy replication in computers. In support of this contention he developed a complicated argument based on Godel's Theorem [Penrose 1989]. Godel's Theorem is one of the most abstruse mathematical arguments ever devised. However, Penrose's treatment of Godel's ideas seemed somewhat suspect even to someone, like myself, without specialist knowledge of mathematics. Penrose developed the argument further in a second book entitled "Shadows of the Mind" (SOTM).

The distinction between algorithmic and non-algorithmic procedures is important because it is known that if a procedure is algorithmic, it must be possible to program a computer to perform that procedure. The central point of Penrose's thesis is that the human brain is capable of some forms of thinking which cannot be replicated by a computer. There are no known examples of non-algorithmic procedures. Indeed, it is difficult to understand how the existence of such a thing could ever be demonstrated without (in the process of explaining it) converting it into an algorithmic procedure.

Penrose's Godelian argument

16.17

Subsequently, in a review of SOTM, Penrose's Godelian argument has been heavily criticised by Feferman - an acknowledged expert on Godel's Theorm and an authority to whom Penrose himself referred and deferred in the development of his argument. After a long and detailed analysis of several technical mistakes in Penrose's treatment (in SOTM) Feferman writes -

"I have not detailed all the occurrences of technical errors that Penrose makes in connection with Godel's Incompleteness theorems in Ch2, many of which propagate through Ch 3. Given the weight that Penrose attached to his Godelian argument, all these errors should give one pause. One has here lots of more of the "slapdash scholarship" that Martin Davis complained about in his commentary on EMH (1993, p116) and they suggest that Penrose may stretch that scholarship perilously thin in areas distant from his own experise. The main question, though, is whether these errors undermine the conclusion that he wishes to draw from the Goldelian argument. I don't think that they do, at least in themselves. This is, I think that the extended case Penrose

makes from section 2.6 on through the end of Ch 3 would be unaffected if he put the logical facts right; but the merits of the case are another matter."

[Feferman 1995]

16.18

Although Feferman declares himself to a sceptic on the issue of machine intelligence he also adds these words -

"How is it that they [mathematicians] actually arrive at proof is through a marvellous combination of heuristic reasoning, insight and inspiration (building of course, on prior knowledge and experience) for which there are no general rules, though some patterns have been discerned by Polya and others; there is no formula for mathematical success. It is only when one arrives at a proof that one can check (mechanically in principle, but not in practice) that it does indeed establish the theorem in question."

Fererman's reference to heuristics, in that second quotation, is interesting. A heuristic is an algorithmic procedure which will often yield valid results but is not guaranteed to do so. This contradicts the claim made by Penrose about the unfailing reliability of mathematical insight,

In a forthright online article called "Penrose is Wrong", Drew McDermott listed a number of famous occasions when the mathematics community was fooled into believing a particular conclusion, which was later shown by formal proof procedures, to be unsound [McDermott 1995].

16.19

I cannot claim to have spotted any technical mistakes in Penrose's detailed treatment of Godel's theorem. But I did feel uncomfortable as I read it - mainly because it appeared to me to be irrelevant and because the claims he makes for his argument seem overblown. It seemed to me that we are being asked, by Penrose, in a very convoluted way (obscured behind a fog of daunting mathematical symbolism) to accept that non-algorithmic procedures exist merely because, in some circumstances, for some thought process, these cannot be proven conclusively to be algorithmic - proof by absence of disproof.

In Chapter 4 of ENM Penrose gives a very long analysis of Godel's theorem (plus extensions). But it is not until chapter 10 that he starts to draw conclusions. The chapters between 4 and 10 are filled with discussions covering almost every esoteric concept in mathematical physics imaginable.

And then, in chapter 10, Penrose writes -

"As I have stated earlier, a good part of the reason for believing that consciousness is able to influence truth-judgements in a non-algorithmic way stems from consideration of Godel's Theorem."

[Penrose 1989 p416]

I could not see that. What I could see was that in chapter 4 he had not actually proven that result at all. He had merely asserted the result. That assertion, moreover, did not "arise" from consideration of Godel's Theorem at all. It was squeezed into the middle of a discussion about Godel's theorem. See for example page 110 where he says -

"All this shows that the mental procedures whereby mathematicians arrive at their judgements of truth are not simply rooted in the procedures of some specific formal system. We see the validity of the Godel proposition $P_k(k)$ though we cannot derive it from the axioms."

What he has not mentioned is the fact that it is quite easy to create additional axioms that do indeed allow the formal proof, and that, as Feferman suggested, the use of heuristic algorithms is also a possibility.

So far as I could discern, the stuff about Godel's Theorem was acting only as the verbal equivalent of bubble plastic. It enveloped and protected his (unproven) assertion from close scrutiny.

The Penrose/Hameroff Thesis

16.20

Anyway, Penrose and Hameroff have joined forces and have jointly advanced a theory that within the microtubules in nerve cells, various quantum effects can take place which would enable information to pass from one nerve cell to another over distances which, according to experts in quantum physics, are improbable. The Penrose/Hameroff idea is that the network of microtubules can act like a second QM-brain within the conventional brain.

However, there are two things about that idea that are really odd.

16.21

First: Even if it turns out to be true, that there is a QM-brain operating within our ordinary macro-brains, the implication would be that the mechanism of consciousness is still just a physical mechanism, albeit at the micro-QM level.

Although attempts to construct QM computers are now taking place, there is as yet no suggestion or hint that they would be able to do anything more than conventional computers are able to do (but at blindingly fast speeds).

Second: Even if a secondary QM computer does exist and is able to process information, it is still clear that the information which it needs to process, depends upon, and is obtained from, the known physical mechanisms of the brain, such as the mechanism of our sensory perceptions. Close your eyes and the conscious aspect of the QM-brain (if it exists) shuts down as firmly as the other known macro-brain.

It is also clear that the known physical mechanisms of the brain also process all that information, and distribute the results of that analysis over all parts the macro-brain. Further - when the macro-brain initiates action, it again acts at a cellular level, to make muscles contract.

So even if there is a QM-brain acting alongside the macro-brain, how does it get information about what the macro-brain is doing? And how does it intervene to ensure that its own decisions are put into effect? Within the macro-brain each cell or synapse contains only a tiny fraction of the knowledge possessed by the whole brain. Does the information pass between the two brains at the level of individual cells, groups of cells, or at some superior all encompassing brain level?

Blindspot

16.22

How is it, for example, that I can demonstrate to my conscious self that there is a blind-spot in the retina of my eyes? Take a sheet of paper. Place a small black dot in the centre of the page. Close one eye and then move the focus of your attention to one side. At one particular point, a few centimetres left or right (depending upon which eye you are using and the distance between your eye and the page), the black dot will disappear. That is because there is a spot in your retina where there are no retinal cells. That is where the nerve fibres dive through the retina to get back to the rest of the brain.

To be able to see that effect (and see it consciously), information about what the macro-brain is observing would need to be passed to the QM-brain from the macro-brain at the level of individual cells. But an individual cell "knows" only one tiny snippet of the information which the macro-brain processes. That processing, as we have seen earlier, involves inter-cell connections which progressively group information into bundles and eventually into concepts. Does the QM-brain do the same? And when it has completed its analysis how does the QM-brain then intervene to force the macro-brain to take action? Does my QM-brain tweak my muscles into action without consultation with my macro-brain?

I stand ready to be corrected, but I predict that no one will be able to show that the presence of a visual blindspot can be consciously detected in a remembered visual scene (if the presence of a blindspot was not detected in the original experience) - even in people with eidetic memory.

16.23

From Penrose's viewpoint the QM-brain idea is attractive because it provides him with a potential locus where his non-algorithmic procedures could be performed (in some unexplained way), but there is a serious problem about the means of information exchange between it and the macro-brain which needs to be addressed before the QM-brain idea can be taken seriously.

16.24

NOTE: Providing an explanation for one mystery by suggesting that it is buried out of sight inside another and equally obscure mystery, seems an odd way to try to "explain" anything.

Higher Order Theories

16.25

The on-going debate about consciousness has recently acquired yet another talking point - the so-called Higher-Order Theories (or HOT). The basic idea seems to be that one part of the brain can "observe" another. In the jargon, the part, which does the observing, is called a "Higher Order" mechanism.

I have reservations about that word "*observe*". I think it has more than one meaning. If we are talking about a person observing the external world then the act of observation can refer to two linked procedures –

(1) The acquisition of information (from the external world).

(2) The processing of that information to gain an understanding about the external world.

However, used formally the word can refer exclusively to the first of these operations while used informally it can refer mainly to the second procedure.

"*She observed that he seemed unsure*".

In that example we are not told what it was that she actually saw. Was it body language? Was it the movement of his eyes? Or was it a tone of voice? What we are told, however, is the conclusion that she came to as a result. It would appear therefore that the second procedure is definitely included. In some cases the word "observe" can also mean that some statement has been made. These distinctions are not always made in discussions about HOT theories.

When we are talking about a process of observation taking place inside the brain itself, it is not clear what mechanism is supposed to be capable of observation in the first sense. There are no eyes, finger tips, ears, noses or taste buds inside the brain by means of which one part of the brain could gather information about what another part is doing. And even if information could be transferred from one part to another, it is not clear what that second (observing) part can do with the information which could not have been done by the first (observed) part.

In my own account I was careful to describe the procedure which I describe as taking place as the *"construction of a representation"*. In that process, concept structures are fitted together and that representation then is a model of what is happening. It contains a representation of what is happening now, what did happen in the recent past, what is predicted is likely to happen in the near future – and, crucially, what should be done about that to achieve a GOAL state. These consequent aspects of the representation do not need to be calculated as part of a secondary process. Constructing that representation is also the process of understanding.

In an early draft of my book I did use the word "observe". That was an informal use of the word. But when I realised how easily that phraseology could be misunderstood I changed my wording. The informal use of the word "observe" is appropriate only if it is interpreted as a reference to the way concepts representing SELF and SELFMIND are used as components in that construction. In that informal sense the behaviour of these components is *"observed"*.

16.26

Anyway, according to Chalmers the central idea in HOT Theories is that -

"A mental state M is phenomenally conscious if and only if a subject has a higher-order thought about M.

Here a higher-order thought about M should be understood as a thought by the subject with the content 'I am in M'. The thesis will usually be modified and qualified in some way. For example Rosenthal holds that for M to be conscious, the higher-order thought must be brought about in the right sort of way and in particular must be noninferential thought."

[Chalmers 2010]

No attempt is made here to describe how the concept of "i" could be formed, what "I am in M" could really mean, or who or what sentient being is having the thought "I am in M".

Note too the assumption in that quotation above, that we are talking about "*mental states*" and that what we are considering is "*phenomenal consciousness*" (as distinct from "*access consciousness*" which is physical and mechanistic). These assumptions mean that the discussion of HOT ideas must avoid all mention of mechanism if it is to avoid admitting the falsity of these subtle assumptions.

16.27

Despite an apparently superficial similarity concerning self-observation, (a similarity brought about by the ambiguity of the word "*observe*") I find it difficult to relate these ideas to my own. To read these accounts is to be enveloped in a fog of circumlocution. One gets a feeling that one is in an aeroplane which is endlessly circling an airfield while the captain tells the passengers that they will be landing shortly and what weather can be expected. But somehow the craft remains airborne and never quite manages to get its undercarriage on the ground.

Meanwhile theories are analysed into a myriad sub-categories based on tiny distinctions. What is never analysed, however, is that all of these are wrong and for the same obvious reason. A non-material entity cannot communicate with a material entity without thereby re-classifying itself as a material entity.

Hidden within these discussions of HOT theories, is the never-quite-stated assumption that when one procedure observes another one or other of them (or perhaps both) becomes conscious. Exactly how this happens or what being phenomenally conscious means, is a question, which is not even addressed, let alone explained. Instead it is thrust away as "The Hard Problem" for someone else to explain.

Consciousness as an emergent property.

16.28

Those who hold, as I do, that the explanation for consciousness will involved some kind of materialist mechanistic description, often respond to questions about what consciousness is, by saying that it is an "*emergent property*" of the brain mechanism. I do not dispute that claim, but I do think that it is an inadequate response. To see that that is so, we need to consider what an emergent property really is.

In popular parlance it is often claimed that when one is dealing with a very complex mechanism,

"*The whole is greater than the sum of the parts*".

I understand the reasons why people say that, but it is a slipshod idea. The whole of any complex system can never really be greater than the sum of its parts. If not from the parts or from the relationships between those parts, where can the extra property come from? What we do often find, however, is that an emergent property is one which is distributed so widely and so finely, that we have trouble observing it at the level of individual parts and their inter-relationships. So the explanation for those emergent properties is in there at a fundamental level, we just don't see it easily and are surprised by the result. The reason why I find that is inadequate as an explanation, however, is that what property will emerge from those basic properties cannot be predicted unless we do know what the basic properties are, and that is often a very complicated process indeed. We know for example that the chemical properties of various substances can be attributed to the properties of atoms and sub-atomic particles at the quantum level. But actually doing the calculations which demonstrate that, is nearly always much too difficult to contemplate trying. The behaviour of the hydrogen atom can be shown by application of quantum mechanics, to depend upon its electron orbits. But hydrogen has the simplest of all atomic structures. Doing the same thing for more complex atomic structures is not a practical thing to try.

I do not see how calling consciousness an "*emergent property*" gets us very far or explains anything. Consciousness must, obviously, be an emergent property. But having said that we cannot relate the subjective experience of consciousness to the fundamental properties of physical brain components or to the procedure these components carry out. My explanation does that.

Dennett's Multiple Drafts Model

16.29

Daniel Dennett is the best known exponent of a natural explanation of consciousness. He is also the archenemy of the advocates of supernatural accounts and a vociferous critic of those zombie arguments. His book "Consciousness Explained" [Dennett 1991] is frequently cited as a flag-bearer for natural explanations of consciousness.

The explanation which he advanced in that book is called "The Multiple Drafts Model". The basic idea is that within the brain a great many different and semi-independent processes operate simultaneously and compete for attention within a global workspace or working memory. That there is a multiplicity of things happening simultaneously in the brain, is an established fact. However, according to the Dennett thesis, it is, apparently, that competing multiplicity which constitutes consciousness. In another, later book, "Sweet Dreams" he called this idea the "*Fame in the Brain*" model [Dennett 2005]. The analogy suggests that those several procedures are all shouting for attention and whichever one shouts loudest, gets the attention of ... of what exactly? That is not explained. After discussing the idea of "fame" in terms of appearance on television, he remarks ...

16.30

"The basic idea is that consciousness is more like fame than television; it is not a special 'medium of representation' in the brain into which content-bearing events must be transduced in order to become conscious. As Kanwisher (2001) aptly emphasises: 'the neural correlates of awareness of a given perceptual attribute are found in the very neural structure that perceptually analyses that attribute.' Instead of switching media or going somewhere in order to become conscious, heretofore unconscious contents, staying right where they are, can achieve something rather like fame in competition with other fame-seeking (or just potentially fame-finding) contents. And according to this view, that is what consciousness is."

[Dennett 2005]

That sounds as if Dennett and Kanwisher are in agreement with the idea expressed above, that it is the construction of a representation that constitutes understanding. However, I still do not get the analogy with fame.

16.31

The statement "X is famous" does not describe an entity called "X". It describes the mental attitude of other entities - a collective "Y" say - and the regard the member of "Y" have for "X". See sections 12.05 and 12.35 for an explanation of how I think we could construct a representation of "society". I am struggling, however, to identify what it is that Dennett thinks modifies the properties of Y when X is able to become famous (in the mind of Y). It cannot be that he is suggesting that when all those other procedures are clamouring for attention (for themselves), each of them possesses a mind of its own. Dennett recognises and comments on the issue in a way that I find puzzling.

"There is no literal searchlight of attention, so we need to explain away this seductive metaphor by explaining the functional

powers of attention-grabbing without presupposing a single attention giving source. This means we need to address two questions. Not just (1) How is this fame in the brain achieved? but also (2) And Then What Happens? - which I have called the Hard Question (Dennett 1991, p255). One may postulate activity in one neural structure or another as the necessary and sufficient condition for consciousness, but one must then take on the burden of explaining why <u>that</u> activity ensures the political power of the events it involves - and that means taking a good hard look at how the relevant differences in competence might be enabled by changes in status in the brain."

[Dennett 2005 p138]

In the same book, two pages later, he makes this comment -

"... whether or not you become famous can depend on what is going on <u>elsewhere</u> at the same time."

I am also puzzled by the lack of any distinction between the "being conscious" procedure itself, and the content of consciousness (i.e. what the process is conscious of). When a person becomes famous, something new happens within the minds of all the people with whom he or she becomes famous. As a consequence something new also happens to the behaviour of those people. If we are to explain consciousness then we have to describe those new somethings. In particular we have to explain the new behaviour which is engendered

Behaviour is an important consideration because that is what provides natural selection with something to be selected. Without behavioural effects, changes in the brain (or any part of our anatomy), could not be grist to the mill of evolution.

Anyway, it is the collection of these new somethings which constitute fame, together with a famous individual's awareness of that fact. Without doubt there is a multiplicity of unconscious perceptions which are potentially capable of becoming the content of conscious awareness. But there has to be a mechanism which makes that happen and we need to know what it is that happens.

16.32

In the paper to which Dennett refers in that quotation above, Kanwisher describes the identification of particular locations within the brain which seemed to be specifically concerned with the identification and analysis of certain classes of perceptions. A good example is the area concerned with the perception of human faces and the (assumed) emotions (predictors of action) associated with certain facial expressions. A measurable activation within these locations, she explained, did not only correlate with conscious awareness of those perceptions but also with the perception itself. Under certain conditions, when exposure to the visual images of faces was restricted or masked by other, longer-lasting images (which, for example, had no associated emotional expression), her team were able to demonstrate that a brain response to the perception, was not necessarily accompanied by a report of conscious awareness at all. A momentary brain reaction was recorded, but the test subject did not report any conscious awareness of the first (masked) image.

Nevertheless, it could also be demonstrated that that fleeting unconscious response to the masked or obscured image, did have an effect on subsequent behaviour. That indicates that the existence of that brief response was accessible, in some way, to the rest of the brain mechanism.

16.33

According to Dennett's argument, the lack of conscious awareness on those occasions can be attributed to the perception not shouting loudly enough, or persistently enough, to achieve the level of fame required to become conscious. So what happens when a component does become famous? This is what Dennett calls "the Hard Question".

16.34

My own explanation does address that issue. I suggest that consciousness is present when a brain procedure observes its own behaviour and tries to anticipate its own future actions. That self-modelling procedure, I claim, is the enactment of consciousness. And what is happening at that particular moment of consciousness,

I suggest, is that that brain procedure is constructing a new short-term representational structure (of itself) in working memory and is anticipating what emotional urgings it has which will determine its own choice of action.

But where within the brain is this elusive self-representing procedure located? Does it have to be lodged in a particular location? Could it be that the procedure is cobbled together, momentarily, with a switch of attention, in order to construct a temporary representational structure in working memory where it will soon decay unless (and until) it is transferred to a longer lasting memory storage location. In my account that switch of attention means that the activity of self-representation, picks up on some newly perceived data and uses that to construct the self-representation. In terms of my knitting analogy, it is as though the knitter had laid down her needles, had grabbed some new balls of wool, and had started, with another set of needles, to knit some new kind of garment. There is, however, no single unique knitter or knitting procedure. There is only a general knitting capability. That ability can be put to use in a variety of ways. One of these is the self-knitting activity which constitutes being conscious.

16.35

So far as I am aware, experiments with brain imaging apparatus have identified several areas of the brain which contribute to the formation of structures in working memory, but that no firm consensus has been established concerning the involvement of any single location.

My hypothesis is compatible with there being no single identifiable correlate of a "being conscious" procedure. It is also compatible with there being several correlates of the contents of consciousness corresponding to the locations which are associated with particular perceptions. Thus, if we take 'face perception' as an example, the "*being conscious*" procedure will construct a self-representation in working memory.

This, however, will not, I suggest, be a simple representation of an observed face. The "*being conscious*" procedure will NOT be saying to itself

"This is what is being observed".

It will be saying to itself

"This is ME representing a face. This is ME interpreting (understanding) the emotional expression on that face. And this is ME anticipating MY own reaction to the predictable future events which that facial expression enables ME to predict."

16.36

To accompany this explanation I also offer a prediction. It may be possible for brain-scan experiments to identify a particular location in the brain which is associated with the concept of SELF and/or the concept of SELFMIND. Recall that I suggested that the concept of SELFMIND not by observing facial expressions but by identifying the muscular controls associated with facial expressions. I suggest, therefore, that such a particular location associated with the perception of the SELFMIND concept, is likely to be found in regions associated with the motor control of facial expressions. Activation of that part of the brain would, according to my explanation of consciousness, always be a contributing component of reported consciousness. Experimental confirmation of that prediction would be strong evidence in support of my hypothesis.

The neural correlate of consciousness

16.37

I had no intention of discussing the physical structure of the brain in this book and I said so at the outset. However, the advent of brain-scanning techniques, which allow non-invasive investigation of brain activity, has triggered an explosion of experiments on the human brain. Most of the recent and very interesting discoveries about brain function are now coming from that source. It difficult to avoid the topic altogether.

So far, these brain-scanning techniques seem to be restricted to identifying only the location of brain activity. It does not necessarily tell us what is happening at those active locations. However, by clever construction of experimental conditions, and by combining the observed results with the reports provided by psychological experiments, researchers in this field have managed to discover some very interesting facts.

The satellite view analogy

16.38

In many ways brain-scanning is rather like observing the world (at night) from an orbiting satellite. We can see the glowing spots which correspond to the cities of the world, the great centres of commercial activity. If aeroplanes (and internet traffic) also carried bright lights we would also be able to see the lines of communication between those centres. If we could intervene to interrupt or accelerate particular forms of commercial activity, we would then be able to observe an increase in the brightness of the places and communication lines concerned with these particular aspects of commerce.

What we would not be able to observe, however, is the activity of lone or small groups of individuals who might exert a significant influence on the world's economy - perhaps a mathematical genius working alone in some remote location, on a new book which might change everyone's understanding of economics. Individual efforts of that kind would escape our attention until they become collectivised and localised.

And so it is, I suggest, with brain activity. The attempt to find the neural correlates of consciousness depends crucially upon an assumption that consciousness is a brain activity which is located in one particular bit of brain structure and which operates there on a significant scale.

Earlier, in section 06.04, I speculated that if consciousness was indeed the performance of special ephemeral procedures which make use of concepts drawn from different parts of memory, then the search for the neural correlates of consciousness could resemble an attempt to identify the location where snowflakes settle, when they are distributed widely, and when they are settling on to the surface of a warm ocean.

The development of memory

16.39

I suggested earlier that the very first stage of memory storage occurs in phase-layer-1 and that at that early stage it takes the form of the activation condition of single detection units being retained for the duration of a single clock-tick.

I arrived at that idea, by consideration of evolution. The detection of motion is an important survival advantage which must have been an early development in primitive brains. There can be no detection of movement without at least a fleeting ability to store the current condition of a visual scene. The ability to create a duplicate of that current condition implies the ability to press into service some physical storage location and storing there some new item of data which was not there previously. I think we can call that an early example of working-storage.

In my account, the development of short-term memory evolved from that point, by being able to store the momentary prevailing condition or more and more detection units for longer and longer periods of time.

Neuroscience tells us that we have two forms of short-term memory devoted to vision/spatial perception (in the right hemisphere) and to audible/language (in the left hemisphere). There is also a suggestion that the pre-frontal cortex exercises some kind of executive control. However, regardless of the details of physical storage location, the functional result is that more and more data is stored and can then be accessed at a later time. I also remain adamant that what must be stored are various conditions of phase-layer-1, not data which is directly "visual" or "auditory". There cannot be any visible scenes or audible noises inside the brain. What is stored is (i.e. it must be) just data (albeit from different parts of the mechanism of perception).

The police case-file analogy

16.40

The analogy I use for this aspect of brain activity, is the way the police, when investigating a given incident, will assemble a case-file of information consisting of data drawn from a number of separate databases of past cases. This will consist of the modus operandi of known criminals, particular types of illegal drug, fingerprint records, DNA records and all the other technical stuff which is currently collected and examined by forensic scientists.

When a case is closed the relevant case-file is stored along with these assembled contents.

And that is precisely what I suggest the brain does not do. It does not store away the collection of relevant data in the same box. What I claim is that that file has to be re-created, or re-assembled, every time the case is re-examined. In that way the storage space required for memories is minimised. All the constituent parts are stored - but once only and in many separate parts of long-term memory. So what gets placed inside the storage box is a collection of references or associations which will allow the rapid re-assembly of the relevant data.

In an earlier section I discussed the construction of data records and remarked that within the brain there is no explicit storage of "software" in the sense we use that term in computer technology. That is, there is no explicit storage of a chronological sequence of "instructions" which must be carried out. Instead, the brain achieves a functionally equivalent performance by using what we could call a "hardware" solution. The chronological sequence of actions (which are expressed in software) is carried out as pulses travel through a section of brain-matter, making and breaking connections elsewhere within the connected structure of the brain.

That being so, there is no reason why, if the brain is able to construct data records and store them in memory, it should not also be able, just as readily, to construct procedures and store them in a similar way. If that is the case, we might expect the procedures associated with conscious understanding of events to be distributed throughout working long-term memory.

By storing procedures along with memory records, the memory recovery procedure could be accelerated. It would be rather as though, as they storage away the case-file of a closed incident, the police store-keeper had packed inside the file box a demon who knows where to find the relevant data and how to recover it quickly. When the box is opened, the demon goes to work.

This then could be the physical realisation of the "knitting pattern instructions" - the analogy I have used several times in this text.

It is interesting to note that, writing in 1998, and reviewing the work of Ericsson and Kintsch, David Hambrick remarked

"Working memory (WM) refers to the simultaneous and temporary storage and process of information. This definition dictates that the activation of extant knowledge brought to bear on ongoing performance is temporary. For example, the activation of contextual information, gained through previously read text and used to make sense of what is currently being read, is only temporary. Ericsson and Kintsch [1995] challenge this view by focusing on two questions: 1) 'Can mechanisms that account for subjects' limited working memory capacity in laboratory tasks [i.e. temporary activation] also account for the greatly expanded working memory capacity of experts and skilled performers?' and 2) 'How can working memory based on temporary storage account for the fact that skilled activities can be interrupted and later resumed without major effects on performance' (p 211)? The aim in addressing these questions is to show that skilled performers can allow for rapid encoding and retrieval of information in LTM."

[Hambrick 1998]

In a recent article (2012) Guida et al commented on explanations for neuroimaging data on the acquisition of expertise.

"When experts are involved, studies show activations in brain regions typically activated during long-term memory tasks that are not observed with novices. By contrast, when involving novices

and training programs, studies show a decrease in brain regions typically activated during working memory tasks, with no functional reorganisation. We suggest that the latter result is a consequence of practice periods that do not allow important structures to be completely acquired ..."

[Guida et all 2012]

I think that these quotations reinforce my suggestion that what is happening when a person acquires expertise in a given topic is the acquisition of efficient retrieval procedures which enable a given item of data to be augmented by associated and relevant information. I will not venture an opinion on where within the brain this process may occur.

Comments on "A User's Guide to Thought and Meaning" by Ray Jackendoff.

16.41

I added this section to my text recently after reading a book by Ray Jackendoff - *"A User's Guide to Thought and Meaning"*. [Jackendoff 2012]. The author is an acknowledged expert in linguistics and is also a prolific author. Despite differences in terminology the hypothesis he offers has many similarities to my own - and also a few interesting differences.

At the outset of *"A User's Guide ..."* Jackendoff explicitly rules out offering any explanation of elusive phenomenon we call *"a conscious subjective experience"*. In contrast, I have been bold enough (or foolish enough) to offer just such an explanation. As I commented in my introduction, if we do not have an explanation for that, then I think that we do not have an explanation of consciousness at all.

I found Jackendoff's book clear, fascinating, full of valuable insights and funny. He calls his thesis "The Unconscious Meaning Hypotheis" (or UMH). The basic idea is that while we are not conscious of having the mental structures (which represent the meaning of a statement), we are conscious of, what he calls "*character tags*" (which are associated with these meaning structures). He claims that these character tags are "*cognitive correlates of consciousness*". I think that his character tags correspond to what I have called "*extra dimensions*". They append information about the source of items of information and our own reactions to them. I conclude that our ideas about the nature of qualia are very similar.

Jackendoff approaches the issue of concepts (mainly) by giving examples of statements and then reflecting on that these statements tell us about the way people think. At one point he gives an example concerned with the visual recognition of triangles. He offers us three types of triangle. The first two of these conform to the strict mathematical definition of a triangle while the third does not. That third one, however, resembles the first, or archetypical example, much more closely than does the second. Why is that?

I draw his attention to section 03.23 in this book where I describe the strip method of recognising shapes. It is based on the calculation of mass distribution (in all orientations) and therefore solves that particular problem. There are other, much more efficient algorithms available, but mine has the advantage of being easily understood by those who are not mathematicians or computer scientists.

Jackendoff and I appear to have the same or similar ideas about what constitutes the stored structure of a quale experience, also that intuitive reactions to perceived events are due to evolutionary development and that truth is the result produced by a procedure which compares data structures and looks for a match.

His main conclusion is that there is no sharp distinction which we can make between conscious and unconscious thoughts. He thinks that conscious thoughts, in effect, ride on unconscious thoughts. I concur with those ideas.

Where we differ is in the particular issue of consciousness itself. It is not clear to me what he means when he describes character tags as "cognitive correlates of consciousness". Clearly they may be constituent parts of what we are conscious OF, but beyond that I am at a loss to understand the significance of that description.

For my own part I think that it is the dynamic process of incorporating these items of data into interpretations of experiences, which constitutes a conscious experience. I have shown how concepts could be formed. I have also shown that that process has plausibility in evolutionary terms. Specifically I have described how the concept of SELF and of SELFMIND could be formed from perceptible events. The incorporation of these concepts into an interpretation would automatically bring about the inclusion of self-ascribed motivations for the actions observed and recorded. Consciousness in this view is not an extraordinary addition to brain activity which has no identifiable utility value. It is an essential extension to existing abilities which make possible additional insights into future events that would otherwise be impossible. I think all of these abilities are possessed by mammals. I think that Jackendoff ascribes too much importance to language. Language, of the sophisticated form used by humans is a technique by means of which we achieve a consensus view of the world which would otherwise be restricted to a personal perspective.

CHAPTER 17

NOTES and Clarifications

Supervenience

17.01

According to the Oxford Dictionary of Philosophy, supervenience is

"... a term introduced by Hare to describe the relationship between ethical properties and other psychological and natural properties of things".

[Blackburn 1994]

I understand that the term was really introduced earlier than that. It has also been adopted by others since, and the meaning has been expanded to cover other circumstances. Dietrich and Hardcastle (2004) gave a list of different usages. These included the causal relationship between the engine of a car and the motion of its road wheels. That is not a usage which I find helpful at all. It throws away the most important characteristic that the two phenomena - a mechanism and its effects - cannot be isolated from one another.

In an earlier text I used the term (*"supervenience"*) in a more restricted sense when I referred to the relationship between consciousness and its underlying physical mechanism. That usage is the same one that we would use when talking about the relationship between the chemical properties of molecules and the properties of sub-atomic particles. Each is just a way of looking at, and describing a mechanism - the same mechanism - at two different levels. For that reason they are inseparable. It was in that sense that I used the term *"supervenience"* and, since I took care to define that meaning carefully, I thought that philosophers, of all people, would understand. That was not to be, however. I was criticised for using a term which had other interpretations. To avoid any repetition of that misunderstanding, for this text, I switched to using the terms "*inside view*" and "*outside view*" and drew attention to the known relationship between temperature and the kinetic activity of molecules.

I maintain however, that "*supervenience*" is a useful and appropriate term when it is used and understood in the way I stated.

Blindsight

17.02

When part of the human visual cortex is damaged, either by a severe accident or as a result of a surgical operation to treat some life-threatening condition, it is sometimes found that the patient loses conscious awareness of one part of the visual field. That means that when the patient is looking straight ahead, a flashing light or any other visual stimulus introduced into, say, the left visual field, is not seen. The odd thing about that, however, is that when asked to "guess" where that stimulus is, some patients seem to be able to indicate the position approximately [Weiskrantz 1987].

The implication is that despite the brain injury, the brain has in fact received information about the visual stimulus but that the information is not accessible to the part of the brain that is concerned with conscious visual conscious awareness.

In terms of my own brain model we could say that the mechanisms of phase-layer-1 and phase-layer-2 are operating as normal. We have to include phase-layer-2 because the patient has to be able to recall the location of the unseen stimulus. But phase-layer-3 is unable to access that information correctly.

The situation is made more complicated by the fact that the verbal communication between the patient and the experimental scientist, must take place at a conscious level. The difficulty, which the patient then has, is to be able, with conscious control, to access the more primitive mechanism of unconscious memory storage. That would require the patient to be able to de-code the "fuzzball" (or some other form of the same information at an earlier stage), to discover the location of the stimulus, and do so in an unusual way. In terms of my own model, what cannot be accessed are the additional "dimensions" such as colour, location, the concept of SELF etc. That might explain why the patient's guesses are not very accurate.

Based on that analysis I made a prediction. If phase-layer-1 is operating fully without impairment, the unconscious automatic stimulus-response mechanism should be fully operational. In that case a patient exhibiting those blindsight symptoms would still be able to carry out an unconscious automatic reaction to the stimulus, such as blinking, if something threatens the eye from the blindsight visual field. The important point of that experiment is that no spoken communication would be involved. The patient would be operating entirely within the phase-layer-1/phase-layer-2 stage.

A quick consultation with Google on the Internet established that it has been known since 1936 that a blink-reflex is exhibited by monkeys which have undergone surgery to remove much of the visual cortex and have therefore been rendered apparently consciously blind as a result [Kluver 1936].

Synaesthesia

17.03

Another example of abnormal brain function, is synaesthesia. This condition (which affects some people and is not necessarily associated with any kind of trauma to the brain), produces unexpected sensory perceptions - of colour, sounds, for example, triggered by other forms of sensory experience. Some people synaesthetics see various colours when they hear musical notes or when they see (or even just think about) particular numbers. Colour synaesthesia seems to be the most common, but other mixed sensory perceptions or "cross-wirings", have been observed.

When it was first described there was some reluctance to accept the observations as real. There is no doubt, however, that the reports are genuine. There have been unsuccessful attempts to acquire synaesthetic associations artificially. There is also some information that there is a genetic link to the condition. The prevalence is 1 in 2000 in the population, there is a sex ratio (6:1 female:male) and its prevalence is family-clustered [Baron-Cohen 1996].

Viewed in the context of my proposed brain model these observations suggest that the condition is brought about by a genetic mutation which causes particular and unusual connections within phase-layer-1. If that is the case, then these connections will be built in to the internal representation of the external world and that these connections (or extra dimensions) will be incorporated first into the "fuzzball" representation, and thence into concepts as they are formed. If that is the case then it would not be surprising to find that even thinking about a particular concept (say a number) is sufficient to conjure up an associated unusual synaesthetic experience.

One can suppose that if - let's say the synaesthetic association of numbers with colours - provided some survival advantage - say a superior ability to think in numeric terms, and that that was a life-preserving ability in some circumstances, that natural selection would eventually ensure that a substantial proportion of the human population would experience these synaesthetic associations.

Synaesthesia is useful antidote to the common mistake of thinking that colours are something observed in the external world. In these instances, the presence of a colour within a particular "quale experience" is very obviously something added to the experience by the brain itself. If we recognise that, the puzzlement about what a colour really is, tends to evaporate. Colour is nothing more mysterious than an added dimension.

Since it is labelled as having a visual source, it has to have a specific location within the system of visual perception and it has to be different from other features within that system. And it has to be different from an experience such as a musical note. Each quale is not a visual scene. It is an understanding of an experience, or a confrontation with some aspect of the external world (see section 08.09).

The Libet Experiment

17.04

In 1979 Benjamin Libet conducted an experiment which appears to contradict the idea that our behaviour is controlled by our conscious thoughts [Libet 1979]. He asked his experimental subjects to "lift a finger", at a time of their own choosing, and at the same time to record the instant at which they were aware of their intention to act. They did this while their brain activity was being monitored. The results indicated that brain activity started a short time before the subjects were aware of their intention to act. This result has been widely interpreted as an indication that the brain activity, which is the trigger for a decision to act, is not under conscious control.

Experiments of a similar kind, but with minor variations of experimental design, have been repeated many times and have yielded similar results. The interpretation of the results have also been disputed.

For example, it could be the case that I decide (consciously) that I will react to any signal which reaches me from elsewhere, without taking any action to specify what that trigger should be. If I am lying comfortably in bed, I may decide that I will rise and get ready for work, when I hear a train arriving at the local railway station. I do not cause that train to arrive, but I am responsible (consciously) for the fact that the sound it makes becomes the trigger for my action. It could be any loud unusual noise.

When viewed from my own perspective, however, these results are not very surprising. Earlier I suggested that the upper phase-layers of the 5-phase-layer model, were able to initiate action by inserting instructions, to that effect, into phase-layer-1.

Consider this analogy - If I ask the telephone exchange to wake me with an early morning alarm call, it has to be the case that some activity must take place within the telephone exchange shortly before I am roused from sleep. In these circumstances, would it be appropriate for someone to say that I had not consciously initiated that alarm call?

Clearly the interpretation of the Libet experiment depends upon the meaning we attach to the words we use. In this case the crucial word and concept is "responsibility". If we insist that I am responsible only for actions of which I have conscious awareness at all times, then I cannot be responsible for any activity that happens inside the telephone exchange while I am asleep. But if we accept that I can be responsible for activity which I initiate at some earlier time, and then leave for automatic completion to be undertaken by others, then that is not a proper interpretation.

It seems to me that the much discussed Libet experiment is not really so surprising and is not as significant as many people think. What it does do is to draw attention to the dangers of having too simplistic a model of brain mechanisms which forces us to think that the unconscious brain mechanism lies outside and beyond the control of the conscious SELF. It also draws attention to the need to make a distinction between "being conscious" and "being conscious OF something".

If we think of consciousness as a static mental state which overtakes or envelops the whole brain, then everything the brain does during that conscious state would be an object of conscious awareness. That idea creates difficulties. If consciousness is a static mental state then when we are conscious everything which happens within the brain at that time, must be part of the conscious experience.

But if we take the view, as I have done here, that consciousness is a procedure - and the analogy I have used frequently is of a process which knits an understanding of events - then we are bound to make a clear distinction between "being conscious" (i.e. doing the procedure) and "what we are conscious of" (i.e. the garment being knitted). A person who is knitting a pullover, creates that pullover. She does not also create the equipment, the knitting needles, which are being used to complete the task. These are part of the process of knitting and, in terms of my analogy, they would not be part of what she would be conscious of.

Creativity

17.05

A passing thought on another issue, which is often raised toward the end of a book on artificial consciousness. The tenor of these discussions is usually to offer consolation to those who feel that the concept of artificial consciousness, in some way, threatens the self-esteem of humans. The consolation is provided by the difficulty in seeing how an artificial mind could be creative. Haikonen did suggest that that might not be so but was not very clear about the mechanisms involved.

I have a suggestion, however, and it comes as a straight forward development of dream-consciousness.

Recall the suggestion I made earlier - that dreams are related to the mechanism with which concepts are indexed, as it were "off-line", and then stored for ease and speed of retrieval during "on-line" processing. I also suggested that the information stored in the longer-lasting secondary memory, before it has been identified and indexed, is stored in a format which is (by analogy) akin to a set of knitting pattern instructions. The attractive aspect of that, is that if we split sets of instructions of that kind, into component parts, recombined those parts in a new way and then tried to knit the pattern which resulted, it is quite likely that some object would be created. The likelihood is that the object would be bizarre and would not correspond to anything which could actually be worn. But it would, nevertheless, be recognisable as a physical object. It would occupy space. It would have a unique and recognisable shape. It would be recognisably made of wool.

Sometimes, however, on a very few occasions, something would emerge from such a process that could be worn. It would not be like any garment ever worn before. Even less likely, but still possible, would be the production of something both new and useful. The trick, of course, would be the recognition of that fact, and the realisation that with a few appropriate amendments the new object could be converted into something very useful indeed.

What I am suggesting, therefore, is that creativity in humans, is associated with dream-sleep, either night time dream-sleep or semi-conscious dream-sleep which is interwoven with conscious mental processing. Significantly it would be likely to occur only when the mind was in a relatively quiet and reflective mood. Creativity of that kind would give free reign to the dream mechanism and at the same time be watchful for the rare moments when something useful emerged. It would be productive when the mind had recently been thinking hard and continuously about some particular problem and its solution. If that was the case, the bits and pieces accessed and utilised by current dreams would be likely to have been retrieved from recently stored concepts and also old ones. In these circumstances it is not so unlikely that what might emerge from the creative process would be recognised as a possible solution to a problem currently being considered.

This explanation of creativity is compatible with the experience that thinking hard about a problem is often unproductive until one relaxes the effort and thinks about something else, perhaps of less significance. That would give brain-space for an interwoven form of dream-sleep to take place. It is often found then that a solution appears to "pop out" from nowhere.

Obviously, if this explanation is correct, there will be many different types of creativity. Some would be focused on the solution of particular technical problems. Others would be more free ranging and we might describe the results that produces as "artistic". Note how the process demands two contrasting abilities - the ability to create unconsciously, and the ability to recognise consciously the potential of what has been created.

A prediction - those who do research with brain-scanning equipment, will find that the neural correlates of dream-sleep, if these are known, will also correlate with creativity and successful problem solving.

Before you dismiss my idea I suggest you go and sleep on it for a while.

CHAPTER 18

Reflections

18.01

I recall, as a child, looking out at the world and asking myself - why these eyes? Why not the eyes of some other person? Why is it that the person who is myself, is tied so irrevocably to the physical entity that is my body? I could also look at my own condition - the state of my hunger, my thirst, the tiredness of my muscles, my pleasure, my pain. That was a form of looking out too. For although these things were in my body, they were not where I was. They were not inside ME. The only thing inside ME was ME. But where is that ME-place exactly?

I have a particular reason to mention these childish musings. Those who propose the supernatural or metaphysical account of consciousness, often accuse their opponents of "not understanding" that consciousness is more than the physical mechanism of the brain. It seems that the main evidence for that intuitive belief, is the lack of an alternative explanation which the supernaturalists find credible - when judged, of course, by the standards of their own intuition.

I offer the comments above as proof that, not only do I understand their position, but once, a very long time ago, I thought as they do.

A telescope helps us to look at the stars. It fails miserably when we try to use it to look at something close. So it is with the instruments of the mind. When we try to use that telescope of the mind (i.e. our intuition) to look inwards, at the SELF, it also fails miserably.

Words based on intuition

18.02

The words I use to describe that experience reflect the expectation of looking out. I use the word "looking" even when it is not my eyes, but my ears, or my fingertips, or my tongue, or my nose, which does that "seeing". If you try to explain something to me, and I understand, I may then try to express that comprehension by saying, "I see".

I don't really "see" at all. I hear your explanation and I absorb the meaning of your words into my mind. Something then happens inside my brain, which constitutes an "understanding". The word "understanding", however, does not help me understand what is really happening. The word speaks only of a net result, the consequence of that internal mechanism. It speaks of how I behave as a consequence of having been informed of the meaning of your words. "Understanding" is what we could call "a package-word". It wraps up the concept of the mechanism as a complete package and delivers it without inviting internal investigation. It is also an outside view word.

Observation and understanding

18.03

I have sometimes described consciousness as a procedure that is engaged in observation of itself. Let's think about what that means. If X observes Y, then X receives, reads or gains information about Y. X forms a mental construct X(Y) which represents Y and then notes that the behaviour of X(Y) corresponds in some way to the behaviour of Y. If X, by using X(Y), predicts some kind of behaviour, the same behaviour is observed in Y. X can then anticipate the behaviour of Y.

S: We then say that X "understands" Y.

Careful! If we take that last sentence S as part of the explanation of understanding, then S must be describing the next thing that X must do. But if that is the case then S does no more than bring us back to our starting point. Yet again we have some indeterminate thing trying to understand what is happening. We would then have to start all over again explaining what is the meaning of "understanding".

A better way to look at the explanation above is to consider the sentence S as standing apart from the explanation. It acts as a summary of the whole explanation - but is not part of it. That way, our explanation of "understanding" ends with the sentence before S. It ends with the way X forms X(Y) and provides itself with predictions of how Y will behave. And if X and Y are the same thing, then that is what self-observation is. We do not need to conjure up some additional entity which looks at the end product and once more "understands" what is going on.

When we get to the end of the explanation sequence, we must recognise that fact, and stop. We must not go on and on down an infinitely regressing series.

And let's not be fooled by the word "observe" into thinking that the event we are describing involves one part of the brain mechanism "looking" (with eyes, or ears, or fingertips or whatever) at another part of the brain mechanism. That is not what is going on - at least not in my proposed model.

Note: it is that misuse of the word "observe" that is the basis for my criticism of HOT theories of consciousness - see section 16.25.

Phase-layer-1 uses the mechanisms of perception to gain information about the external world. It then records the recognition of various features present within that external world. (If you prefer, it ticks the boxes on a pre-prepared form.) The higher phase-layers gather up those ticks, recognise a particular pattern of ticks (which will include action-response ticks) identify a more elaborate pattern (a concept) which is a compendium of several previous similar experiences and which include predictions about future events, and then it integrates that enhanced pattern, along with all its predictions, into its representation of the experience.

And that's it.

It's a bit complicated, I admit. But I am not asking anyone to accept something supernatural. No quantum mechanics. No multiple drafts which regard one of their number as famous. Nothing needing the involvement of virtual machines. It is just a complicated way of dealing with data (or that pattern of ticks) to make possible predictions about the system's own behaviour.

If the original information comes, not through vision, or touch or scent, but through hearing the words spoken by another, then the process which happens is nearly the same. It has one extra stage. The words are heard. Phase-layer-1 ticks those boxes. The pattern of ticks is recognised. Another, enhanced pattern of ticks is slotted into place and that pattern will contain the pattern of action ticks which correspond to the way those words are uttered.

So now it has the words and, by following association connections, their associated meanings. So once again a new pattern of ticks is slotted into place and once again the system has an enhanced interpretation of the events described. And that process, not the structure itself, but the process of creating that structure, is the system's understanding.

Go no further than that. There is no requirement for the system to "make up its mind" whether or not to believe its own representation of events. Things are complicated enough. We do not need yet another unopened package, another mind to get involved. The system has to believe. It has no choice. That construction process is the system's belief.

The enhanced pattern of ticks includes a representation of the concept SELF, of SELFMIND and of the action (that that SELFMIND is likely to initiate). That is self-observation. That is self-prediction. That is conscious awareness of itself and its own actions. And if it attributes its own actions to an emotional drive like "*wanting*" to do something, then that is okay. If that is an imagined emotion then it is also a trick of imagination that works. It believes that it "*wants*" to do something.

Analogy: the square root of minus one

18.04

I introduced this idea in section 09.12. The square root of minus one (or "i" as it is often denoted) is a mathematical concept which is hard to understand. However, it is also extremely useful. Using that concept as a tool, mathematicians can solve problems that would otherwise be unsolvable. Coincidentally, "i" is said to be an "imaginary number". There is no actual number which when multiplied by itself yields the result minus one. So "i" fails the basic prediction test of existence. However, it can be used in calculations. When it is used in that way it can enable electronic engineers to make accurate predictions about how the universe operates. So in that restricted sense it does pass the prediction test for existence. Perhaps we could designate that a form of "quasi-existence". There are many other mathematical concepts which have similar properties - useful but failing in some respect with regards having an existing counterpart in reality.

I think that those emotional drives are like "i". I cannot say what they are exactly. But I can say what they represent - a collection of causal precursors which (with moderate accuracy), can predict certain forms of behaviour. I also suggest that those concepts are used by the brain to anticipate its own behaviour. The concepts do that job successfully. Evolution, driven by natural selection, could not ignore that success.

Pain and Pleasure

18.05

And what of pain and pleasure? That is the crunch issue, isn't it? Pain and pleasure (the emotional drives for actions) cannot be directly perceived. But they can be predicted. If a particular pattern of "ticks" (recognised features) includes action-response ticks which indicate a spontaneous avoidance action, or a seeking of repetition, then that condition will be classified as either a painful experience or a desirable one. What else is feasible?

I touch a hot flame. An interrupt signal stops all my other actions. My hand jerks away. I avoid repetition. The condition is a unique cocktail of dimensions (or distributed signals, or character tags).

I need an explanation. For the purposes of prediction, I need to understand why that was my reaction. I interpret that composite condition as one that is "painful", a condition I do not "want". How else can I interpret it?

The mechanism can recognise that experience and that behaviour and interpret the experience (and others) as being "*painful*" or "*pleasurable*". It will do that consciously. It will identify these emotional "feelings" as the causal precursors of the actions just as mathematicians identify "i" as the thing which can produce the square root of minus one.

Thus the consciousness mechanism could, on occasions, recognise if and when an automatic instinctive reaction is ill-advised. Do not freeze. Do not panic. Do not blink. Do not allow your knee to jerk when I tap it with a hammer. Keep cool and act deliberately in some non-instinctive way. In these circumstances, could the conscious mechanism stop its normal instinctive reaction? Since conscious reactions operate more slowly than instinctive ones, the brain can intervene to stop an instinctive reaction only if it can anticipate it in time get ready for it and shut off the automatic reaction before it happens.

Is that also a marginal survival advantage - the ability to anticipate automatic reactions and force an alternative calculated response, which led to its being chosen by natural selection? Is that also a characteristic form of behaviour which a real zombie could never ever reproduce?

Conscious and unconscious parts

18.06

Another diagram. Here, once again, we see the five phase-layers of the system being proposed as an explanation of consciousness. This time, however, I have divided the phase-layers into two groups. The lower group is labelled "UNCONSCIOUS PART". That part (consisting of the SRA and the MEMORY phase-layers) has no form of consciousness. All it has is an "awareness" (in the special sense I described earlier 04.02) of the environment and an ability to respond to stimuli with actions which have proved beneficial over countless years to various ancestors.

The three upper phase-layers in the diagram are labelled "CONSCIOUS PART" because all three contribute to the conscious procedure being performed.

And then there is that arrow marked with a question mark. That represents the "puzzlement" of the conscious process as it tries to understand the way its own unconscious reaction decisions are taken. It has to take an outside view despite the fact that it is doing so from inside the mechanism.

Fig 18.06 The five phase-layers again

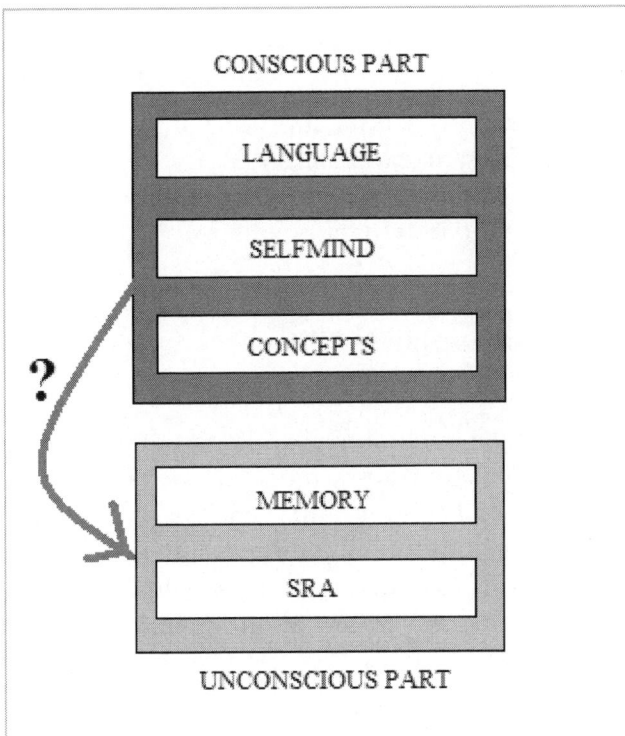

Beware of the word "puzzlement" (which I have put into scare quotations). The upper part of the system does not have a self-contained mind of its own with which it can feel anything resembling puzzlement. It has a mechanism which constructs a representation of the lower layers. That representation includes sub-structures which represent SELF and SELFMIND. And that representation also contains predictions on the basis of which the mechanism may act. But the representations of SELF and SELFMIND do not contain any mechanistic representation of the mechanism of action-decisions. Instead it contains a false representation of an autonomous emotional urges which act in certain ways. These are the simplified rules-of-thumb for predicting action. The mechanism has no alternative way of predicting actions.

What then must be the way intuition will represent itself? It has to take the view that those lower phase-layers are not part of its own knowable mechanism - hence the intuitive view is that the brain is a duality.

And that's it. That's my explanation of consciousness. That is why our intuition gets the explanation of its own behaviour so wrong (in a precise sense) and correct (in the general sense of being able to make useful pragmatic predictions).

Multiple models and multiple realities

18.07

A traditional debate in philosophy is the issue of "*realism*" versus "*idealism*". The question which that debate raises is this one. If our model of reality is internal, and that is all we have to consider, how "*real*" is the external world? Does it "really" exist?

Once again we are caught in an argument about the meaning of words. What exactly do we mean when we ask that question - "Does it *really* exist?". The answer we give to that question cannot be separated from the meaning of the words "*real*" or "*reality*" or "*exist*".

We need to take a general position which covers all of these issues so that a single answer applies to them all, and resolves them all, simultaneously.

A curious thing about the explanation of consciousness, which I offer, is that it suggests that there is not one, but a sequence of internal models, each of which offers a version of reality, and each of which offers its own definition of the word "exist".

To analyse the situation I need a notation or terminology which allows me to identify them separately.

Let E = external reality
>   M1 = the internal model developed by phase-layer-1
>   M2 = the internal model developed by phase-layer-2
>   M3 = the internal model developed by phase-layer-3
>   M4 = the internal model developed by phase-layer-4
>   M5 = the internal model developed by phase-layer-5

Six models in all, five of which are internal. Only E is external and to make things even more confusing E is a component of all of the others. And that is the crux of the matter. The external location of E is a "fact" which owes its factual condition to its presence within the other internal models.

M1 is formed automatically by phase-layer-1. It happens without our conscious involvement and has operated that way for a very long time. Phase-layer-1 has an inventory of "features" which were produced by evolution. In effect, phase-layer-1 examines E and ticks-off, each feature which is identified by its internal network of detection units. It then inserts additional information into the model which includes time, priority, and many other properties including those instinctive action responses.

Phase-layer-2 then examines M1 adds a time dimension (to record past events) and in that way creates a new model M2.

Phase-layer-3, compresses M2. That makes it possible for the system to store that model in a smaller space. By doing that it finds that it has, as a side effect, developed the ability to construct model M3. In effect it chops the M2 model into pieces which can be re-assembled into representations of new configurations of circumstances which have not occurred previously. M3 is that re-constructed multi-component model. It allows the system to "understand" (in an ephemeral way) the experience it is currently having.

Phase-layer-4, augments M3 to produce M4 by adding the concept of SELF and of SELFMIND. It is therefore able to "understand" the world and its own contribution to that world, in terms of motivation. M4 also contains the concept MIND/SELFMIND and in that way it can expand M3 to include the various internal mental models possessed by itself and its fellow creatures.

Phase-layer-5 expands M4 even further by enabling other creatures to communicate their own versions of M4. When these different versions of M4 are put together into a single model, M5 is the result. M5 is a "consensus model". It does not rely only on the evidence available to a single individual. In that respect it conforms to the formal specifications of the scientific method by insisting that the only acceptable evidence is required to be third-party accessible.

Each of the other models - E, M1, M2, M3 and M4 - is a component of M5. We could say that they are "nested" within M5. What I derive from that is a notion of "existence" which is defined in terms of an individual model. So we can have $EXIST_{M1}$, $EXIST_{M2}$, $EXIST_{M3}$, $EXIST_{M4}$ and $EXIST_{M5}$. Five kinds of existence. The most significant of these is $EXIST_{M5}$ but $EXIST_{M4}$ also has a role because it is also part of the fully conscious mechanism. If a person operates exclusively within the context of M4, then the truth of any belief will be dependent upon that belief being able to improve the sense of personal well-being. A person who operates within the context of M5, will include the consensus view of society as a factor.

The context-dependent idea of existence is less fixed and more ambiguous than most people would like. The intuitive notion of existence would give it properties which are immutable and independent of any human mental model. It is a global concept of existence. But that too is dependent upon the concept of E having an independent existence irrespective of our presence and our mental models.

Unfortunately for that view, however, we do operate with internal models and it is hard to see how we can ever step outside the internal mental world and "*see*" the world as it "*really*" is.

The view I take is based on the idea that anything that exists must be a component of a given model and the justification for inclusion as a component depends upon how useful its inclusion in that proves to be.

That criterion of "usefulness" does not correspond to what most people think of when they consider the meaning of "*existence*", and yet it is hard to see how we can escape from that conclusion.

Consider the point I made in an earlier chapter about the postulation that there are two extra forces of gravity. These, by being equal in strength and opposite in direction, can never be detected because each cancels out the observable effects of the other. This illustrates the need for a definition based on utility. What would be the point of including the idea of these two extra forces in our inventory of the things which may exist? If we included them in M4 or M5 say, our ability to predict future events would not be improved in any way at all. If we include the possibility of their existence in E, that would also open up the possibility of an infinite number of extra inclusions as we postulate the existence of four extra gravitational forces, six, eight, ... and so on - all of which would be completely useless.

What I like about this use-relevant, context-dependent view of existence, is the way it provides satisfactory answers to traditional questions about reality. That external model of reality - the one which I called "E" - does it really exist?

E is one component of M5. According to my definition it exists if, by being included in M5, it provides us with an ability to predict future events with greater accuracy. It certainly does that. It explains why it is that the consensus model (M5) is feasible. Each of us is able to experience the opinions expressed by other people, and can interpret these statements (usually) as expressing agreement about what can be observed. That is exactly what the inclusion of E within M5 enables us to predict. M5 tells us that we are all looking out at the same external world and so our reports of what we see will be similar.

Therefore, the inclusion of E as a component of M5 is justified. We are then able to declare that E *"really exists"* (i.e. it EXISTS$_{M5}$). And that, I think, is a satisfactory result.

David Hume

18.08

When David Hume addressed the same problem he despaired of finding a neat solution.

"This sceptical doubt, both with respect to reason and the senses, is a malady which can never be radically cured, but must always return upon us every moment, however we may chase it away, and sometimes may appear entirely free from it. It is impossible, upon any system, to defend either our understanding or senses; and we but expose them further when we endeavour to justify them in that manner. As the sceptical doubt arises naturally from a profound and intense reflection on those subjects, it always increases the further we carry our reflections, whether in opposition or conformity to it. Carelessness and inattention alone can afford us any remedy. For this reason I rely entirely upon them; and take it for granted, whatever may be the reader's opinion at this present moment, that an hour hence he will be persuaded there is both an external and internal world; ..."
[David Hume. A Treatise of Human Nature, Posthumous edition 1777]

The model I have proposed provides a way to reconcile the apparent conflict between opposing realities - internal and external. Hume's puzzlement arises from the disparity between the internal model he uses and a definition of existence, which is relevant to E (which therefore assumes the existence of E). My proposal enables an internal model to define and accept the concept of an external reality, without any conflict at all. External reality (and the definition of existence that comes with it) is a component of the internal model, M5 - and it is a useful one.

Why be conscious?

18.09

Basic to my thesis is the idea that the brain mechanism started out on its evolutionary journey to our current condition, as a stimulus-response automaton. In most circumstances the automatic responses to various conditions which evolution has programmed into our behaviour patterns, are still operational, must have been appropriate for survival or will have been at one time. But there will have been some occasions when that was not the case. The survival advantages which accompany evolutionary steps, are a statistical tendency, not a certainty. Consciousness, however, as it operates in parallel with those more primitive behaviour patterns, provides us with a mechanism which enables us to anticipate our own behaviour and therefore it enables us to inhibit those automatic reactions which might, in current circumstances, be ill-advised. We can then substitute something more appropriate.

The Board Game analogy

18.10

Imagine that you are playing a board game - like chess. But this game is not like any other game you have ever played. The board, the various squares on it and all the pieces, represent the place where you are at present, they represent the other people around you and the situation in which you currently find yourself.

Moreover, one of the pieces on the board, is YOU. Let's call it the SELF-piece. You also find that when you move that SELF-piece, the various other pieces move themselves, spontaneously, without you needing to touch them. You find, moreover, that when you put out a hand to move that SELF-piece to a new position, there are times when it appears to resist the move that you intend to make.

More. You also find that if you are not thinking hard about the game and about the best move to take, that SELF-piece just moves itself to a new position. However, if you pay attention and push hard you can sometimes overcome that tendency. And then sometimes you cannot. You push, but it goes in some other direction. You might be tempted to say to some other person in the room - "This SELF-piece seems to have a mind of its own". Or maybe you would just think that to yourself. And then again, maybe that SELF-piece does have a mind of its own.

So which mind are you taking about when you say what YOU want to do?

You are not sure? Recall that YOU are watching YOU wanting to do something while YOU want to do something else. That's YOU on the board. That's YOU feeling a big hand picking YOU up and moving YOU to some place where YOU did not want to go. Which one of those YOUs is really YOU? Both of them? Does that situation have a "feel"? Is there *something that it is like* to be in this situation?

If another piece makes a move which, according to the rules of this strange game, seems to threaten the SELF-piece (i.e. to take it off the board, or to "kill" it), you may then find, when you try to move the SELF-piece in some way, that something strange suddenly happens. It is as if a stun-grenade has gone off. All your planned actions are paralysed. And then, when you have recovered, you find the SELF-piece has jumped to a new position, where the threat is less direct. At a time less urgent, when you touch that SELF-piece, you can feel the action it seems to want to take, pressing against your hand.

And remember, this SELF-piece is YOU. You regard it as yourself. It is your understanding of yourself. So according to the rules of this game, what it "wants" to do is what you think YOU want to do. And vice versa. If YOU want to do something then that is what IT wants to do.

According to those same rules, the surprise YOU felt at that moment is also what the SELF-piece felt at that moment. You know it has done what it wants, but YOU do not know why it wants to do any of these things. All you know is that it does appear to have wants of its own which sometimes overwhelm its (or YOUR) own carefully planned actions.

When YOU construct this representation of what is happening, YOU are not constructing a representation of what that SELF-piece is thinking or what is motivating the behaviour of that SELF-piece. What your are constructing is what YOU are thinking - what motivates YOU. YOU are behaving this way because YOU are scared, YOU are angry, pleased, excited ... etc. These concepts may not exist in reality, but, like the square root of minus one, they help you to make predictions which are accurate enough, on most occasions, for practical purposes.

How would you describe that situation? *A subjective experience* perhaps? "*Experience*" is really the wrong word. Too passive. This is not a subjective *experience*. It is a subjective *performance*. It is certainly strange and disconcerting. What is worse - YOU need to know what YOU are going to do before YOU can decide what YOU are going to do. It is only when you know that (or think you know that) that you will know what it is you will need to deal with in the future that you are trying to predict.

This crazy YOU-inside-YOU predictive game is the closest illustration, that I can think of, which represents the convoluted self-representing situation which I suggest is the performance of the procedure that we call "being conscious".

The Zombie Test

Here is a test of consciousness which a genuine zombie could never pass. Explain to it that to prove that it is conscious it must refrain from blinking. Explain too, that there will be a special signal given which will indicate when it is to take control of its blinking reaction. And here is the catch – we do not tell the person who has programmed the zombie, what that signal will be. It could be a snap of the fingers. It could be the command "Do not blink". It could be a wave of the hand. It could also be any one of a zillion different signals including those which do not mention blinking explicitly, but just ask for a task to be performed for which non-blinking is a logical requirement. So the programmer of this particular zombie cannot program a specific trigger-signal into its mechanism to act as a stimulus for its controlled non-blinking reaction. Note that that is the same condition which is used in standard examinations. The examinee is not allowed to know the questions before they are asked.

And then we run the test. First, we establish, with a number of experiments, that the system does have an instinctive blink reaction. Then we give the special signal and try again. A conscious human being could meet that requirement. I challenge zombie enthusiasts to explain how an _unconscious_ system could be programmed to achieve that result. I think that I have shown in this book how a mechanism could be programmed to do that – but then, I maintain that a mechanism programmed in that way would, in fact, be fully conscious.

APPENDIX

A Shape Recognition Program

AP.01

This appendix is included to support my claim that simple silhouette shapes of objects can be identified using a method constructed from the more elementary ability to recognise short line segments, their density and orientation.

Ap.02

The program was written in the computer language PERL. Perl is a free language system which can be downloaded from the Internet. It is compatible with Unix, Linux and with various Microsoft Windows systems. Superficially it has some similarity to the syntax of the C language.

AP.03

I offer these programs with some diffidence. For visual recognition, much faster and more efficient software systems are available. My concern here is merely to demonstrate that the approach is viable and produces the results I claim. The initial problem, which I confronted, was how I could prepare simple images in the form of a two-dimensional array using only the facilities which I had available. Within the Windows XP system, I also had the MS application PAINT and that typically produces BMP files with each pixel represented by 24-bit arrays. So I wrote a program which is called "process_image". It opens a file of that kind, reads the header record data, discovers the X-Y co-ordinates of the image and creates a Perl array of the same size. My programs generally are so slow that I found it best to restrict the size of each image to something like the size of a postage stamp - or maybe the size of a typical Christmas stamp. A minor complication is that in the BMP files produced by PAINT, the origin (the position represented by the co-ordinates 0,0) is at the top left hand corner and not the bottom left hand corner as is normal in mathematics.

Once a Perl array of that kind had been prepared, various subroutines were able to process it. It could be assumed that there was only one shape present and that it consisted of one continuous silhouette.

Diagram.

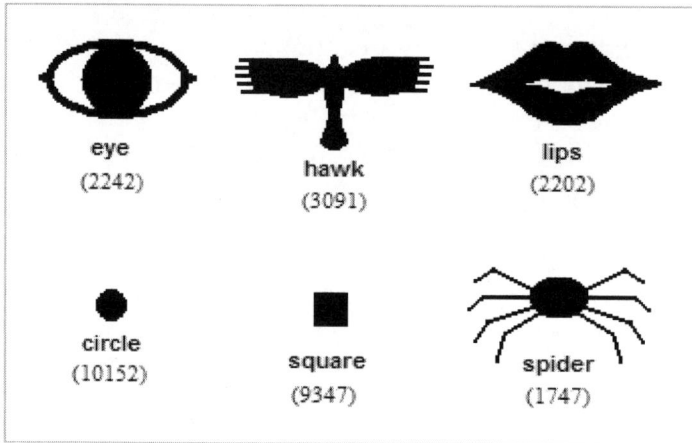

eye
(2242)

hawk
(3091)

lips
(2202)

circle
(10152)

square
(9347)

spider
(1747)

BUG

Program Text

AP.05

Here is the text of the program.
NOTE: In Perl a hash symbol "#" indicates a comment
Many lines have been commented out and these need to be
re-established for various stages of testing

```perl
use Tk;
use Win32::OLE;
#use Win32::OLE::Const 'Microsoft Word';
use IO::Handle;
use FileHandle;
use English;

use testsubs;

$IMAGENAME="";

# ============================IMAGE ANALYSIS
STORES========================================

%ALLIMAGES=(); # a hash of all image arrays
%STDIMAGES=(); # a hash of every standard image array
%FINDIMAGES=();

# ============================SET SHADE
VALUES=============================================
  $white=  4278190080;
  $palegrey=3221225472;
  $darkgrey=2147483648;
  $black=  0;
# ===========================SET
ARRAYS==================================================
==

@M=([0],[0]);      # holds the test array of the image which is to be identified
@ROTARRAY=([0],[0]); # holds an array after it has been rotated
@STANDARD=([0],[0]); # holds the standard array against which the test
array is matched
```

```
#===========================IMAGE
ANALYSIS===================================================
=

    $ANGLE=0.414213562; # radians = 22.5 degrees

#============================================================
================================

#process_image("bird",\@M);
#analyse(\@M,\%ALLIMAGES);
#process_image("square",\@M);
#analyse(\@M,\%ALLIMAGES);

@M=([0],[0]);
process_image("circle",\@M);   # process the image array for "circle" and put it
into @M
analyse(\@M,\%ALLIMAGES);      # analyse @M and put the resulting
"fingerprint" into %ALLIMAGES

#process_image("triangle",\@M);
#analyse(\@M,\%ALLIMAGES);

@M=([0],[0]);
process_image("spider",\@M);
analyse(\@M,\%ALLIMAGES);

#process_image("cross",\@M);
#analyse(\@M,\%ALLIMAGES);

@M=([0],[0]);
process_image("hawk",\@M);
analyse(\@M,\%ALLIMAGES);

@M=([0],[0]);
process_image("bug",\@M);
analyse(\@M,\%ALLIMAGES);

#process_image("rect",\@M);
#analyse(\@M,\%ALLIMAGES);

@M=([0],[0]);
process_image("ellipse",\@M);
analyse(\@M,\%ALLIMAGES);
```

```
@M=([0],[0]);
process_image("wedge",\@M);
analyse(\@M,\%ALLIMAGES);

#process_image("lozenge",\@M);
#analyse(\@M,\%ALLIMAGES);

@M=([0],[0]);
process_image("bird2",\@M);
analyse(\@M,\%ALLIMAGES);

@STANDARD=([0],[0]);
process_image("spider0",\@STANDARD);
analyse(\@STANDARD,\%STDIMAGES);

@STANDARD=([0],[0]);
process_image("hawk0",\@STANDARD);
analyse(\@STANDARD,\%STDIMAGES);

@STANDARD=([0],[0]);
process_image("eye0",\@STANDARD);
analyse(\@STANDARD,\%STDIMAGES);

@STANDARD=([0],[0]);
process_image("lips0",\@STANDARD);
analyse(\@STANDARD,\%STDIMAGES);

#@STANDARD=([0],[0]);
#process_image("tiger0",\@STANDARD);
#analyse(\@STANDARD,\%STDIMAGES);

@STANDARD=([0],[0]);
process_image("square",\@STANDARD);
analyse(\@STANDARD,\%STDIMAGES);

@STANDARD=([0],[0]);
process_image("circle",\@STANDARD);
analyse(\@STANDARD,\%STDIMAGES);

@STANDARD=([0],[0]);
process_image("wedge",\@STANDARD);
analyse(\@STANDARD,\%STDIMAGES);

identify("bug",\%STDIMAGES);
```

```perl
printanalysis("hawk",\%ALLIMAGES);
printanalysis("hawk0",\%STDIMAGES);
printanalysis("eye0",\%STDIMAGES);
printanalysis("circle",\%STDIMAGES);
printanalysis("circle",\%ALLIMAGES);


#===========================================================
================================
#=========================================------======SUBROUTINES===
================================
#===========================================================
================================

sub process_image
{
$IMAGENAME=$_[0];
$IMAGEARRAY=$_[1];
$infile="$IMAGENAME"."."."bmp";
# =========================------======OPEN
FILE=================================================
# print("IMAGE FILE = ");  $infile=<STDIN>;
# chomp($infile);

# $subname=$infile;
# $pos=index($subname,'.',0);
# substr($subname,$pos,1)=",";
# ($IMAGENAME,$ext)=split(",",$subname);
#===========================================================
==================================
  open (INFILE,"<".$infile);
  $ENDOFFILE=eof INFILE;
  binmode INFILE;
# ==========================------======PROCESS THE INFILE HEADER
STRUCTURE=============================------===
  $unpackheader="a2La2a2L";
# ===========================================------======READ THE
HEADER================================------===
  $bytes=read(INFILE,$header,14);
  ($signature,$filelength,$res1,$res2,$offset)=unpack($unpackheader,$header);
# ===========================================------======PRINT THE HEADER
DATA ON SCREEN=====================------===
# =====(the printout os for diagnostic purposes and will be commented out
later)================------===
  #print("\nHEADER DATA\n\n");
```

382

```perl
#print("signature=".$signature."\n");
#print("file length=".$filelength."\n");
#print("res1=".$res1."\n");
#print("res2=".$res2."\n");
#print("offset=".$offset."\n");
#====================================PROCESS THE INFO
HEADER STRUCTURE=========================
# Necessary values
#    colour bit-count=24
#    compression=0 (or "BI_RGB") ie no compression
#    colour map size=0
#--------------------------------------------------------------------------------
  $unpackinfoheader="LLLSSLLLLLL";
  $bytes=read(INFILE,$info,36);

($IHsize,$width,$height,$planes,$bitcount,$compress,$imgsze,$Hpixper,$Vpix
per,$Ctable,$import)=
    unpack($unpackinfoheader,$info);
#--------------------------------------------------------------------------------
#    print("\nINFO HEADER\n\n");
#    print("Info header size=".$IHsize." bytes\n");
#    print("\n image width=".$width."\n");
#    print("image height=".$height."\n");
#    print("planes=".$planes."\n");
#    print("colour bit count=".$bitcount."\n");
#    print("Compression=".$compress."\n");     # BI_RGB (not compressed),
BI_RLE8 (run_length), BI_RLE4
#    print("Image size=".$imgsze."\n");
#    print("Horizontal pix/metre=".$Hpixper."\n");
#    print("Vertical pix/metre=".$Vpixper."\n");
#    print("color map size=".$Ctable." zero means no map\n");
#    print("Importance count=".$import."\n");
#====================================PROCESS THE COLOUR
PALETTE=========================================
#  Necessary values
#    The colour palette should be exactly four bytes, all zero.
#============================================================
======================
  $bytes=read(INFILE,$palette,4);
  $unpackpalette="B8B8B8B8";
  ($P1,$P2,$P3,$P4)=unpack($unpackpalette,$palette);
#============================================================
========================
#    print("palette=".$P1.",".$P2.",".$P3.",".$P4."\n");
```

```
#
=============================================================
====================
# ==================CALCULATE FILLER
SIZE======================================
  $words=$width/4;
  $intwords=int($words);
  $oddbytes=($words-$intwords);
  $wholebytes=$oddbytes*4;
  $FILLER=round($wholebytes);
#  print("\nFILLER SIZE = $FILLER\n\n");
# ==========================READ THE FILE AND FILL THE M-
ARRAY===========================
  $x=0;
  $y=0;
  do
    {
    do
      {
        $bytes=read(INFILE,$threebytes,3);
      $ENDOFFILE=eof INFILE;
          #----------------------------
          ($char1,$char2,$char3)=unpack("B8B8B8",($threebytes));

$pixel=unpack("I",pack("B32","00000000000000000000000".$char1));
          #-----------------------------------------------------------------
          if   ($pixel<$darkgrey) {$$IMAGEARRAY[$x][$y]="3"}   # BLACK
          elsif ($pixel<$palegrey) {$$IMAGEARRAY[$x][$y]="2"}   # DARK
GREY
          elsif ($pixel<$white)   {$$IMAGEARRAY[$x][$y]="1"}   # PALE
GREY
          else                 {$$IMAGEARRAY[$x][$y]="."};  # WHITE
          #-----------------------------------------------------------------
          $x++;
          #-----------------------------------------------------------------
        }
      until ($x>=($width));
      $bytes=read(INFILE,$fillerpadding,$FILLER);
      $ENDOFFILE=eof INFILE;
      $x=0;
      $y++;
      }
  until $ENDOFFILE;
  close (INFILE);
#printarray(\@$IMAGEARRAY);
```

```perl
} # end of process_image


sub analyse
{
 my $MARRAY=$_[0];
 my $IMAGESTORE=$_[1];
 local $STORE=[];
#=====================================================
===================================
# WITHOUT ROTATION
#=====================================================
===================================
  $TOP=findtop(\@$MARRAY,$width,$height);
  $BOT=findbottom(\@$MARRAY,$width,$height);
  $LEFT=findleft(\@$MARRAY,$width,$height);
  $RIGHT=findright(\@$MARRAY,$width,$height);
  #-------------------------------
  $MTOP=$TOP;
  $MBOT=$BOT;
  $MLEFT=$LEFT;
  $MRIGHT=$RIGHT;
  #-------------------------------
  twos(\@$MARRAY,0,$width,$TOP,$BOT);
  threes(\@$MARRAY,0,$width,$TOP,$BOT);
  fours(\@$MARRAY,0,$width,$TOP,$BOT);
  fives(\@$MARRAY,0,$width,$TOP,$BOT);
#=====================================================
===================================
# ROTATE 22.5 degrees
#=====================================================
===================================
  $ALPHA=$ANGLE;
  rotate(\@$MARRAY,$ALPHA,$MLEFT,$MRIGHT,$MTOP,$MBOT);
#--------------------------------------------------------------------
  $TOP=findtop(\@ROTARRAY,$width,$height);
  $BOT=findbottom(\@ROTARRAY,$width,$height);
  $LEFT=findleft(\@ROTARRAY,$width,$height);
  $RIGHT=findright(\@ROTARRAY,$width,$height);
#-----------------------------------------------
  twos(\@ROTARRAY,0,$width,$TOP,$BOT,);
  threes(\@ROTARRAY,0,$width,$TOP,$BOT);
  fours(\@ROTARRAY,0,$width,$TOP,$BOT);
  fives(\@ROTARRAY,0,$width,$TOP,$BOT);
```

```
#==================================================================
==================================
# ROTATE 45 degrees
#==================================================================
==================================
  $ALPHA=$ANGLE*2;
  rotate(\@$MARRAY,$ALPHA,$MLEFT,$MRIGHT,$MTOP,$MBOT);
#------------------------------------------------------------------
  $TOP=findtop(\@ROTARRAY,$width,$height);
  $BOT=findbottom(\@ROTARRAY,$width,$height);
  $LEFT=findleft(\@ROTARRAY,$width,$height);
  $RIGHT=findright(\@ROTARRAY,$width,$height);
    #-----------------
#print("TOP=$TOP\nBOT=$BOT\nLEFT=$LEFT\nRIGHT=$RIGHT\n");
    #-----------------
  twos(\@ROTARRAY,0,$width,$TOP,$BOT);
  threes(\@ROTARRAY,0,$width,$TOP,$BOT);
  fours(\@ROTARRAY,0,$width,$TOP,$BOT);
  fives(\@ROTARRAY,0,$width,$TOP,$BOT);
#==================================================================
==============================
# ROTATE 67.5 degrees
#==================================================================
==============================
  $ALPHA=$ANGLE*3;
  rotate(\@$MARRAY,$ALPHA,$MLEFT,$MRIGHT,$MTOP,$MBOT);
#------------------------------------------------------------------
  $TOP=findtop(\@ROTARRAY,$width,$height);
  $BOT=findbottom(\@ROTARRAY,$width,$height);
  $LEFT=findleft(\@ROTARRAY,$width,$height);
  $RIGHT=findright(\@ROTARRAY,$width,$height);
#-----------------------------------------------
  twos(\@ROTARRAY,0,$width,$TOP,$BOT);
  threes(\@ROTARRAY,0,$width,$TOP,$BOT);
  fours(\@ROTARRAY,0,$width,$TOP,$BOT);
  fives(\@ROTARRAY,0,$width,$TOP,$BOT);
#==================================================================
================================
# ROTATE 90 degrees
#==================================================================
================================
  $ALPHA=$ANGLE*4;
  rotate(\@$MARRAY,$ALPHA,$MLEFT,$MRIGHT,$MTOP,$MBOT);
#------------------------------------------------------------------
  $TOP=findtop(\@ROTARRAY,$width,$height);
```

```
  $BOT=findbottom(\@ROTARRAY,$width,$height);
  $LEFT=findleft(\@ROTARRAY,$width,$height);
  $RIGHT=findright(\@ROTARRAY,$width,$height);
#------------------------------------------------
  twos(\@ROTARRAY,0,$width,$TOP,$BOT);
  threes(\@ROTARRAY,0,$width,$TOP,$BOT);
  fours(\@ROTARRAY,0,$width,$TOP,$BOT);
  fives(\@ROTARRAY,0,$width,$TOP,$BOT);
#=================================================================
===============================
# ROTATE 112.5 degrees
#=================================================================
===============================
  $ALPHA=$ANGLE*5;
  rotate(\@$MARRAY,$ALPHA,$MLEFT,$MRIGHT,$MTOP,$MBOT);
#----------------------------------------------------------------
  $TOP=findtop(\@ROTARRAY,$width,$height);
  $BOT=findbottom(\@ROTARRAY,$width,$height);
  $LEFT=findleft(\@ROTARRAY,$width,$height);
  $RIGHT=findright(\@ROTARRAY,$width,$height);
#------------------------------------------------
  twos(\@ROTARRAY,0,$width,$TOP,$BOT);
  threes(\@ROTARRAY,0,$width,$TOP,$BOT);
  fours(\@ROTARRAY,0,$width,$TOP,$BOT);
  fives(\@ROTARRAY,0,$width,$TOP,$BOT);
#=================================================================
===============================
# ROTATE 135 degrees
#=================================================================
===============================
  $ALPHA=$ANGLE*6;
  rotate(\@$MARRAY,$ALPHA,$MLEFT,$MRIGHT,$MTOP,$MBOT);
#----------------------------------------------------------------
  $TOP=findtop(\@ROTARRAY,$width,$height);
  $BOT=findbottom(\@ROTARRAY,$width,$height);
  $LEFT=findleft(\@ROTARRAY,$width,$height);
  $RIGHT=findright(\@ROTARRAY,$width,$height);
#------------------------------------------------
  twos(\@ROTARRAY,0,$width,$TOP,$BOT);
  threes(\@ROTARRAY,0,$width,$TOP,$BOT);
  fours(\@ROTARRAY,0,$width,$TOP,$BOT);
  fives(\@ROTARRAY,0,$width,$TOP,$BOT);
#=================================================================
===============================
# ROTATE 157.5 degrees
```

```
#==================================================================
====================================
  $ALPHA=$ANGLE*7;
  rotate(\@$MARRAY,$ALPHA,$MLEFT,$MRIGHT,$MTOP,$MBOT);
#-----------------------------------------------------------------
  $TOP=findtop(\@ROTARRAY,$width,$height);
  $BOT=findbottom(\@ROTARRAY,$width,$height);
  $LEFT=findleft(\@ROTARRAY,$width,$height);
  $RIGHT=findright(\@ROTARRAY,$width,$height);
#---------------------------------------------
  twos(\@ROTARRAY,0,$width,$TOP,$BOT);
  threes(\@ROTARRAY,0,$width,$TOP,$BOT);
  fours(\@ROTARRAY,0,$width,$TOP,$BOT);
  fives(\@ROTARRAY,0,$width,$TOP,$BOT);
#==================================================================
====================================
# ROTATE 180 degrees
#==================================================================
====================================
  $ALPHA=$ANGLE*8;
  rotate(\@$MARRAY,$ALPHA,$MLEFT,$MRIGHT,$MTOP,$MBOT);
#-----------------------------------------------------------------
  $TOP=findtop(\@ROTARRAY,$width,$height);
  $BOT=findbottom(\@ROTARRAY,$width,$height);
  $LEFT=findleft(\@ROTARRAY,$width,$height);
  $RIGHT=findright(\@ROTARRAY,$width,$height);
#---------------------------------------------
  twos(\@ROTARRAY,0,$width,$TOP,$BOT);
  threes(\@ROTARRAY,0,$width,$TOP,$BOT);
  fours(\@ROTARRAY,0,$width,$TOP,$BOT);
  fives(\@ROTARRAY,0,$width,$TOP,$BOT);
#==================================================================
====================================
# ROTATE 202.5 degrees
#==================================================================
====================================
  $ALPHA=$ANGLE*9;
  rotate(\@$MARRAY,$ALPHA,$MLEFT,$MRIGHT,$MTOP,$MBOT);
#-----------------------------------------------------------------
  $TOP=findtop(\@ROTARRAY,$width,$height);
  $BOT=findbottom(\@ROTARRAY,$width,$height);
  $LEFT=findleft(\@ROTARRAY,$width,$height);
  $RIGHT=findright(\@ROTARRAY,$width,$height);
#---------------------------------------------
  twos(\@ROTARRAY,0,$width,$TOP,$BOT);
```

```
  threes(\@ROTARRAY,0,$width,$TOP,$BOT);
  fours(\@ROTARRAY,0,$width,$TOP,$BOT);
  fives(\@ROTARRAY,0,$width,$TOP,$BOT);
#========================================================
====================================
# ROTATE 225 degrees
#========================================================
====================================

  $ALPHA=$ANGLE*10;
  rotate(\@$MARRAY,$ALPHA,$MLEFT,$MRIGHT,$MTOP,$MBOT);
#-------------------------------------------------------------
  $TOP=findtop(\@ROTARRAY,$width,$height);
  $BOT=findbottom(\@ROTARRAY,$width,$height);
  $LEFT=findleft(\@ROTARRAY,$width,$height);
  $RIGHT=findright(\@ROTARRAY,$width,$height);
#--------------------------------------------
  twos(\@ROTARRAY,0,$width,$TOP,$BOT);
  threes(\@ROTARRAY,0,$width,$TOP,$BOT);
  fours(\@ROTARRAY,0,$width,$TOP,$BOT);
  fives(\@ROTARRAY,0,$width,$TOP,$BOT);
#========================================================
===================================
# ROTATE 247.5 degrees
#========================================================
===================================

  $ALPHA=$ANGLE*11;
  rotate(\@$MARRAY,$ALPHA,$MLEFT,$MRIGHT,$MTOP,$MBOT);
#-------------------------------------------------------------
  $TOP=findtop(\@ROTARRAY,$width,$height);
  $BOT=findbottom(\@ROTARRAY,$width,$height);
  $LEFT=findleft(\@ROTARRAY,$width,$height);
  $RIGHT=findright(\@ROTARRAY,$width,$height);
#--------------------------------------------
  twos(\@ROTARRAY,0,$width,$TOP,$BOT);
  threes(\@ROTARRAY,0,$width,$TOP,$BOT);
  fours(\@ROTARRAY,0,$width,$TOP,$BOT);
  fives(\@ROTARRAY,0,$width,$TOP,$BOT);
#========================================================
===================================
# ROTATE 270 degrees
#========================================================
==================================

  $ALPHA=$ANGLE*12;
  rotate(\@$MARRAY,$ALPHA,$MLEFT,$MRIGHT,$MTOP,$MBOT);
#-------------------------------------------------------------
```

```
  $TOP=findtop(\@ROTARRAY,$width,$height);
  $BOT=findbottom(\@ROTARRAY,$width,$height);
  $LEFT=findleft(\@ROTARRAY,$width,$height);
  $RIGHT=findright(\@ROTARRAY,$width,$height);
#----------------------------------------------

  twos(\@ROTARRAY,0,$width,$TOP,$BOT);
  threes(\@ROTARRAY,0,$width,$TOP,$BOT);
  fours(\@ROTARRAY,0,$width,$TOP,$BOT);
  fives(\@ROTARRAY,0,$width,$TOP,$BOT);
#====================================================
=================================
# ROTATE 292.5 degrees
#====================================================
=================================
  $ALPHA=$ANGLE*13;
  rotate(\@$MARRAY,$ALPHA,$MLEFT,$MRIGHT,$MTOP,$MBOT);
#-----------------------------------------------------------
  $TOP=findtop(\@ROTARRAY,$width,$height);
  $BOT=findbottom(\@ROTARRAY,$width,$height);
  $LEFT=findleft(\@ROTARRAY,$width,$height);
  $RIGHT=findright(\@ROTARRAY,$width,$height);
#----------------------------------------------

  twos(\@ROTARRAY,0,$width,$TOP,$BOT);
  threes(\@ROTARRAY,0,$width,$TOP,$BOT);
  fours(\@ROTARRAY,0,$width,$TOP,$BOT);
  fives(\@ROTARRAY,0,$width,$TOP,$BOT);
#====================================================
=================================
# ROTATE 315 degrees
#====================================================
=================================
  $ALPHA=$ANGLE*14;
  rotate(\@$MARRAY,$ALPHA,$MLEFT,$MRIGHT,$MTOP,$MBOT);
#------------------------------------------------------------------
  $TOP=findtop(\@ROTARRAY,$width,$height);
  $BOT=findbottom(\@ROTARRAY,$width,$height);
  $LEFT=findleft(\@ROTARRAY,$width,$height);
  $RIGHT=findright(\@ROTARRAY,$width,$height);
#--------------------------------------------
  twos(\@ROTARRAY,0,$width,$TOP,$BOT);
  threes(\@ROTARRAY,0,$width,$TOP,$BOT);
  fours(\@ROTARRAY,0,$width,$TOP,$BOT);
  fives(\@ROTARRAY,0,$width,$TOP,$BOT);
#====================================================
=================================
```

```
# ROTATE 337.5 degrees
#====================================================
================================
  $ALPHA=$ANGLE*15;
  rotate(\@$MARRAY,$ALPHA,$MLEFT,$MRIGHT,$MTOP,$MBOT);
#----------------------------------------------------------------
  $TOP=findtop(\@ROTARRAY,$width,$height);
  $BOT=findbottom(\@ROTARRAY,$width,$height);
  $LEFT=findleft(\@ROTARRAY,$width,$height);
  $RIGHT=findright(\@ROTARRAY,$width,$height);
#----------------------------------------------
  twos(\@ROTARRAY,0,$width,$TOP,$BOT);
  threes(\@ROTARRAY,0,$width,$TOP,$BOT);
  fours(\@ROTARRAY,0,$width,$TOP,$BOT);
  fives(\@ROTARRAY,0,$width,$TOP,$BOT);
#====================================================
================================
# ROTATE 360 degrees (not required)
#====================================================
================================
  $$IMAGESTORE{$IMAGENAME}=$STORE;
}


#==============================================
#==============================================


sub nonwhiteline
  {
  $AA=$_[0];
  my $y=$_[1];
  my $maxx=$_[2];
  my $x=0;
  my $res=0;
  do
    {
    if ($$AA[$x][$y]!=0) {$res=1};
    $x++;
    }
  until (($res==1)||($x>$maxx));
  return($res);
  }

sub nonwhiterow
```

```perl
  {
  my $AA=$_[0];
  my $x=$_[1];
  my $maxy=$_[2];
  my $y=0;
  my $res=0;
  do
    {
    if ($$AA[$x][$y]!=0) {$res=1};
    $y++;
    }
  until (($res==1)||($y>$maxy));
  return($res);
  }

sub findtop
  {
  $AA=$_[0];
  my $maxx=$_[1];
  my $maxy=$_[2];
  my $y=-1;
  do
    {
    $y++;
    }
  until (($y>$maxy)||(nonwhiteline(\@$AA,$y,$maxx)));
  #print("TOP=$y\n");
  if ($y>$maxy) {return(-1)} else {return($y)};
  }

sub findbottom
  {
  $AA=$_[0];
  my $maxx=$_[1];
  my $maxy=$_[2];
  my $y=$maxy+1;
  do
    {
    $y--;
    }
  until (($y<0)||(nonwhiteline(\@$AA,$y,$maxx)));
  #print("BOT=$y\n");
  if ($y<0) {return(-1)} else {return($y)};
  }
```

```perl
sub findleft
   {
   $AA=$_[0];
   my $maxx=$_[1];
   my $maxy=$_[2];
   my $x=-1;
   do
     {
     $x++;
     }
   until (($x>$maxx)||(nonwhiterow(\@$AA,$x,$maxy)));
   if ($x>$maxx) {return(-1)} else {return($x)};
   }

sub findright
   {
   $AA=$_[0];
   my $maxx=$_[1];
   my $maxy=$_[2];
   my $x=$maxx+1;
   do
     {
     $x--;
     }
   until (($x<0)||(nonwhiterow(\@$AA,$x,$maxy)));
   if ($x<0) {return(-1)} else {return($x)};
   }

sub twos
   {
   $AA=$_[0];
   my $minx=$_[1];
   my $maxx=$_[2];
   my $miny=$_[3];
   my $maxy=$_[4];
   my $halfy=(($maxy-$miny+1)/2);
   my $wholey=int($halfy);
   my $cut=$miny+$wholey;
   my $fracty=($halfy-$wholey);
   my $TOPHALF=0;
   my $BOTHALF=0;
   my $WHOLE=0;
   my $DATA=0;
   my $extra=0;
   my $x=0;
```

```perl
    my $y=0;
    for($y=$miny;$y<=$maxy;$y++)
        {
        for($x=$minx;$x<=$maxx;$x++)
            {
            $extra=$$AA[$x][$y];
            if   ($y<$cut)                {$TOPHALF=$TOPHALF+$extra}
        #-----------------------------------------------------------------------
            elsif (($y==$cut)&&($fracty>0))
{$TOPHALF=$TOPHALF+($extra*$fracty);
                                    $BOTHALF=$BOTHALF+($extra*(1-$fracty))}
        #-----------------------------------------------------------------------
            elsif (($y==$cut)&&($fracty==0))
{$BOTHALF=$BOTHALF+$extra}
        #-----------------------------------------------------------------------
            else                      {$BOTHALF=$BOTHALF+$extra}
            }
        }
    $WHOLE=$TOPHALF+$BOTHALF;

$DATA=[round(100*$TOPHALF/$WHOLE),round(100*$BOTHALF/$WHO
LE)];
    storedata(\@$STORE,\@$DATA);
    }

sub threes
    {
    $AA=$_[0];
    my $minx=$_[1];
    my $maxx=$_[2];
    my $miny=$_[3];
    my $maxy=$_[4];
    #------------------------------
    my $thirdy=(($maxy-$miny+1)/3);
    #------------------------------
    my $wholey=int($thirdy);
    my $cut1=$miny+$wholey;
    my $fracty=($thirdy-$wholey);
    #------------------------------
    my $twothirdy=($thirdy+$thirdy);
    my $whole2thirdy=int($twothirdy);
    my $fract2y=($twothirdy-$whole2thirdy);
    my $cut2=$miny+$whole2thirdy;
    #------------------------------------
    my $TOPTHIRD=0;
```

```perl
  my $MIDDLE=0;
  my $BOTTHIRD=0;
  my $extra=0;
  my $x=-1;
  my $y=-1;
  for($y=$miny;$y<=$maxy;$y++)
    {
    for($x=$minx;$x<=$maxx;$x++)
      {
      $extra=$$AA[$x][$y];
      if   ($y<$cut1)                {$TOPTHIRD=$TOPTHIRD+$extra}
    #------------------------------------------------------------------------
      elsif (($y==$cut1)&&($fracty>0))
{$TOPTHIRD=$TOPTHIRD+($extra*$fracty);
                            $MIDDLE=$MIDDLE+($extra*(1-$fracty))}
    #------------------------------------------------------------------------
      elsif (($y==$cut1)&&($fracty==0))  {$MIDDLE=$MIDDLE+$extra}
    #------------------------------------------------------------------------
      elsif (($y>$cut1)&&($y<$cut2))    {$MIDDLE=$MIDDLE+$extra}
    #------------------------------------------------------------------------
      elsif (($y==$cut2)&&($fract2y>0))
{$MIDDLE=$MIDDLE+($extra*$fract2y);
                            $BOTTHIRD=$BOTTHIRD+($extra*(1-
$fract2y))}
    #------------------------------------------------------------------------
      elsif (($y==$cut2)&&($fract2y==0))
{$BOTTHIRD=$BOTTHIRD+$extra}
    #------------------------------------------------------------------------
      else                    {$BOTTHIRD=$BOTTHIRD+$extra}
      }
    }
    $WHOLE=$TOPTHIRD+$MIDDLE+$BOTTHIRD;

$DATA=[round(100*$TOPTHIRD/$WHOLE),round(100*$MIDDLE/$WHOL
E),round(100*$BOTTHIRD/$WHOLE)];
    storedata(\@$STORE,\@$DATA);
  }

sub fours
  {
  $AA=$_[0];
  my $minx=$_[1];
  my $maxx=$_[2];
  my $miny=$_[3];
  my $maxy=$_[4];
```

```perl
#-----------------------------
my $quady=(($maxy-$miny+1)/4);
#-----------------------------
my $whole1quady=int($quady);
my $cut1=$miny+$whole1quady;
my $fracty=($quady-$whole1quady);
#-----------------------------
my $twoquady=($quady+$quady);
my $whole2quady=int($twoquady);
my $fract2y=($twoquady-$whole2quady);
my $cut2=$miny+$whole2quady;
#-------------------------------------
my $threequady=($quady+$quady+$quady);
my $whole3quady=int($threequady);
my $fract3y=($threequady-$whole3quady);
my $cut3=$miny+$whole3quady;
#-------------------------------------
my $TOPQUAD=0;
my $TOPMIDDLE=0;
my $BOTMIDDLE=0;
my $BOTQUAD=0;
my $WHOLE=0;
my $DATA=0;
my $extra=0;
my $x=-1;
my $y=-1;
for($y=$miny;$y<=$maxy;$y++)
  {
  for($x=$minx;$x<=$maxx;$x++)
    {
    $extra=$$AA[$x][$y];
   #------------------------------------------------------------------------
    if  ($y<$cut1)              {$TOPQUAD=$TOPQUAD+$extra}
   #------------------------------------------------------------------------
    elsif (($y==$cut1)&&($fracty>0))
{$TOPQUAD=$TOPQUAD+($extra*$fracty);
                        $TOPMIDDLE=$TOPMIDDLE+($extra*(1-
$fracty))}
   #------------------------------------------------------------------------
    elsif (($y==$cut1)&&($fracty==0))
{$TOPMIDDLE=$TOPMIDDLE+$extra}
   #------------------------------------------------------------------------
    elsif (($y>$cut1)&&($y<$cut2))
{$TOPMIDDLE=$TOPMIDDLE+$extra}
   #------------------------------------------------------------------------
```

```
        elsif (($y==$cut2)&&($fract2y>0))
{$TOPMIDDLE=$TOPMIDDLE+($extra*$fract2y);
                                $BOTMIDDLE=$BOTMIDDLE+($extra*(1-
$fract2y))}
        #-------------------------------------------------------------------
        elsif (($y==$cut2)&&($fract2y==0))
{$BOTMIDDLE=$BOTMIDDLE+$extra}
        #-------------------------------------------------------------------
        elsif (($y>$cut2)&&($y<$cut3))
{$BOTMIDDLE=$BOTMIDDLE+$extra}
        #-------------------------------------------------------------------
        elsif (($y==$cut3)&&($fract3y>0))
{$BOTMIDDLE=$BOTMIDDLE+($extra*$fract3y);
                                $BOTQUAD=$BOTQUAD+($extra*(1-
$fract3y))}
        #-------------------------------------------------------------------
        elsif (($y==$cut3)&&($fract3y==0))
{$BOTQUAD=$BOTQUAD+$extra}
        #-------------------------------------------------------------------
        else                            {$BOTQUAD=$BOTQUAD+$extra}
        }
    }
    $WHOLE=$TOPQUAD+$TOPMIDDLE+$BOTMIDDLE+$BOTQUAD;

$DATA=[round(100*$TOPQUAD/$WHOLE),round(100*$TOPMIDDLE/$W
HOLE),

round(100*$BOTMIDDLE/$WHOLE),round(100*$BOTQUAD/$WHOLE)];
    storedata(\@$STORE,\@$DATA);
    }

sub fives
    {
    $AA=$_[0];
    my $minx=$_[1];
    my $maxx=$_[2];
    my $miny=$_[3];
    my $maxy=$_[4];
    #-----------------------------
    my $fivey=(($maxy-$miny+1)/5);
    #-----------------------------
    my $whole1fivey=int($quady);
    my $cut1=$miny+$whole1fivey;
    my $fracty=($fivey-$whole1fivey);
    #-----------------------------
```

```perl
    my $twofivey=($fivey+$fivey);
    my $whole2fivey=int($twofivey);
    my $fract2y=($twofivey-$whole2fivey);
    my $cut2=$miny+$whole2fivey;
    #-------------------------------------
    my $threefivey=($fivey+$fivey+$fivey);
    my $whole3fivey=int($threefivey);
    my $fract3y=($threefivey-$whole3fivey);
    my $cut3=$miny+$whole3fivey;
    #-------------------------------------
    my $fourfivey=($fivey+$fivey+$fivey+$fivey);
    my $whole4fivey=int($fourfivey);
    my $fract4y=($fourfivey-$whole4fivey);
    my $cut4=$miny+$whole4fivey;
    #-------------------------------------
    my $TOPFIVE=0;
    my $TOPMIDDLE=0;
    my $MIDDLE=0;
    my $BOTMIDDLE=0;
    my $BOTFIVE=0;
    my $WHOLE=0;
    my $DATA=0;
    my $extra=0;
    my $x=-1;
    my $y=-1;
    for($y=$miny;$y<=$maxy;$y++)
      {
      for($x=$minx;$x<=$maxx;$x++)
        {
        $extra=$$AA[$x][$y];
      #-------------------------------------------------------------------------
        if   ($y<$cut1)              {$TOPFIVE=$TOPFIVE+$extra}
      #-------------------------------------------------------------------------
          elsif (($y==$cut1)&&($fracty>0))
{$TOPFIVE=$TOPFIVE+($extra*$fracty);
                              $TOPMIDDLE=$TOPMIDDLE+($extra*(1-
$fracty))}
        #-------------------------------------------------------------------------
          elsif (($y==$cut1)&&($fracty==0))
{$TOPMIDDLE=$TOPMIDDLE+$extra}
        #-------------------------------------------------------------------------
          elsif (($y>$cut1)&&($y<$cut2))
{$TOPMIDDLE=$TOPMIDDLE+$extra}
        #-------------------------------------------------------------------------
```

```
          elsif (($y==$cut2)&&($fract2y>0))
  {$TOPMIDDLE=$TOPMIDDLE+($extra*$fract2y);
                              $MIDDLE=$MIDDLE+($extra*(1-$fract2y))}
       #-----------------------------------------------------------------
          elsif (($y==$cut2)&&($fract2y==0))  {$MIDDLE=$MIDDLE+$extra}
       #-----------------------------------------------------------------
          elsif (($y>$cut2)&&($y<$cut3))     {$MIDDLE=$MIDDLE+$extra}
       #-----------------------------------------------------------------
          elsif (($y==$cut3)&&($fract3y>0))
  {$MIDDLE=$MIDDLE+($extra*$fract3y);
                              $BOTMIDDLE=$BOTMIDDLE+($extra*(1-
  $fract3y))}
       #-----------------------------------------------------------------
          elsif (($y==$cut3)&&($fract3y==0))
  {$BOTMIDDLE=$BOTMIDDLE+$extra}
       #-----------------------------------------------------------------
          elsif (($y>$cut3)&&($y<$cut4))
  {$BOTMIDDLE=$BOTMIDDLE+$extra}
       #-----------------------------------------------------------------
          elsif (($y==$cut4)&&($fract4y>0))
  {$BOTMIDDLE=$BOTMIDDLE+($extra*$fract4y);
                              $BOTFIVE=$BOTFIVE+($extra*(1-$fract4y))}
       #-----------------------------------------------------------------
          else                        {$BOTFIVE=$BOTFIVE+$extra}
          }
       }

  $WHOLE=$TOPFIVE+$TOPMIDDLE+$MIDDLE+$BOTMIDDLE+$BOTFI
  VE;
     $DATA=[
         round(100*$TOPFIVE/$WHOLE),
         round(100*$TOPMIDDLE/$WHOLE),
         round(100*$MIDDLE/$WHOLE),
         round(100*$BOTMIDDLE/$WHOLE),
         round(100*$BOTFIVE/$WHOLE)
         ];
     storedata(\@$STORE,\@$DATA);
     }

  sub rotate
     {
     $BB=$_[0];
     my $theta=$_[1];   #angle of rotation
     #----------------
     my $minx= $_[2];
```

399

```perl
  my $maxx= $_[3];
  my $miny= $_[4];
  my $maxy= $_[5];
  #print("\n left=$minx, right=$maxx, top=$miny, bot=$maxy\n\n");
  #---------------------------
  for ($x=0;$x<=$width-1;$x++){for
($y=0;$y<=$height;$y++){$ROTARRAY[$x][$y]=".";}}
  #------------------------------------------------------
  # ---- calculate the origin with backward x
  $ORIGX=$width+1;
  $ORIGY=0;
  #-------------------------------------------------
  my $halfx=(($maxx-$minx+1)/2);
  my $halfy=(($maxy-$miny+1)/2);
  #-------------------------------------------------------
  my $OX=($minx+$halfx); # origin of rotation
    $OX=$ORIGX-$OX;      # origin of rotation (backward coords)
  my $OY=$miny+$halfy;   # origin of rotation (Y)
  #print("backward: OX=$OX, OY=$OY\n");
  #-------------------------------------------
  my $psi=0;       #angle subtended by each point
  #-------------------------------------------
  my $x=0;         # coords in input array BB
  my $y=0;
  #-------------------------------------------------
  my $xx=0;        # modified coords (with backward x)
  my $yy=0;
  #-------------------------------------------------
  my $newx=0;      # coords in ROTARRAY
  my $newy=0;
  #----------------------------------------------------------------
  for($x=$minx;$x<=$maxx;$x++)
    {
    for($y=$miny;$y<=$maxy;$y++)
      {
      #-----------------------------------------
      $xx=$ORIGX-($x+0.5);
      $yy=$y+0.5;
      #-----------------------------------------
      $dispx=$xx-$OX;
      $dispy=$yy-$OY;                 # displaced X and Y (with new origin)
      #-----------------------------------------
      $psi=atan2($dispy,$dispx);      # polar psi from the new origin
      #-----------------------------------------
      $R=sqrt(($dispx**2)+($dispy**2)); # polar R from the new origin
```

```
#----------------------------------------
$newpsi=$psi+$theta;              # the new psi after rotation
$newx=$R*cos($newpsi);            # the new x after rotation
$newy=$R*sin($newpsi);            # the new y after rotation
#----------------------------------------
$dispnewx=$ORIGX-($newx+$OX);     # return x to the old origin
$dispnewy=$newy+$OY;              # return y to the old origin
#----------------------------------------
$dispnewx=round($dispnewx-0.25);  # integer value
$dispnewy=round($dispnewy-0.25);  # integer value
#----------------------------------------
$ROTARRAY[$dispnewx][$dispnewy]=$$BB[$x][$y];
#----------------------------------------
        }
    }
#printarray(\@ROTARRAY);
}
```

#--------------end of program text---------------------------

The images used and referred to in the program text are shown in the diagram above. To run the program you must prepare .bmp files - one file per shape - and place each in the same directory/folder as the program text. You should not include the name or the surrounding frame shown in the diagram. Check the program text to make sure that the file names agree with the program text. If any reader seriously wants to try my program (not recommended) the PERL download recommendations (available on the Internet) should be followed carefully.

REFERENCES

[Aleksander 2000], "How to build a mind", Aleksander Igor, Weidenfeld and Nicholson 2000.

[Baars 2013], "Fundamentals of Cognitive Neuroscience" Baars B.J. and Gage N.M, AP/Elsevier 2013

[Baron-Cohen 1996], "Synaesthesia: prevalence and familiality" Baron-Cohen S. Burt L. Smith-Laittan F. Harrison J. Bolton P Perception 25(9) 1073-1079 (1996)

[Blackburn 1994] "Oxford Dictionary of Philosophy", Blackburn S. OUP 1994.

[Blakemore and Cooper 1970], "Development of brains depends upon the visual environment" Blakemore C and Cooper G.F. Nature 280, 313-314, 1970.

[Brooks 1990], "Elephants don't play chess", Brooks R.A. Robotics and Autonomous Systems 6, 3-15, 1990.

[Carey 1980], "The development of face recognition - a maturation component?" Carey S, Diamond R and Woods B., Developmental Psychology, 16, 257-269. 1980.

[Chalmers 2010], "The Character of Consciousness", Chalmers D.J. Oxford University Press. 2010

[Chalmers 2002], "Consciousness and its Place in Nature", Chalmers D.J. from The Philosophy of Mind, ed Stich and Warfield, Blackwells Guide to Philosophy of Mind Blackwell 2002.

[Chomsky 1971], "Syntactic Structures", Chomsky Noam, Mouton

& Co N.V 1971.

[Conway Morris 2003], "Life's Solution: Inevitable Humans in a Lonely Universe" Conway Morris, Simon. Cambridge Univ. Press. 2003.

[Davies 2006], "The Goldilocks Enigma", Davies P. Allen Lane 2006.

[Dawkins 1986], "The Blind Watchmaker", Dawkins R. Longmans 1986.

[Dennett 1991], "Consciousness Explained", Dennet Daniel C. Little Brown & Co 1991.

[Dennett 2005], "Sweet Dreams: Philosophical Obstacles to a Science of Consciousness", Dennett Daniel C. MIT 2005.

[Dietrich and Hardcastle 2004], "Sisyphus' Boulder, Consciousness and the limits of the knowable", (introduction), Dietrich E. and Hardcastle V.G. John Benjamins Pub.

[Ericsson and Kintsch 1995], "Long-term working memory" Ericsson K.A. and Kintsch W. Psychological review, 102, 211-245, 1998

[Feferman 1995] - "Penrose's Godelian Argument" Feferman S. available online at http://psyche.cs.monash.edu.au/v2/psyche-2-07-feferman.html

[Feldman 2003] "The Simplicity Principle in Human Concept Learning", Feldman, J. Current Directions in Psychological Science V 12, No 6 Dec 2003],

[Fodor 1975], "The Language of Thought", Fodor J. Cambridge, Harvard Univ. Press

[Fodor 1981], "The Current Status of the Innateness Controversy", Fodor J. A. in Representations, Cambridge. MIT Press 1981.

[Fodor 1977], "Semantics: Theories of Meaning in Generative Grammar", Fodor J.D. Harvester Press 1977.

[Gabrilovich and Markovich 2009], "Wikipedia-based Semantic Interpretation for Natural Language Processing.", Gabrilovich E. Markovich S. Journal of Artificial Intelligence Research 34, (2009) 443-408.

[Haikonen 2003], "The cognitive approach to Conscious Machines", Haikonen P. Imprint Academic 2003.

[Hambrick 1998] "Ericsson and Kintsch 1995", Hambrick D. Cognitive Science Summaries. http://www.jdavies.org/summaries/

[Hare et al 2000], "Chimpanzees know what conspecifics do and do not see", Hare B, Call J. Agnetta B and Tomasello M. Animal Behaviour 2000, 59, 771-785.

[Hebb 1961] "Distinctive features of learning in the higher animal", Hebb, D.O. in "Brain Mechanisms and Learning" ed Delafresnaye J.F. OUP, 1961.

[Horowitz and Sahni 1978], "Fundementals of Computer Algorithms", Horowitz E, Sahni S, Pitman Pub Co. 1978.

[Hume 1739/40], "On Human Nature and the Understanding", Hume D. 1739/40

[Hutchins 1971] "the generaion of syntactic structures from a semantic base", Huchins, W.J. North-Holland 1971.

[Iacoboni 2008], "Mirroring People", Iacoboni, M. Farrar, Straus and Giroux 2008.

[Jackendoff 1992], "Languages of the Mind", Jackendoff R. MIT Press 1992.

[Jackendoff 2012], "A User's Guide to Thought and Language" Jackendoff R. OUP 2012

[Jackson 1982], "Epiphenomenal Qualia" Jackson F, Philosophical Quarterly 32: 127-136 1982.

[Kahneman 2011] "Thinking, Fast and Slow". pub Farrar, Straus and Giroux 2011, (also Allen Lane and Penguin)

[Kluver 1936], "Analysis of the effects of the removal of the occipital lobes in monkeys" Kluver H. J. Physiol 2 49-61 (1936).

[Lakoff 1987], "Women, Fire and Dangerous Things", Lakoff G. Univ of Chicago Press 1987

[Libet 1979], "Subjective referral of the timing for a conscious sensory experience". Libet, B Wright E.W. Feinstein B. Brain 102, 193-224, 1979.

[Locke 1690], "An Essay Concerning Human Understanding" Locke J. 1690

[Loftus and Palmer 1974], "Reconstruction of auto-mobile destruction: An example of the interaction between language and memory" Loftus E.F. and Palmer J.C. Journal of Verbal learning and Verbal Behaviour, 13, 585-589, 1974

[Lorenz 1952], "King Solomon's Ring" Lorenz, K. pub Methuen & Co, 1952

[MacCarthy 1980], "Circumspection: A form of non-monotonic reasoning" MacCarthy J, Artificial Intelligence, 13, 27-39.

[McDermott 1995], "Penrose is Wrong" available online at

http://psyche.cs.monash.edu.au/v2/psyche-2-17-mcdermott.html
McDermott D.V.

[McDermott 2001], "Mind and Mechanism", McDermott D.V.
MIT 2001

[Nagel 1974] "What is it like to be a bat?", Nagel T. Philosophical
review 83: 4435-450, 1974 Cornell University Press. Reprinted in
Philosophy of Mind ed Chalmers, p219-226 2002.

[Ng 2013], available online at "http://robotics.stanford.edu/~ang/"
Ng A. 2013

[Noble 1988], "Natural Language Processing", Noble H.
Blackwell Scientific Publications 1988. (also available as an online downloadable text - www.tartanhen.co.uk)

[Noble 2005], "Operational Consciousness" Noble H. Tartan Hen
Publications 2005.

[Noble 2008], "Reasoning Beyond Reason" Noble H. pub Tartan
Hen Publications 2008.

[Penn and Povinelli 2007], "On the lack of evidence that non-
human animals possess anything remotely resembling a 'theory of
mind'". Penn D.C. and Povinelli D.J.. Philos Trans R Soc Lond B
Biol Sci, 2007 April 29, 362(1480) 731-744.

[Penn et al 2008],   "Darwin's mistake: Explaining the
discontinuity between human and nonhuman minds", Penn D.C.
Holyoak K.J. Povinelli D.J. Behaviour and Brain Sciences (2008)
31, 109-178.

[Penrose 1989], "The Emperor's New Mind", Penrose R., Oxford
Univ. Press, 1989.

[Penrose 1994]. "Shadows of the Mind" Penrose, R. Vintage 1994

[Philips 1992], "The role of eye contact in goal detection: Evidence from normal infants and children with autism or mental handicap" Philips W, Baron-Cohen S, and Rutter M.Development and Psychopathology 4 (1992) 375-383.

[Pinker 1994], "The language Instinct", Pinker S., William Morrow & Co inc/Allen Lane/Penguin Press 1994.

[Plotkin 1994], "The Nature of Knowledge", Plotkin H. Allen Lane 1994.

[Prinz 2002], "Furnishing the Mind", Prinz, J. MIT Press 2002.

[Quine 1960], "Word and Object", Quine W.V.O. MIT 1960.

[Quirk et al 1972] "A grammar of contemporary English" Quirk R. Greenbaum, Leech G. and Svartvik J. Longman House 1972.

[Range 2009], "Absence of reward induces inequity aversion in dogs". Range, F. Horn, L. Viryani Z. and Huber L., Porc. Nat. Acad of Sc. Jan 6, 2009, vol 106, No 1, 340-3345.

[Range 2011], "Development of Gaze following abilities in Wolves (Canis Lupus)", Plos ONE 6(2) e16888 published 2011.

[Reisenhuber and Poggio 2003], "How the visual cortex recognises objects. The tale of the standard model", Riesenhuber M and Poggio T. In The Visual neurosciences, ed Chalupa and Werner. MIT press 2003.

[Rendell 1985], "Substantial constructive induction using layered information comprerssion tractable feature formation in search". Rendal L.A., Proc. Ninth Int. Conf on AI, 18-23 Aug 1985, Los Angeles, Calif. Vol 12 pp650-658].

[Searle 1983] "Can computers think?", Searle J. from Minds,

Brains and Science, Harvard University Press 1983.

[Serra 2002], "Theory of mind in children with lesser variants of autism: a longitudinal study", Serra M, Loth FL, van Geert PL, Hurkens E, Minderaa RB. J Child Psychol Psychiatry 2002, Oct 43(7): 885-900

[Silk et all 2005], "Chimpanzees are indifferent to the welfare of unrelated group members", Silk J.B. Brosnan S.F. Vonk J. Hendrich J. Povinelli D.J. Richardson A.S. Lambeth S.P. Mascaro J. Shapiro S.J. Nature 437, 1357-1359 Oct 2005.

[Turing 1936], "On computable numbers, with an application to the Entscheidungsproblem" Turing A. M., Proc. of the London Mathemaatical Society, Second Series, Vol 42 (1936) pp 230-265.

[Venter 2012], available online at http://www.jcvi.org, (Ventner Institute) Venter J.C. 2012

[Vigo 2011], "Representational information: a new general notion and measure of information" Vigo R., Information Sciences 181, 4847-4859, 2011

[Warneken et al 2007], "Spontaneous altruism by chimpanzees and young children", Warneken F, Hare B, Melis A.P. Hanus D, Tomasello M. available at Plos Biology 2007

[Warneken 2010] "On the origins of altruism on ontogeny and phylogeny", Warneken, F. Boston University Dialogues 2010.

[Watt 2001], "Demonstration of concept formation in the Horse" Lisa M.W. McDonnell S.M. Univ of Pennsylvania School of Veterinary Medicine, Equine Behaviour Laboratory, Interim report Aug 2001. (Available online).

[Weiskrantz 1987], "Neuropsychology and the nature of consciousness". Weiskrantz L. .in Mind Waves ed C. Blakemore and S. Greenfield, Blackwell, Oxford 1987

[Wolff 2001], "Information compression and multiple alignment as unifying concepts in AI and computing." Wolff, G. Expert Update 4(3) 22-36, 2001, bulletin/magazine of the SGES, the British Computer Society Specialist Group on Knowledge-based systems and applied artificial intelligence 2001.

INDEX

413